Happy 75th Birthday mom!
Love Bruce Judy Jen & Don

Frank Ney

A Canadian Legend

Paul Gogo

Paul Gogo

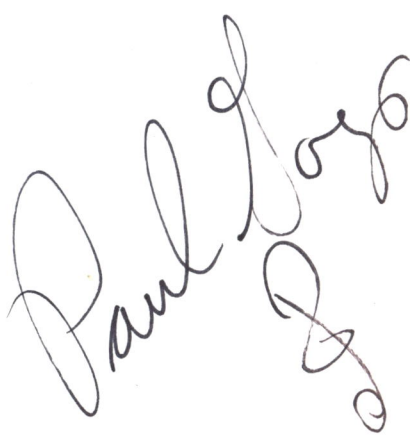

Frank Ney

A Canadian Legend

Paul Gogo

Sunporch Publishing
Vancouver Island, B.C.

Canadian Cataloguing in Publication Data

Gogo, Paul, 1965 -

Frank Ney

Includes index.

ISBN 0-9699468-0-5

1. Ney, Frank, 1918-1992. 2. Nanaimo (B.C.)—Biography.

3. Mayors—British Columbia—Nanaimo—Biography. 1. Title.

FC3849.N35Z49 1995 971.1'204'092 C95-910499-2

F1089.5.N35G63 1995

FIRST EDITION

This book is a 100% Canadian product.

No public (government) funds were used in the making of this book.

Acknowledgments

This book was researched, written and compiled by Paul Gogo.

A special "Thank you" to those who made it all happen...

Cover Design	Dave Wotherspoon *DesignHouse Type & Graphics*
Book Layout	Marty Shepard *DesignHouse Type & Graphics*
Map (inside cover)	Rod Krell *Creative Ink Design*
Assistance in editing	Muriel Loftus
Assistance in publication	Teresa Albert
Printed in Canada by	Hignell Printing Limited
Photographs courtesy of	The Nanaimo Centennial Archives *(Pages 53, 82, 121, 131, 173)* Joyce MacMillan *(Pages 309, 311, 329)* Theodora and Ken Gogo *(Page 125)* The Ney Family *(All other photographs)*

All quotes and submissions have been published courtesy of those being quoted. Thank you to everyone for being a good sport. The Ney family in particular showed much support, generosity and love over the duration of this publication. Paul Gogo would like everyone to know that their kindness is very much appreciated.

Comments or questions regarding Sunporch Publishing and/or the late Frank Ney may be directed to:

FNACL
427 Milton St.
Nanaimo B.C.
Canada V9R 2K9

For information pertaining to the World Championship Bathtub Race and/or The Nanaimo Marine Festival please contact:

Loyal Nanaimo
Bathtub Society
51 A Commercial St.
Nanaimo, B.C.
Canada V9R 5G3.

Bill McGuire (Commodore) is available at (Fax) 604-753-7244 or (Tel) 604-753-7223

The Ney Family Military Artifacts may be viewed at:

Vancouver Island
Military Museum
Rutherford Rd.
Nanaimo, B.C.
Canada V9T 4K6.

Ted Brothers (President) or Richard Copland may be reached at 604-756-2554

Many of Frank Ney's notes and photographs are now available for public viewing at:

Nanaimo
Community Archives
100 Cameron Rd.
Nanaimo B.C.
Canada V9R 2X1.

Volunteers may be contacted at 604-753-4462

"It is very pleasant to have a large family, but my milk bill alone is a $100 a month."

Frank Ney,
March 1976

Contents

Preface

THE SUN IS SHINING. The birds are singing. The warm summer breeze sweeps past the boats in the calm harbour. Children play and swim in the ocean that surrounds the Island. Everywhere there are signs of life. People are happy to be living in such a magnificent place.

The city of Nanaimo sits on the foot of a mountain that towers above the sea. It sparkles on the sheltered side of Vancouver Island, a location that never fails to charm people with its diverse natural splendour. Every year sees more and more people visiting this special place.

This is a boater's paradise. There are dozens of islands and very favourable conditions. Pleasure boat people have noticed a few strange things regarding maritime activity in these parts. It is no secret that Nanaimo's harbour occasionally becomes stirred up by a regiment of floating bathtubs. What is even more striking is the fact that one boat in particular circulates around blasting Scottish bagpipe music. Beside the piper on the bow stands a respectable, fully clad pirate from another century. His sword is held high.

Lately, our society has been a little bit numbed to worldly curiosities by the onslaught of the constant media assault we all experience. We have all seen the craziness of our world from one angle or another and it becomes more difficult all the time to excite people. All that taken as a given, people still love the idea of a first-class pirate in the later part of the twentieth century.

A nearly neon jacket is the perfect accent to this pirate with a twist. This one is not here to rape and pillage; rather to greet all with the friendliest smile on the coast. With megaphone in hand Black Frank welcomed the world with "WELCOME TO NANAIMO! JEWEL OF THE WEST! SUNPORCH OF CANADA!" He would look you in the eye and holler it to your face as his boat passed by on its way to being within hearing range of the next spectator.

Frank Ney A Canadian Legend

All the world really was a stage for Frank Ney. As mayor he would love to have you sign the guest book at city hall. Any questions about the town? He would gladly sell you any piece of the Island that you like. If money was a problem, he would gladly lend you some. If it's just enough to cover an emergency, don't worry; it's covered. Enjoy! Be happy! Frank was everything to everyone all the time.

Life was a lot of fun for him. His image now stands with sword in hand to welcome anyone who dares to visit our shores. This pirate is slightly taller and as solid as brass. Not many people get honoured with a statue any more. Frank was always the exception; throughout his life and beyond.

Frank's memory has been best served through the stories people tell about him. The man had thousands of friends, fans and acquaintances, yet few really knew him. Many were left to wonder what he was really all about. Why did he work so hard? How could he be everywhere at once? In his lifetime he answered every question with his actions. All we know is that love is always the answer and that life is for living!

Early Days

The Major

WHERE DOES A GUY LIKE FRANK COME FROM? Millions of television viewers saw a very eccentric man waving a plastic sword every year. One might only guess that he had been born either on a time-warped pirate ship or backstage at a circus. People who saw him in person may have guessed that he entered this world into the arms of a very wealthy and sophisticated family. Truth be known, he was the product of a conservative British military family.

The Major: Portrait of a World Traveler

The father of Frank Ney was a prim and proper Englishman. This distinguished gent was born into the age of Victorian pride. There was no dressing as a pirate or dancing down the street to be had for this Major Frank Alfonso Ney. "The Major", or "Pop", as he was later to be known, was quite a serious man in his youth. He was said not to have been a comic by any stretch of the imagination.

The Major was born and educated at Rye, Sussex on the south coast of England. His academic training was followed with a post as teacher at St. Aidan's school at Carlisle, England and by 1910 he was assisting in the Overseas Education League, a project founded by one of his three brothers. He had three sisters as well, all of them forever to reside in England.

Frank Ney A Canadian Legend

The Ney family in Europe knew what it was like to have a famous name. Frank was a descendent of a French military man known as Marshal Michel Ney. This dynamic Frenchman was also known as "Napoleon's right hand man". Marshal Ney was a major figure during the notorious Napoleonic War in Europe. This man had shown solid humanity when he rescued an infant whose mother had thrown the baby from a sled. Marshal Ney promptly brought this boy up as his own.

The question of whether Marshal Ney was executed after the war or whether it was a hoax and he escaped to America remains a mystery. There have been plenty of movies made about Napoleon since the war. If ever the main actor calls out to a big red-headed man, he is not saying "No!", rather "Ney!'.

During his bachelorhood, Frank Alfonso traveled to Nicosia, Cyprus and to Canada. He first caught sight of Canada when he was offered a teaching post in Winnipeg. He was quite happy to be teaching on the Prairies until the First World War broke out. Frank Alfonso joined the 90th Rifles of Winnipeg and went overseas. These war years were very hard for everyone. Having served in England and France, he was wounded and then hospitalized for many years. His military career was commemorated by his being awarded the Military Cross for conspicuous bravery at Regina Trench at the Second Battle of the Somme.

Ethel & baby Frank. 1918
Ethel had grown up as the daughter of a railway engine driver in a happy home.

The Major was ready for a change. He had lived

through two completely separate careers so far and had no children to tell his tales to. He was an impressive intelligent man of the world; certainly an eligible bachelor. It was in England during the war when he met a beautiful young lady by the mane of Ethel Vizard. Ethel was a very sweet and friendly lady from the Stourbridge sub-district of Staffordshire. Everyone who met her liked her and had good things to say about her easy-going personality. She was playing her part in this terrible war by running a lathe in a munitions factory in London and was also ready for a more fulfilling life.

When the Major met his dream girl, they fell in love and were married. Their first born was christened Frank James William Ney in London May 12, 1918. When the war was over the young couple brought the baby to Canada to start a new life for themselves.

Prairie Kids

NOW THAT THE MAJOR WAS BACK IN this time with a wife and child, it was time for him to adjust to his life as a civilian. In those days no exams were necessary to qualify insurance salespeople and he soon found himself joining the actuarial staff of the London and Lancashire Insurance company. As with his other ventures, success was his and soon the Major became independent by opening his own insurance and real estate company.

The family grew in 1921 with the arrival of William Beresford Ney. The three-year-old Frank could not have wished for a nicer and more supportive brother. The Ney brothers were very close throughout Frank's life.

Life with Frank…
Brother Bill Ney

We lived in a house one block away from the prairie that goes on for a long, long way.

Although Frank was three years older than me he took an interest in myself and my pals. He would organize us to do things. He would take us on what we called a "hike"on the prairie, which was really a picnic with sandwiches. He would get us to build a fort, play "cowboys and indians" or just chase gophers.

Bill Ney, Frank's brother

Life with Frank…
Cousin A. E. Swaine

I met Frank in 1925 when the family came to England on leave. Frank and Bill Ney, Ethel, plus an aunty and her son Jack came to tea. We four boys were told to play in my room with my trains and the three women went somewhere else to natter. Frank was known to have a quick temper in those days and liked his own way. He and Jack both wanted the same toy at the same time, which resulted in a fight in which one or the other put his foot on one of my railway wagons, which resulted in tears all round. Ethel gave Frank a smack bottom.

It was during this leave when Frank and Bill's parents were seeing as many shows as they could that Frank got lost. We were all living in London at the time. So that the adults could get out off to the theatre, Ethel took to giving Frank the old nip of Guiness at bedtime to make him sleep.

In the twenty's it was usual to find that London pubs had seats sat out on the pavements for the wives of the working class to use whilst their men folk were in the pub drinking as women were not usually welcome. When we were called to the lunch table there was no

Frank. He could not be found and a general search was organized which ended with Frank being found outside the "Load of Hay", (a very famous pub outside Paddington Station) climbing onto the seats outside the pub and helping himself to the dregs left in the empty glasses.

Major A. E. Swaine, Frank's cousin

Frank Ney A Canadian Legend

Like most Canadian boys on the prairies the Neys found hockey. During those early winters in Winnipeg a child could skate at every district. The parks board would level a corner of every school ground and section off a square with shiplap supported by pegs. Every two or three weeks this would be flooded with water from a fire hose. A portable shack complete with a woodstove was moved to a spot beside this new ice rink. The local kids considered it an honour to help the caretaker with the chores of scraping the ice and keeping the fire going.

Each one of these rinks had its own hockey team for kids twelve and under. Frank played on the Queenston School team and as he became a teenager he began to organize and run the team. Although Frank was not much older than the boys he was coaching, there was not any problem in getting the action onto the ice.

When the ice melted there was work to be done and some money to be made. The crops in the local fields would ripen and Frank would join the other local teen-agers in helping the farmers with the harvests. The boys told jokes and discussed ambitions as they walked down the highway until a farmer would wave them down and call them in to work. The boys proved to be an important part of the agricultural process and always received their fair pay. It was, however, not a whole lot of money as it was the early 1930's and the great depression was in full swing.

Schooling was not completely lost amongst all the activities this young Frank involved himself in. Frank Ney was a bright student who sat at the top of his class, even though it was pointed out that he could have placed even better had he not been distracted by wanting to do a hundred things other than his homework. He took his education further than most young men of the era by graduating from Calvin high school and completing the first year of University. He continued to coach the local hockey players through all of this while getting enough ice time to develop himself into a fine player.

Frank, pictured here on the right, leads the Alpine skating team.

For the first time in his life, young Frank found himself working in an office. His father had hired him to work in his office in downtown Winnipeg. The Major was brokering stocks as well as insurance and Frank was to go out and sell. When he wasn't selling, he was at a typewriter. He later said that he was pulling in $30 per week for a

Frank learned how to drive after turning a crank by the front bumper.

while at this job. The Major was also employing a stenographer as well as the recently graduated young Frank.

Everyone who lived through the Great Depression on the Canadian Prairies will speak of how devastating it was to their lives. Frank never dwelt on it so much in later years, but in truth the Ney family was never immune to the mighty hand of a horrible economy. The people who could afford to buy the Ney's products did so and those who couldn't did without. Finally there was not enough money circulating to support the insurance business and it folded.

When the Major lost his business, both he and Frank became unemployed. Bill didn't get the chance to graduate and the family lost their house. All of that stress led to the Major suffering a heart attack. With no loss of pride the homeless family decided to move back to England. The Major was old enough to retire and felt that he could live off the pension offered by the army.

The story of the Ney family is a true testament to the concept that families of the early part of the century stuck together. Their British relatives had told the Major of the state their Great Uncle Billy was in. Uncle Billy had been a bachelor all his life and at eighty was still living alone. It was suggested that the Neys move in with the old fellow and keep an eye on him. The Ney family said good-bye to their River Heights home and headed back to England and became citizens of Rye, Sussex.

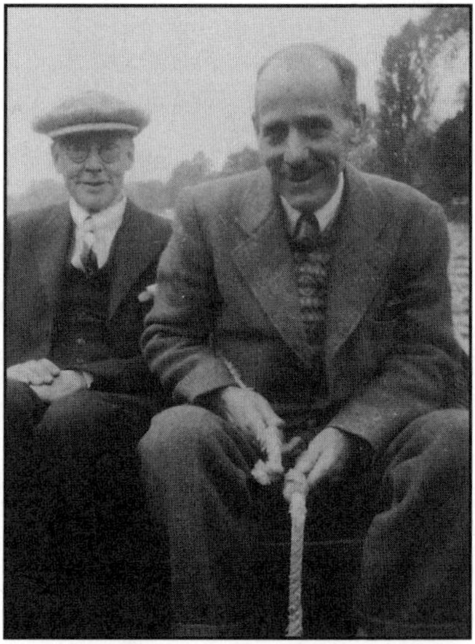

Great Uncle Billy and the Major relax by the English seaside.

One of the first jobs Frank got in England was that of a demolition man. He was ripping apart a

Life with Frank…
Frank's Cousin, A. E. Swaine

We next met again when the whole family came back to live in Rye. I was at school then and Frank and Bill worked for Gwen's husband who farmed and grew apples, for about a month whilst they were deciding what to do. We met most days and I remember being taught poker by Algy (their dad's nickname).

Major A. E. Swaine, Great Britain

five story building that housed the Singer sewing machine factory. This is somewhat ironic because Frank was not only scared of heights but he also later said that he was the "most unlikely one to be wielding a hammer." In those days jobs were hard to come by and Frank accepted that he was to be up five stories with a hammer in his hand.

The Great Depression was an international phenomenon. There was political unrest in Europe, and England's economy was not at its best by a long shot. The British government was running a program for suitable young men called the "short service commission." Frank found himself participating in this six month pilot training course. The idea was that if a war was to break out there would be a good list of capable pilots to enlist in the efforts. Frank was excited about flying and did very well at it. The course enabled him to become a fighter pilot with the Royal Air Force.

It was during his training that Frank somehow made it over to British Columbia for the first time. "I went fishing off of Nanaimo and I fell in love with it at first sight."

The Major was never told of the circumstance that led to Frank's dismissal from the Royal Air Force. It was decided that he would not approve of the report that Frank was out "buzzing the *Queen Mary*." The *Queen Mary* at that time was one of the fastest, and finest ships afloat. She was also the largest ship at sea with accommodations for 2038 passengers. Frank got a rare up-close aerial view of the superlative transatlantic liner while flying a biplane over Southampton harbour.

Frank recalled the story from a cafe in 1980, "Actually, all that happened; it was a lovely summer afternoon and I went out with two other young cadets at that time and we flew over the *Queen Mary*. Unfortunately my plane was the only one they caught the numbers on and that was the end of my career in the Air Force at that time."

Ney on Ice

WHAT ARE TWO CANADIAN BROTHERS to do in England? Frank found the answer in London. There were two open air skating rinks side by side. One had morning, afternoon and evening skating sessions. There were also three sessions for dancing. Londoners would enjoy the ten step, the waltz, foxtrot and three others. Frank loved to dance and managed to find the time to indulge in a social skill that would last his lifetime.

It was the second of the two ice rinks where Frank found his place in pre-war Europe. This rink had plenty of spectator seats and was used for hockey. It was not instant fame and fortune for Frank as he landed himself a job doing the work that had to be done in the rinks. His salary matched the very best of times in Winnipeg, but that in itself was not enough to keep him out of the spotlight.

Bill was only fifteen years old, but when he noticed that his fellow Brits were a lot smaller than him he passed as being twenty-five.

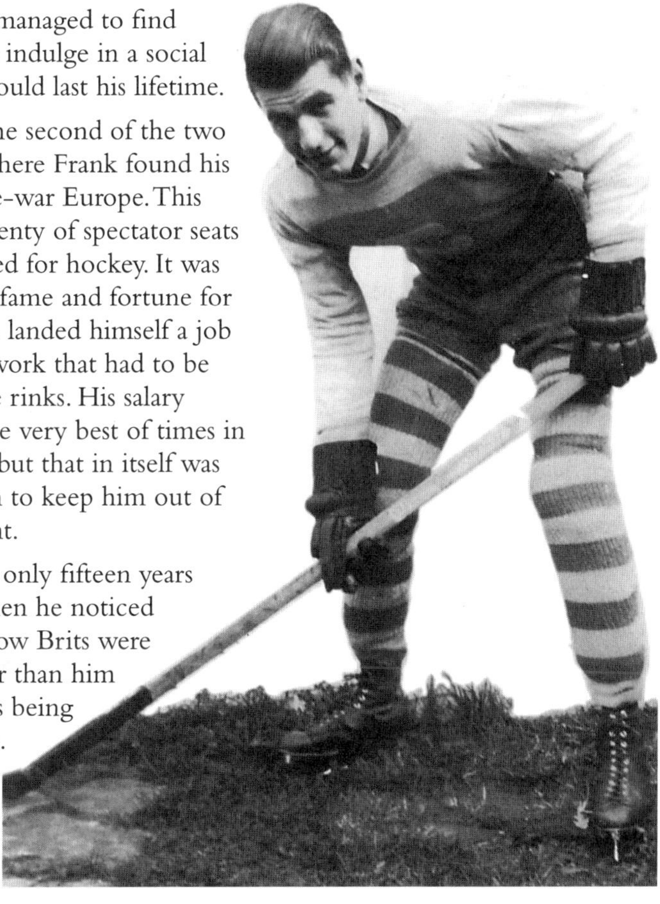

In the 1930's, hockey players wore no helmets. The game wasn't quite as rough as it is today, but it was still very fast-paced.

By the time Bill made it to London to join Frank in the rinks, four or five months had passed and Frank had switched to playing hockey for a living. He had been granted a $10 per week raise in the very short time he was employed at the rinks. Taking a gamble he quit his secure job and joined a hockey team. Bill was also a good skater but decided not to be featured on the ice. Instead he became foreman at the rinks and eventually an icemaker.

Some of the best Canadian players went to England at that time to help build up ice hockey as a major sport. Even though Frank had been a notable player in Canada he still felt some pressure when he signed on with the Wembley Lions. Frank always loved to live in his uniform. He proudly pranced around town in his hockey jersey with a huge number on his back.

After only one month with Wembley he got kicked off the team. "They said I wasn't good enough." This was a disappointing start to a remarkable career. Never to be defeated, he simply joined another team. There were two positions, forward and defence, and in keeping with Frank's approach to life, he was playing forward.

The aggressive Canadian played for six or seven teams in a league that had the stature in England that the NHL now has in Canada. Stature didn't always mean equal pay in those days and the young hockey player decided to moonlight in an industry that was brand new for England.

Door to door sales were very novel and vacuum cleaners were not yet available when Frank became a sales representative for the Fuller Brush Company. In those pre-vacuum days Frank would knock on an unsuspecting door and dazzle the occupant with a variety of brushes designed to clean all parts of the home.

Frank packed up his stick, skates and suitcase full of brushes and headed into Northern Scotland near the end of 1936 with the intention of gaining experience and playing more hockey. He became popular as a player with Glasgow's Mustang team and travelled all over the country with the big players of the era. He enjoyed a full two years as professional athlete in Scotland and gained a tremendous respect for Scottish customs that he treasured throughout his lifetime. He found that he was quite at home wearing a kilt.

It was always Frank's wish to retain Canadian domicile. He had an ongoing file in the immigration branch office in London. He was proud to be a Canadian and convinced the commissioner that he was absent from the country only for temporary purposes. Frank was granted the extensions that he requested. He had it somewhere in his mind that he had not seen the last of Canada. These feelings met with good company when he joined the Canadian ice hockey team. It was during this victorious trek through Europe when Frank first experienced the beauty of Poland.

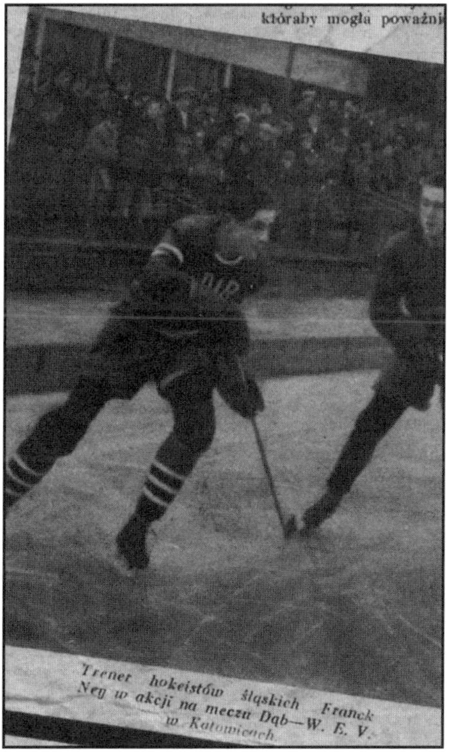

Much to Frank's dismay, the only English words the Polish players knew were all popular swear words. Frank felt this reflected poorly on him as a leader.

Everyone in Poland was aware of the fact that Canadian children grow up on the ice with a puck and a stick. Canadian players were regarded around the world as the very best players, and for very good reason. By Christmas of 1938 Frank had bid farewell to his fellow Canadians and was boarding a train for a 48-hour run back to Poland.

Frank was an instant celebrity as he stepped onto the platform of the train station. The newspaper reporters were there to capture the moment. The tall, smiling Canadian was draped in a long thick overcoat with his hand extended. The man who was shaking Frank's hand also tipped his hat, while the other smiling men helped form a circle around the Canadian. The Polish Councillor immediately gave Frank a visa. In usual circumstances the Polish government received some fee for this transaction, but the arrival of the Canadian hockey star was enough to warrant a free visa.

The young player didn't have to work his way up the ranks in the world of pre-war Polish professional hockey. Frank was immediately signed on as coach as well as player for the KS Debe; the Sports Club Oak. The timing was perfect. The hockey season was just beginning. The Polish team won its first game with Vienna 4-0. This was publicly credited to "Canadian Ney, best on the team." He also "demonstrated beautiful play" in the 5-4 victory over Austria.

Frank was "like gold" as he scored the only two goals in one game. He was regarded as "handsome and elegant" in Polish newspapers. This "very intelligent player" had the time and the skills needed to joke on the ice. He would "make crazy with the other guys" during a game. He would play any position he wanted to, dance around on the ice and generally do whatever he wanted to. The spectators were crazy about him. Immediately he was recognized as "the best player on the ice." The stage had been set for his personality to shine in a game he had mastered as a child.

This Polish ice hockey team was centered in a city called Katowicach, the third largest city in the country with one million residents. The steel industry was very prominent and there were plenty of jobs to support the population. In this city of many coal mines there was a large, enthusiastic sports audience. It could not have been easy for anyone to step into this country and learn the language at such a tense point in history. The people were wanting to be entertained with a good sporting event. These hard-working individuals also wanted to be proud of their homeland, as it defeated other cities and other nations in a very competitive game of physical skill.

All eyes were on Frank Ney, the tallest player on the team at 6'1". It was his job to make all these people happy. He was a better player

Ney on Ice

An extremely rare 1938 Polish newspaper. Most printed material was destroyed as Poland fell to Hitler. This cover survived Frank's suitcase ride through World War II.

and all around leader than these people could have hoped for. The local hero was well compensated for this challenge at $220 per month. This respectable salary closed the door on Frank's brush sales forever.

Frank's salary was soon boosted up an additional $40, as his duties grew to include arranging training programs, ice schedules, and picking from the 185 players he managed. He worked to arrange a Polish National Team and coached them to world championship standards, all the while putting a number of teams together. He had one team on the side that was comprised entirely of women. This was all good news for Poland, but it wasn't enough to win a game with the Canadian SmokEaters ice hockey team when they rolled back into Poland.

Even Frank couldn't save the day when the Canadian Trail Smoke Eaters played their final match with Poland before World War II. He was credited as being a great help to the Polish team, but Canada still maintained it's reputation as the nation that dominates the world of ice hockey.

It is safe to say that Frank enjoyed being a young hockey star in Poland. He was making more money and receiving more press than he ever had previously. His social life flourished as he existed as a famous and important sports figure for the country.

Frank found the time to visit and made very good use of the fabulous yet relatively unknown ski hills of Poland. He kept one pamphlet of a breathtaking resort in his suitcase and it remained with the few possessions he held onto through the war and through his life. He liked to be reminded of the good times, and skiing in Poland was certainly one of those.

Is is interesting to wonder what might have become of Frank Ney had a war not broken out. He was in the prime of his youth and in remarkable physical condition. Obviously very talented, he had a variety of skills. His gift as a leader had made him the coach of the team that represented the entire nation. Perhaps if the war had never happened his life may have been more centered on the Polish people.

Frank and the other Canadian hockey players in Europe made hockey the international sport that it is today. The equivalent of Frank's success could only be represented today by that of a wealthy

Life with Frank... Flyers Teammate Don Ross

Like Frank, Don Hamilton and I grew up in the River Heights area of Winnipeg, coming into the world to make our way in the post depression era of the thirties. Frank was a younger member of the area, and our first close association came in 1938 when Don and I bought one way tickets to Britain to play with what we hoped would be a Scottish team.

Frank was away in Poland when we arrived, but we learned his whereabouts through other Winnipeg fellows we met. We worked out of Glasgow teams and could have been placed on other Scottish teams but the rule limiting the number of Canadian imports caused us problems until one of the Winnipeg fellows suggested we write to Bristol as his cousin, who was a famous goaltender, was forming a team there. Most of the fellows were also working for the Bristol Airplane company so it was a good set-up once the season was open.

Just after we arrived, we got a letter offering us jobs playing hockey in Amsterdam plus Poland. The letter was of course through Frank. We were tempted to go to Poland but decided we had been travelling around enough and would stay put in Bristol for 38/39 then to Poland the next year and perhaps catch up with Frank once again. However, as you know Poland was blitzed by Hitler so who knows what might have happened to us at that time.

Frank wrote us a few times and I was thrilled to get one letter prior to the European tour of the Trail Smokeaters (world amateur champions at that time) and he said they were scheduled to play them twice! - and all he was expected to do was score half a dozen goals each time!! When it was over, he wrote and said they lost the first game about 7-2 and he got both goals and in the second they had a "hellish" goal keeper and the score was in double digits for Canada.

Don M. Ross, Retired

athlete. He certainly never struck it rich as a sports celebrity, but his notoriety did provide him with the benefits of extraordinary life experiences. He always loved people, and the Poles were never an exception to this. He never did lose his love for the Poles. During many later points of his life he was heard exclaiming "JA KOCHAM POLSKIE DJIEWCZYNKI!" (I LOVE POLISH WOMEN!)

Frank continues the story, "I started playing professional hockey in Europe and I got over to Poland. I was going with the German Consul's daughter and living at the Katowicach. I was getting on quite well there and she kind of indicated that I should take a holiday. Which I did, and when I got back I was in Paris when the war broke out." Frank's last hockey game in Poland was ten days before the country was invaded. Three days before the tanks rolled in, Frank rolled out. "We knew what was happening, and we sort of drifted out one by one."

Frank went on to Zurich, Berlin, Paris and Italy as a player with the Winnipeg team and finally to Scotland where his athletic career reached its highest point and ended. Once again he travelled all over the major centers of Scotland. He was by then mainly a defenceman, only playing a forward position in the odd game. These were very

LIFE WITH FRANK...

Don Ross

Frank came back from Poland and stayed with us for a few days hoping to be able to play a few games with the Bristol Bombers, but our season was ending, so he proceeded to Scotland and spent part of the 1939/40 season with the Kircaldy Flyers. Nowadays ex - NHL'ers play in those leagues. None of us made a fortune but it was a wonderful experience and many of us kept in touch in a loosely knit way. Don Hamilton and I returned to Canada in August and joined the RCAF.

Don Ross

good times for Frank. In Scotland during 1939 he played with a team called the Kirkcaldy Fife Flyers out of the town of Kirkcaldy.

The Fifes were enjoying a great season by April 1940. The spectators at some of these matches were treated to thrilling exhibitions of local skaters before the game commenced. The crowds loved every minute of these proceedings. Frank was having a ball playing against some of the teams he used to be a member of. When the Wembley Lions rolled into town he would party with both teams.

The Kircaldy Fifes became involved in the 1939 Scottish ice hockey competition. Frank loved the Scottish countryside and enjoyed having this opportunity to experience it one more time. The Fifes were an excellent team and a great bunch of friends. The team

LIFE WITH FRANK... *The Newspapers*

"WE WANT FRANK NEY."

Frank Ney, Flyer's young defenceman, was on the ice for exactly two minutes in Thursday's game against the (Dundee) Tigers. He was not called upon at all in the first and last periods and his brief appearance took place midway in the second session. Repeatedly during the game there were cries of "We want Frank Ney" from large sections of the supporters which is some indication of the popularity of this young player, who may be lacking in some respects but not in enthusiasm. And, after all he has played his part in Flyer's league success. In the words of one supporter, "Flyers played themselves a man short" and it certainly does seem strange to have any player don his uniform for such a brief appearance on the ice.

The Fife Free Press, Saturday, April 6, 1940

Kirkcaldy Fife Flyers Scottish Champions 1939-1940 Great fame for Frank (third from left), but not a lot of money.

morale got higher with every game they won. There was no stopping the Fifes as they went on to win the championship.

Frank was very proud to have played with the best team in the country. He always held on to a copy of the programs from the games they played in various cities. He dropped them into his suitcase along with the copies of Polish newspaper reviews that showed him in his prime. He wasn't so interested in keeping souvenirs of other teams in other countries. He had weaved his way through so many teams without having the time to develop the comradery the Fifes had. It was this fellowship that meant more to Frank than anything else. Because of this, the Fifes were his number one team for life. The official team photo was the only one that Frank framed and had as a reminder of his prolific and demanding career as a European hockey star from Canada.

Many of the team members remained in touch with Frank over the years and even during the last year of his life he had team mates coming over to stay the weekend with him. Considering that he was only twenty one when they won the championship, he maintained more than a fifty-year friendship with these fellows. His old friends were very special to him. He never lost his passion for hockey and attended as many games by local teams of youngsters as he could over the decades.

Hit the Skies

WHILE IN SCOTLAND he was registered on the unemployment list and got a letter saying that he was being conscripted into the British infantry. Frank had no reservations about contributing his bit to the cause of freedom, but felt that he would make a better pilot than a foot soldier. It made sense because he was already a fully qualified pilot. He jumped the first train to London to sort it all out.

It was Frank's wish that he immediately become a member of the Royal Canadian Air Force. That wasn't to be for most of the war. He had been trained in Britain and he still stood on British soil. The Royal Air Force in Britain needed pilots, and that's where Frank signed his name on the dotted line.

He remembered, "When I went back to join the Air Force again, I never told them that they kicked me out before and I went solo in five hours and flew all through the war."

Bill and Frank Ney... two brothers whose paths always managed to cross.

"There was a lot of luck in it. I remember one squadron, a training squadron, to which we were all posted. Within three weeks nearly all those that went to the low level squadron (flying low level into Holland) were dead. In those days five trips made a tour but most of them never made the five trips. Other ones would get posted to another place where there was nothing going on, but the thing that really impressed me was the courage, the quiet courage that men would, you know, just light a cigarette, put it out and jump in a plane knowing that the odds of coming back were just 50/50.

Very casual. Those guys that were out there, they were good guys. They went in there and risked their lives. They were Canadians that were at the front. Good Canadians that were fighting for their country - Canada. I take my hat off to them 100 per cent."

The Ney family in England was preparing for another major change in their lives. Great Uncle Billy, with whom they had been living, soon passed away. It was time for Ethel and the Major to move on. They found themselves welcome in London with Ethel's relations. The war brought Frank's dad out of his retirement. He ended up serving with the supply and services corps in northern Scotland while Ethel stayed in London and worked in an aircraft factory. She was helping to build the planes that her son was flying. Bill meanwhile joined the Canadian army in England and was serving in France and Italy.

In the last year of the war, Frank finally got his earlier wish and was transferred from the Coastal Command to the Royal Canadian

In the 1940's, girls loved men in uniform – as Frank discovered.

Air Force. He finished his service with the rank of Flight Lieutenant in 1946. His dream of returning to British Columbia after the war helped him through some extremely stressful situations.

Many hours were spent calculating complex navigational problems.

Frank and his colleagues had spent many hours defending British shores and it was felt that some of these pilots needed a change of venue. Frank was soon stationed in Canada where he accepted the position of flight instuctor. Three winters and two summers were spent in the maritine and prarie provinces bringing young pilots to new heights. This also proved to be a stressful position for him.

LIFE WITH FRANK…
Major A. E. Swaine

The last time I saw Frank was in January 1942 when he was Sergt pilot in the RAF awaiting transfer to the RCAF and I was 2 lieut in the Queens Royal Regt on embarkation leave prior to leaving for the Middle East. We went to a dance together in Chelmsford on the last day of my leave and I expect that I saw him at breakfast the following morning.

Frank has always been in a hurry and gave the impression that he was off to put out a fire somewhere. He was a man of considerable charm in very much the same mold as Algy of whom I was very fond. Walking back from that famous dance I remember Frank was full of ideas as to how he could make a fortune after the war. That night he and I were going turkey farming in Alberta or somewhere but that never materialized. It could be said that Frank was feeling homesick. He had a strong sense of nostalgia mixed with a healthy curiosity towards the west. He vowed he would return to Nanaimo.

Major A. E. Swaine, Great Britain

Life with Frank...
Rocky Cameron

I was a student pilot in Weyburn, Saskatchewan - an RAF Station - and Frank was my instructor. He about drove me crazy but it was all done - unbeknownst to me - for a very good reason.

Thanks to Frank's teaching I received my wings and I think I can safely say the reason I got through the rest of my flying career safely.

My wife and I visited with Frank in 1979 and enjoyed a day with him on the Blue Girl. He was one hell of a guy - Per Ardua Ad Astra Frank...

R.G. Cameron "ROCKY"
Ex. Pilot Flying Officer, Auburn, California

Although he was not in direct combat, he strongly felt his responsibility towards the safety of his students.

2745 hours were spent flying. Frank was assessed "Above the Average" as an instructor.

At the outbreak of the war the airlines had been on the verge of providing transatlantic service. With the war over, regular service commenced with the propeller planes making relatively slow and tiring trips. It was a new budding industry and Frank really wanted to get involved as a commercial pilot. He was offered a course with Air Canada that would lead him to the job that he was after, so he went to Winnipeg to await the starting date. The job as co-pilot would pay $800 per month, raised up to $1200 once promoted as a pilot. That was an excellent wage for the late 1940's.

Frank had developed an ulcer during the war. When the Air Canada course started up, so did Frank's ulcer, and he decided not to go through with it. His ulcer was bad enough to land him in a number of military hospitals in different towns before he ended up at Shaugnessy Hospital in Vancouver. This medical condition put an end to the dream Frank had of returning to the world of professional hockey. The war had changed everything for everyone. News of big pre-war hockey stars quickly became old news as people worked to bring their lives back together.

With the war finally over, Bill returned to Winnipeg with the army. When Winston Churchill was voted out, Major Frank Alfonso Ney and his wife also hopped on the next boat back to Canada.

There was plenty of travelling time for Frank to catch up on his reading. By the time he hit the west coast of Canada he had sifted through and let go of many of the books he had read. However, one novel struck him strong enough to gain a firm place in his mind, and in his suitcase amongst his medals and memorabilia.

The Townsman, is the story of a man's life which has a very strong parallel with Frank's. Uprooted from England as a boy, he set out to create the best possible environment in the new world. He put his community first, and over his life time created the best possible environment in which people could settle, work, raise, and educate their children. The townsman was a modest man much like Frank, who had vision and compassion beyond others. His community in return held him in the highest esteem and felt fit to honour him with the dedication of a new school.

With much interest Frank read of the effect that the Townsman had on people. His life was both enhanced and hampered by the demands he had placed upon himself. A local lawyer fell in love with and stole the heart of his wife. The Townsman became a living legend yet rejected the people's dream of a large bronze statue in his honour. During his lifetime he didn't want his physical image to overshadow his message. Fiction is what dreams are made of, and Frank had enough time alone in planes, trains and hospitals to meditate on what was yet to become real.

Frank Ney's Military Career

ROYAL AIR FORCE (Britain)

Oct. 22, 1940 - Jan. 1, 1942

Units: *R.A.F.V.R. / PADGATE / West Kirby / Kenley / Stratford On-Avon / NO 5 ITW Torquay /*
No. 22 EFTS CAMBRIDGE / No. 10 EFTS Weston
No. 4 SFTS CAMBRIDGE / No. 29 EFTS Clyffe
No. 2 PDC WINSTON / Bergenfjord
First recorded flight - May 23, 1941
6 hrs. 30 min. - learning in the Link Trainer
First recorded solo flight - June 2, 1945
10 hrs. 40 min - training in the Tiger Moth
Total RAF flight time - *576 hours 40 minutes*

ROYAL CANADIAN AIR FORCE (Canada)

Jan. 1, 1942 - Mar. 30, 1944

Units: *No 31 P.D.C. Moncton / No 2 Manning - Brandon*
No 31 EFTS Dewinton / No 34 EFTS Assiniboia
No FIs Trenton / No 37 SFTS Calgary
No 41 SFTS Weyburn / No 31 P.D. Moncton

ROYAL CANADIAN AIR FORCE (Britain)

Mar. 30, 1944 - Nov. 2, 1944

Units: *H.M.T.S. Andes / No 1 P.D. West Kirby /*
No 20 AFU Kidlington / No 22 AFU Kidlington
1519 BAT Flight Feltwell / No AFU Weston - on - the green
#3 S of GR Squires Gate / 59 Soon - Ballynessy
Total RCAF Flight Time
2167 Hrs 30 mins as an instructor
plus 40 Hrs 35 mins as a passenger
plus 48 Hrs 35 mins learning in link trainer

Main aircraft flown *DH 82 (GIPSY MAJOR) / HARVARD (WHITNEY PRATT) / TIGER MOTH plus HAGISTER (GIPSY MAJOR) / CORNELL (RANGER) OXFORD (JACOBS) / ANSON (JACOBS)*

Last recorded RCAF flight June 30 1945
on a navigation exercise in a liberator out of Ballykelly

Last recorded flight June 5 1949
in a Cessna around Gabriola Island

Welcome to Nanaimo

Frank Ney didn't like to tell stories of his days spent in military hospitals. His ulcerous stomach wasn't healing quickly. Like many nights in other towns, his first ones back in Nanaimo were spent in a hospital bed. Fate had somehow landed him in the town he had dreamed of returning to. On the surface this little old-fashioned blue collar mining town didn't have much to offer a man who had "conquered" the western world. Frank had been to Paris, New York, Vienna, all the hot spots. He had already seen all the bright lights. So far his adult life had been a fast-paced one. Why would such a man settle in a quiet, unknown corner of the world?

The biggest reason Frank had for staying in Nanaimo was a very simple one. He fell in love with the place. Vancouver Island was basically a pristine natural paradise. A meandering tree-lined road that served as a highway was virtually a paved magic carpet from one spectacular spot to the next. The waters in the many rivers and lakes were swimmable, drinkable, and crawling with fish. Land was cheap and the local people were quite content. Restrictions were few and the Vancouver Islands presented themselves as a picture of opportunity. Frank had seen most of the developed world and instantly recognized the potential of the west coast. Few industries were monopolized. It was all there for the taking.

Frank was an unemployed Veteran with his father's old leather suitcase in hand. This well-used suitcase, with all its stateroom baggage-check stickers exposed for the world to see, had made its last stop. It was a miniature museum of one man's hectic and fiercely competitive existence. Flight log books were now resting with the hockey clipping and programs from days gone by. The suitcase also represented present day survival. Frank's wardrobe was not extensive, but it was all there. These few worldly possessions, and a positive attitude now served as Frank's ammunition in landing on a new career. He had already faced plenty of challenges tougher than that.

Frank Ney A Canadian Legend

Frank was a young man with life experience usually found only in a much older man. One ongoing experience was a communication problem with the Department of Veterans Affairs, which involved the question of his compensation money. He was entitled to receive some, but no one was in a hurry to send any.

The main objective for Frank was to find a place to live

Frank was always good at meeting people and managed to stay a few days here and there. He was certainly not becoming known as one to sit at his friend's house all day and relax. It was summer and the war was over. It was exciting for Frank to have arrived at the place he had spent so much time dreaming about. All he needed now was a job, and his stomachache to go away.

Frank was not the first Ney to inhabit the west coast; in fact real estate was already becoming a family tradition by the time he stepped foot on the Island.

Frank's Uncle Reg, or "Reginald Osbourne Ney" as he was better known, had lived in Africa previously. Like his brothers, he was an army officer during the First World War. It was during this war that he got his first exposure to the dark continent. It had a certain appeal to him and he stayed there after the war.

From 1920 until 1940 Reginald Ney and his wife raised coffee, sugar, and six children in Mombasa, the major seaport for Kenya. The family owned a lot of land in Kenya, and Reg would help secure parcels for other Englishmen who wanted to settle there. When the Second World War broke out, it became apparent that it was not the place for them to live anymore. They crossed the Pacific towards a new life in Vancouver, British Columbia.

This family had only been in Kerrisdale, Vancouver for six months when they heard about a 70-acre farm on Departure Bay Road in a town called Nanaimo. It was time for another move. The Neyland

Road area of Nanaimo then played host to the Neys' chickens, cows and pigs.

During the war, the Japanese residents were all rounded up and interned. When all of their possessions came up for sale, Reg bought one of their fishing boats and added commercial fishing into his life of farming.

The war provided a chance for Reg to sell Victory Bonds. Having a number of incomes allowed him to buy more farms, and as he didn't need this much land for his personal use some of it was sectioned off and sold. The people working on his farm were soon building houses for him. All these collective activities eventually resulted in a real estate company.

A man named Barraclough helped Reg start Bastion Realty. By the time Frank Ney showed up in town, Uncle Reg was rocking and rolling in real estate, insurance, and mortgages, with a new company he named after himself. Nanaimo had basically stood still since the 1890's. With soldiers now returning from overseas, it was the perfect time to start selling land. None of this was a big surprise for Frank. He had visited his uncle during his first trips to the coast. This time around Frank arrived with plenty of experience in general sales. He knew his way around an office.

One thing Frank had never sold was land. This didn't worry him or his uncle, who offered the young man a job. The office was right in the center of town and not too far away from the dairy. Frank was drinking as much milk as he could to soothe his ulcerous stomach. Everyone noticed right away what a great salesman Frank was. Naturally Uncle Reg was glad to have such an energetic fellow on his team.

R.O. Ney himself was a very persistent salesman. He never gave up on anything. His clients became his friends, and his boating companions. The fish boat doubled as pleasure boat for real estate clients until it was sold and replaced by a cruiser that was better suited for the purpose.

LIFE WITH FRANK... *Hugh Ney*

He used to come out to our house on Neyland Road and he and I used to play checkers. I was only about 7 years old or so. He'd start beating me so I'd say "let's switch to 'giveaway'." He'd start beating me at giveaway so I'd say "let's switch to checkers." By this kind of means I sometimes beat him but of course he was a lot smarter than I was.

Hugh Ney, son of R.O. Ney

Frank later explained that in those days you could buy a lot in the very best district of Nanaimo for $500, with city water. If you went three more blocks and dug a well you could buy a lot for $50.You could buy brand new homes for $4500-5000 at 4 ½ per cent interest.

A three bedroom home that today would sell in the neighbourhood of $200, 000 listed for $6500 in the late 40's This type of house had a full basement, hardwood floors, everything a person could want. A brand new smaller house would sell for $3300. Frank would take home half of the 5% commission he would earn on these types of sales.

LIFE WITH FRANK... *Bob Grey*

Frank and Bill and I worked in the office of R.O. Ney. We were the three salesmen there. Frank was on leave from the army, I don't think that at that time he had accepted his discharge, or if he had he hadn't gotten around to buying civilian clothes. He was still wearing his uniform when he was selling for awhile.

Bob Grey,Retired

Welcome to Nanaimo

Frank found himself a place to sleep at the Vendome Rooms on the top floor of the building that stood where the Royal Bank now stands on Commercial Street. This was right across the street from the office of R.O. Ney. All he had to do was wake up each morning and continue where he left off the day before. He found his new work to be "just as challenging and renumerative as flying Air Canada." Frank had landed on the career that would fuel his drive through life. "In those days," he said, "you just had to sign an application and you became a salesman." This presented the first opportunity for Frank to be mentioned in a Canadian newspaper.

CANADA'S VANCOUVER ISLAND

Retire In Paradise Retreat At Low Cost

Your land and home, your security. New, fully modern 4 room bungalows, near sea. $3700. Write us today for particulars on our exclusive seashore orchard estate subdivision. Located on a beautiful panoramic setting in one of the loveliest parts of the island.

R. O. NEY & CO. Real Estate and Insurance
Nanaimo B.C. (Recognized Island Property Specialists)

Our representative Frank J. Ney
will be at St. Charles Hotel until December 10th.

It was determined that Frank's ulcer was not going to heal on its own, and in an operation that may not have been necessary today, half of Frank's stomach was removed. The doctor told him to stay in bed for a whole week and not do anything. Frank had other ideas and immediately arranged for two telephones to be installed by his bed. There was business to be done and there was no time like the present. The doctor was not impressed when he discovered this. He was remarkably quick at removing the phones from the room.

This was the beginning of Frank's crusade in which he invited his friends to share in the healthy benefits of drinking buttermilk everyday. He was generally never a very big eater after his operation.

R.O. kept Frank working by directing his potential clients right to his hospital bed. The letters Uncle Ronnie sent out to potential clients helped set the course for the massive post-war expansion experienced on the west coast. It is funny to think that B.C. didn't simply sell itself back then as it certainly does now. Sending a letter (such as the one below) to someone who might be interested in buying a house in such an unknown place as Vancouver Island seems rather quaint today.

Capt. H. J. Chandler,
R.C.O.C.Fort Osborne
Barracks,Officers' Mess,
Winnipeg, Man.

Dear Sir:

I have to thank you for your favour of the 27th ultimo. I am having a few of our listings prepared for dispatch, but I am writing to let you know that we are One Hundred per cent a Veterans' Firm, and that one of our members is now in Deer Lodge Hospital, Winnipeg, and if you can possibly get out to see him, I'm sure he will give you some interesting information. I am referring to my nephew F/ Lt., Frank J. Ney.

I am quite sure that we will have no difficulty in finding you a small place where you can retire. May I seriously suggest that you consider being out here by the sea where you will get better fishing than you will be able to find in the lakes. As you probably realize, the Gulf of Georgia, with its hundreds of islands, provides sheltered water and such a place cannot be found anyplace in the world. I would also like to point out that the climate on the Island is far superior to that of the mainland and the best climate on the Island is between Maple Bay and Nanaimo.

When you write next time, will you please let me know if you are prepared to utilize four or five acres in any way, or, if it is your desire to retire completely. You are probably aware that both chickens and turkeys do very well out here and they are profitable, particularly on the island.

Hoping to have the pleasure of hearing from you again in the near future, and Wishing you Compliments of the Season.

Yours very truly,
R. O. Ney

Once Frank was out of the hospital he found that he also enjoyed taking people out in his uncle's boat. He would take his nephews and nieces as well as clients for a cruise. Of course it was not all work and no play for Ney. He was a very eligible bachelor and many of the women around town had noticed the ex-pilot.

A little sailboat caught Frank's eye one day. He bought it and started taking some of his girlfriends out sailing. The boat was small enough that Frank had to yell "Duck!" when the boom swung by. One girl lowered her head but accidently raised her backside in the air at the same time. As the boom swung by, it hit her in the behind and she flew out into the ocean. This however, didn't scare other girls away from sailing with Frank.

Business was going well for R.O. Ney and he was ready to expand. It was mainly people from the Canadian prairies coming to the west coast that were buying properties. Frank saw what kind of money was being pulled in. But more than this he had a vision of what could be accomplished with the inevitable expansion of the town. Both his father and brother were now living in Nanaimo and working with him under the eye of his uncle. Frank was a top-notch salesman, capable of handling every end of a transaction. He had in one way or another been giving and taking orders over the entire duration of his adult life. When his uncle had expansion on his mind, Frank had other ideas.

Frank was no longer interested in working for other people. He was 27 and ready to do his own thing. After barely a year in with his uncle, he decided to start his own business. Bill and the Major, who had also been working with R.O. Ney, had to decide if they were going to go with Frank or stay with the old company. With Reg they were employees, and did not have the money to buy him out. With Frank they would have a ground floor position on everything. Meanwhile, Reg, with ailing health, wasn't aware of what was in the making.

After signing a lease for an office across the street and investing ten postwar dollars in a business licence, Frank was ready to open the doors to his new company, Nanaimo Realty.

LIFE WITH FRANK...

Ken Gogo

I remember the first time I met Frank. I was still in high school and was having one of those legendary White Owl hamburgers with my friend Ted Jeffs, who was the "chef" at his little coffee shop in the Eagle building where the Spirit-wood book shop is today.

Frank came in the door and sat next to me, extending his hand and introducing himself. He was wearing his R.C.A.F. greatcoat over his suit. Only the buttons had been changed. He informed me that he was working for his uncle R.O. Ney whose real estate and insurance office was next door where the Commercial beer parlour is now. Frank went on to say that his uncle had suggested that he go across the street and rent the vacant office next to the Lotus Hotel, as their office was too small. Frank said that halfway across the street he had the idea to perhaps rent the space himself and start his own company. What I witnessed next was to become a typical Frank Ney routine in later years. He would get an idea while walking down the street, stop for a cup of coffee and ask the person next to him what he or she thought of the idea. My reply to his question was: "If you think Nanaimo needs another real estate office, why not go for it."

Only drinking half his coffee, he stood up, shook my hand and said, "Thanks Kenny," and was off and out the door to give birth to Nanaimo Realty.

Ken Gogo

Nanaimo Realty was also the name of a company that had been in business before the turn of the century, but the former owner had died and the name was up for grabs. Bill joined Frank in the new venture and it wasn't long before the Major stepped in as a senior director and foreman of the insurance division. By December 1945 they all had titles and had incorporated themselves as a company. They were excited to be setting up business in this small town. None of them expected it to be small forever.

The Neys invested a few more dollars in a kerosene heater that barely managed to keep the winter chill out of the office. They rarely ever removed their overcoats. Bill made the company's only sale in the first month of operation. A retired prairie farmer bought both a house and a cottage for $2400 and the Neys collectively earned $50 commission.

Nanaimo Realty was located in a smallish, cramped office in the old Lotus Hotel where the Royal Bank on Bastion Street is now. Bill and the Major did all the typing, but Frank never touched a typewriter. Being a "neat freak", he would take out the vacuum cleaner everyday at 5 p.m. He also liked the public relations part of the business and spent what time he could greeting people at the door. These were work habits that everyone lived with for many years to follow. Frank was terribly excited at having the opportunity to put his talents to work in a new business. He had lived out his worst nightmares during the war and he now felt that it was all clear sailing. He wasn't worried about making mistakes or being laughed at. In fact he wasn't worried about anything. He was a survivor dedicated to seeing his visions come to life.

R.O. Ney was not thrilled about his relatives jumping ship. He had wanted the new office for himself, and was the one who had told Frank about it being available. He felt that he had helped Frank out by giving him his start and was quite upset when he realized that his preferred arrangement was not a permanent one. He was sad to see everyone go. Reg gave up his real estate firm and concentrated more on his farming until he moved to Victoria.

By the time Frank's new business was rolling he had spoken before the commissioners with the department ofVeterans Affairs and successfully managed to have some cheques issued in his name. It had been a year of hard work for the new company. It took a while to build up to the point where there was steady money coming in. However, everyone kept a positive attitude and a sense of humour through it all. With the Neys on the Island, it would never be the same again!

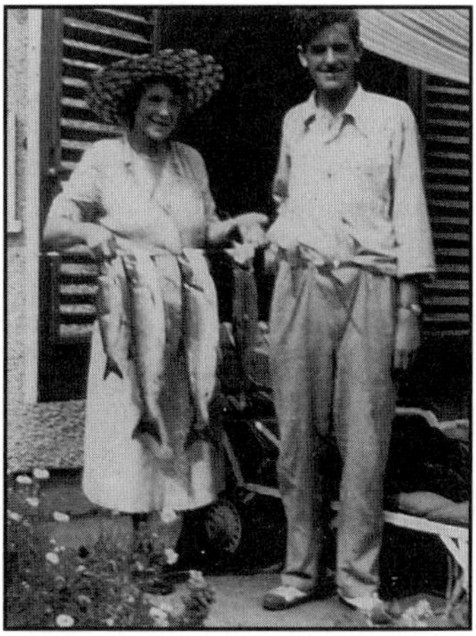

Bringing home fresh salmon to Mom. They indulged in activities not common place for prairie folks.

After working together for three years, the Ney brothers were able to buy a fully furnished house for their parents to live in. Frank had been staying at rooming and boarding houses. He was not ready to settle into any one place and decided that it would be beneficial to all concerned for him to stay with the folks for a while in the new house.

The Ney family had finally settled into a house that would see them through past retirement. Frank was meeting plenty of new people and would often bring them by to see the folks. His new friends would be introduced as "Ambassador of Switzerland," or any other title that danced its way into Frank's imagination. It wasn't long before Frank started to pool his earnings with his friends and found a nice $4500 house on Kennedy Street to speculate on. " I found as a salesman with no training at all I was making as much money as I would as a pilot." It wasn't long before he had a share in a few houses around town.

Uncle Fred joined the Neys living in Nanaimo and Uncle Reg started Victoria Realty and Newstead Realty up Island. Reg never really did retire. Frank did come to an understanding with his uncle and they referred clients to each other up until one month before Reg's death in 1967.

A big jolly fellow named Jim Goodwin moved from Vancouver to Nanaimo in 1948. An advertisement from a marine towing outfit looking for an accountant brought him over to the Island for work. Jim's wife and Frank's wife-to-be both worked for a common lawyer friend. With Frank they became one big group of friends. Jim and Frank became pals for life. They were the kind of friends that could, and did, trust each other to the end.

In 1949 Bill met a girl across the street from the office. Her name was Mary Eby and she soon changed it to Mary Ney. She is a very pleasant and cheerful lady. Bill was always a much more conservative man his brother Frank. He and Jim Goodwin became the much needed stabilizing elements in Frank's life over the years. Frank's ambitions were often very grand, and someone needed to be there to help him with the details.

Frank's first subdivision was the result of a deal he made in 1950. Mr. Wilson was an old prairie farmer who owned five acres on Waddington Road, close to where he lived. The old fellow offered to sell it to one man who in turn had to refuse because he was starting a business at the time. Frank heard about this and stepped into the picture.

Frank's gang was pretty wild. They used to tell a story about Frank driving to Victoria at about 100 miles per hour and shaving at the same time. They said that he couldn't fly his plane anymore so he had to fly his car!

Anonymous

The total purchase price of the lot was $5000. Frank put $500 down and arranged the balance on terms with the vendor. He subdivided into 66' x 132' city lots. Prices had gone up considerably over the turn of the decade and the market value of these lots was around $500 to $700 apiece. Frank loved the idea of being able to make money by helping to fill a growing demand for building lots. Once the project was completed he was out looking for another one.

I was one of the original announcers at CHUB radio back in '49. In my travels I would go in and ask people for advertising on the radio station and all that. That's pretty well where I met Frank. He was a very friendly fellow anyway and was nodding to me even before then.

LIFE WITH FRANK...
Gordon Theedom

When I left the radio station in 1951 I began to work for him selling real estate. He's a workaholic, as you know.

Frank used to take a lot of his customers to the IXL dairy, especially if they had young kids, to have an ice cream cone.

He was in there himself a lot having a milk shake or something. This was instead of going for a coffee in the hot summertime.

He tested us a couple of times on this one: He would come in to the office, I don't know where he got this bright idea but he'd slap the top of the counter as he came around the corner and say, "We're going to start having half-days off. Beginning right now we're all going to have a half day off from real estate."

I said, "How can we do that, Frank? We're all busy here." He said, "Gord, you take the rest of the day off." I told him, "Frank, it's 3:15 now! That's not much of an afternoon off." He said "Well, take it off and next week you'll have a full afternoon off."

We started the new program where we all got half days off and it went on for about two weeks. Next thing you know we were getting phone calls at home on our half days off asking if we were coming back down: "We got some work here for you to do." So we end up back at the office again.

After he did that for about three weeks he came into the office, slapped the counter and said, "We're going to start these half days off again." I'll be damned if he didn't go through the same thing. He told one of the other fellows that time. It was 3:15 again. He must have got the idea from somebody at the ice cream place. I don't know where he got the idea. After a while we all gave up on the idea. There was always that smile on his face when he came up with this new idea, "Half-days off!" He was so serious about it each time.

He was the best guy to work for. Easy going. Nice sense of humor, just the best.

Gordon Theedom,
one of the first Nanaimo Realty Employees

Some salesmen really weren't making much money back then. It was a difficult time because of the huge areas of houses that had well water. It was hard to sell these houses, especially in the summertime. There were about 44 salesmen in town showing people these houses. The houses that did sell were more often than not through Nanaimo Realty, and the salesmen credited what success they had to Frank's leadership.

Frank himself was starting to turn a good profit. He had a very well-established car and house insurance business. He and Bill were actively selling real estate, and Frank did particularly well because he got on with people so well. It was nothing special to see him out selling at 10 or 11 at night. He was. He was on the go at all times.

The Major was carrying much more than just his own weight. He knew his insurance and his real estate inside and out, and was a great office manager.Contrary to his reputation he was found to be very

LIFE WITH FRANK...

Murray Barbour

I moved to Nanaimo in September 1951 to open an automotive wholesale business. All the money was in the business so I tried to rent. Nanaimo was in the throes of industrial development and there was nothing to rent. One shack had a dirt floor, there were a couple others but nothing liveable. I saw a house opposite the old golf course on Wakesiah so we stopped by and some old gent said, "it's for sale with Ney at Nanaimo Realty." So down we go to the office and at that time it was opposite the frontier building, just a long narrow office and the complete staff was Frank, his brother Bill, his dad, a girl receptionist and one salesman, Gordon Theedom. Frank showed us the house, forgot the keys so he went in the window with a ladder.

We play golf and we like the house. I said, "Frank, I can't buy it. All the money's in the business. We'd like to rent it." Frank said he'd talk to the owner and see. The owner did not want to rent.

Frank was good at finding answers and getting to the bottom of things. Problems never seemed too great to him. He said, "Do you own your car?" I said yes. He said, "Car companies are getting into the lease business. See if you can sell your car and lease one. Then you will have money for a down payment." With Frank's perseverance he said, "If that's not enough money, I'll carry a second." In other words he found some way to make the deal. I sold my car and leased one. We raised our family in that house. He always referred to the wife and I as the "Love birds" up till the day he died. The reason was because when we went up the ladder he said, "Just like love birds going into the nest."

Murray Barbour

---

funny. The salesmen found him to be as humourous as Frank but in a much more quiet manner. The old fellow, having travelled all over the world, and having served in both world wars must have had plenty of great stories to tell as he sat behind his desk in a wheelchair.

Frank enjoyed going out and selling real estate, but it was also his responsibility to ensure that there was product available to be sold. It only made sense that he hire more salesmen and concentrate on providing listings. Because he couldn't afford to hire more staff until the company had more to offer, it was time for the new company to raise the capital needed for expansion.

The company found the opportunity to take a big step forward when Frank spotted a large subdivision being designated in the Woodlands part of town. Another company had initiated this 50 or 60 house development but couldn't pull the whole thing together. Frank, Bill and the Major still had no staff other than a couple of salesmen. They knew it would mean a hefty workload if they were to take on this project. Frank wasn't worried about this; in fact he thrived on it.

Frank's biggest responsibility was to raise the money needed for the project. He then hired an engineer and a surveyor to lay it all out. A bulldozer was hired to blast the roads in and a lawyer was contacted to file a subdivision plan. Now the salesmen would have something to sell. It was a big project for Frank and the boys to take over, but they did and it made them a much bigger company.

The properties in the Woodlands subdivision sold very easily when they breezed onto the market. The key to success in this venture lay in the fact that it had its own water system. There was one central well that fed blocks of houses. There was always water pressure because Frank made a point of showing up at midnight every night to prime the pump.

The real estate game was very simple for Frank. He would find a large piece of choice land and suggest to a number of people that they put up enough money to buy it. Frank would take care of the subdividing and selling. This was happening more and more often. Around 1952 he had his eye on a waterfront lot on Departure Bay that stretched all the way up to the highway. This became Beach Estates and Frank didn't pass up the opportunity to buy a waterfront lot on Beach Drive when it hit the market. The home by the sea that Frank imagined was one big step closer.

With all these new areas opening up, some salesmen were starting to make as much money as the average doctor. This was before the independent companies became involved in the multiple listing service and commissions were still 5%. Frank was rolling a lot of his own money back into the company in the way of advertising. There were five or so other companies in town doing basically the same thing and Frank wanted to be on top.

There was a ten piece big band playing at the Pigmy Ballroom downtown every Saturday night. Frank would always be there dancing up a storm. He loved the music and the chance to meet new people. It was in the best interest of his business to be mixing in the community. More important than that he was a raving socialite by nature. He had already wooed the girls on the dance floors of the big cities and knew all the possible graces by the time he blended into the small town social scene. He usually showed up wherever people would gather.

Still relatively new to the west coast, Frank was actively seeking all types of involvement with the community. He wanted to enhance community life and became a volunteer for various organizations.

One of his favorite projects was the Salvation Army Christmas Cheer. He would raise money, food, and toys for the less fortunate. Every year he would help assemble hampers and personally deliver

LIFE WITH FRANK...

Alice Faganello

I first saw Frank Ney on Christmas Eve 1953 or 1954. I was working at Grassick's Jewellers. That afternoon we saw a congo line of maybe eight to ten people coming across the street, extending Christmas wishes to all they met. The line came in one door of Grassick's and out the other. I asked, "Who was that?" I was told by Marg and Mr. Grassick, "Frank Ney and his staff, he has a realty office across the street."

Alice Faganello

them around town. During the deliveries he would acquaint himself with many people who would tell him stories. It was his experiences with these people that made it all worthwhile to him. Soon he was delivering groceries in person. Frank couldn't stand to see people unhappy in such a prosperous age, and the smile he would receive when he handed over a bag of food to a stranger made him feel that much better. He never lost touch with the fact that not everyone's lives were as fortunate as his.

Early into its conception Nanaimo Realty took full advantage of the promotional benefits of initiating and supporting community projects. Often Frank would take things one step further than other sponsors and ensure better press coverage for himself. It is against the rules for the driver of a soapbox to get any help during a derby, but Frank defied this in a publicity stunt. He squeezed inside one of the little home-made racing cars and got got an extra push from a friend as he rode along with the kids in a warm-up run. It was still outrageous enough to see a grown man in a soapbox derby and that was all it took to get B.C. wide newspaper coverage in 1954. Newspaper editors loved that kind of thing back then and gave Frank a chance to mention that he was taking four boys to the B.C. derby "to keep the eyes of the thousands attending on the city of Nanaimo." Frank wasn't just selling his projects, he was selling the town.

As a social worker in Nanaimo during the early 1950's, each Christmas I was there, Frank Ney, privately and quietly donated a number of Christmas hampers to our office requesting they be delivered anonymously to families in need.

Jean Hannon

Once Frank got out of the driver's seat to let the 15 year old Ray Biggs behind the wheel, Nanaimo Realty soapbox went on to win the B.C. championship. The teenager then moved on to Akron, Ohio for the international derby. Frank was warming up for a lifetime of promoting community events for fun, charity and publicity.

Nanaimo has for decades had the honour of having the oldest consecutive Empire Day celebration in Canada. Frank saw an opportunity to make some favourable press while doing something he truly enjoyed and believed in. He became involved in organizing events for the annual spring festivals. As his enthusiasm grew he became the Chairman of the Junior Chamber of Commerce (Jaycees), which handled the Empire Day festivities. His position quickly elevated to that of the Chairman of the Empire Day Committee, a position he took very seriously. He decided to make the Empire Day celebrations bigger than they had ever been.

A big celebration needed some new ideas. Frank organized a "babies parade." Mothers with gaily coloured prams filled the street. The World Championship Corn-on-the-cob Contest followed. Each contestant was allowed 15 minutes to eat as many cobs as possible. The cobs were then closely inspected by the judges. This "extravaganza of all extravaganzas" promised to have "something doing every single moment of Empire Day." The city was designed to be a mecca for those who enjoyed fun.

Large crowds were predicted and expected. Newspapers advertised the events throughout the province, while radio stations gave a round-the-clock build up. The ferries changed their schedules to Vancouver Island in the hope of a strong turnout.

Up to his eyebrows organizing the Empire Days events for 1955. Frank arranged for films to be shown outdoors at night.

The May Empire Day celebrations drew crowds of 45, 000 people from all over Vancouver Island in the mid-1950's. Downtown Nanaimo was literally filled with people. What was the big fuss? People were proud to celebrate their roots. There was plenty of activity to keep the large crowds happy over the four days. The National Bicycle Marathon was a hit, as was the International Logger Sports. The television cameras were on hand to capture the soapbox races and foot race. There was also a salmon derby complete with a barbeque on Newcastle Island where 500 pounds of salmon was consumed. An elegant show at the arena combined ballet, fashion, motorama, music and beauty contest.

As with every year, the May Queen was crowned and a big parade with well over 100 entries went through town. There was music everywhere. Nine bands, numbering more than 500 musicians, filled the streets. These celebrations would be topped off with record-breaking enthusiastic crowds cheering on musical guests such as The Fabulous Dorsey Brothers at the Civic Arena.

The only problem Frank faced in making the Empire Day shows so successful was in making them even bigger the next year. He was overjoyed one day when the Canadian Broadcasting Corporation called. The CBC had been noticing what great results these festivities were yielding and decided to give the event full TV and radio coverage. Movie theatres were still honouring a long set tradition of showing newsreels of current events before movie shows. Unlike today, where captive audiences preview commercials for other movies, 1950's patrons were shown Empire Days celebrations. The Associated Screen News was represented alongside the CBC during the filming of the events. Frank was initiating a long and prolific relationship with the CBC, and the world media in general. He made friends out of reporters.

And there was plenty to report. Danny Sailor, a proud logger, did acrobatics atop a 80' spar tree. It was thrilling! One soapbox driver had his brake cable snap, narrowly missing several people, a telephone pole, and a car before he safely crashed between two trucks. The crowds for the scheduled events were so large that people had to move off their standing ground to let the train go by. Cars filled the streets, making traffic come to a complete halt. Frank's promotions created some of the earliest recorded ferry backlogs in the Island's history.

It was Frank's style to give them a bit of the old and a bit of the new. Nanaimo had never at any point been the location for a fireworks display. Frank changed that by launching the first fireworks display into the sky over the town he loved. This was such a delight for the people that it became an event that was to be held twice every year. Frank helped keep the fire in the sky by directing some Nanaimo Realty cash towards the cause each time.

It was very expensive to set this all up. In 1955 Frank said, "We figure we broke even or even made a little money. We made a profit on every event we produced but each cost us a lot of money." There had to be an admission to most events. Small towns like Nanaimo were not equipped to deal with big crowds. There was no outdoor stadium that could hold 5000 people for a show and that resulted in almost half of them getting in for free or viewing from a hillside. To organize security to block all possible ways of entering the Caledonian grounds was too much to add to the existing work load. This factor, combined with the number of free events that needed attention, brought down the cash earning potential of this venture considerably. It is amazing that the whole thing somehow broke even year after year.

Early in his career, Frank studied for and passed his Notary examinations. This enabled him to present himself as a Notary Public, a role he played for the rest of his career. In this capacity he was qualified to handle legal work connected with real estate transactions, wills and other works of a legal nature, with the exception of appearing in court. Frank was one of the few to be commissioned in this capacity in B.C. since 1947. By the mid 1950's he was appointed vice-president for Central and Upper Vancouver Island for the B.C. Society of Notaries. There is much evidence to suggest that Frank never charged any individual a fee for his services as a notary. He may have charged corporations, but he certainly gave the little guy a break. Frank made large chunks of money on bigger deals and found that his personal relationship with clients improved by not worrying about $5 here and there.

Clients were wanting to invest their money with Frank because he was obviously quite successful. Gone were the days when he actively searched out people with money. He was rolling in projects with a perfectly clean track record.

He used to answer sometimes two or three phone calls at the same time. He used to watch what was happening in the office, take one call, take another call and not lose track of anything.

Allan Deering
Nanaimo Realty 1952-65

The only people in town who had not heard of Frank Ney were the ones who didn't read newspapers or go out much. Almost everyone had some kind of an opinion about him. The 35 year-old Frank was well dressed, handsome and successful and his social life was a very complete one. He was free to carry on as he pleased and was becoming known to some as the "Playboy" of Nanaimo. When he told his buddies about his plans to marry, there were shock waves. Nanaimo's confirmed bachelor was ready to tie the knot.

One thing that almost everyone could agree on was that they couldn't imagine Frank being married with kids. People were placing bets that he was not going to go through with it. This was all in jest of course. Everyone wanted him to be happy and to have all the kids he wanted.

Jocelyn Floyer had shown more than just a little interest in Frank. The date was set, and on Dec. 31, 1953, she was to become a bride. When the New Year's bells had sounded, the happy couple were husband and wife.

The Neys bought a little house on Holly Street and awaited the arrival of their first child. Frank loved the Gulf Islands so much that he intended to name his children after them. Jocelyn worked with the idea and on Oct. 8, 1955, Frank Decourcey Ney entered their lives. They were overjoyed.

Welcome to Nanaimo

It was the perfect beginning to a storybook 1950's family. The Neys were soon to move into their custom built six bedroom waterfront house on Departure Bay. It was a picturesque neighbourhood; the result of Frank's vision as a developer. It was here that the Neys were blessed over and over again with elevan children. Bradley Cortez Ney, Peter Pender Ney, and Todd Douglas Ney all carry middle names rumoured to be synonymous with the local island each was conceived on. Almost all the girl's middle names are Lynn; Jocelyn's last syllable.

For several years I was cleaning lady for Jocelyn, his wife. They were very kind to me - I worked all day Fridays and all day on Saturdays, and often missed my bus from Beach Drive to home. Frank would see me walking towards town and pick me up and drive me to the south end. Frank and Jocelyn gave me a turkey each year, and imagine my surprise when he himself delivered a 26 lb. bird for me and my three sons! Wonders never ceased where he was concerned!

Anonymous

Family life didn't change Frank's life in the community at all. He was becoming a better public speaker through his involvement with the Toastmasters and was actively seeking more things to get involved with. The Jaycees didn't stop after the Empire Days Events. They were busying themselves in many areas during the '50's.

Under Frank's direction a United Nation's Ball was presented to the community and attended by representatives of every national and racial group in the city and surrounding area. The overcapacity crowd listened to a variety of excellent speakers tell of democracy, co-operation and peace. Frank, as master of ceremonies, led the guests towards dinner and raffles. Instrumental as well as vocal music from all points of the globe was performed by many of the guests. Traditional dances in colourful ethnic costumes enhanced the musical numbers. Scottish dancers made way for square dancers, and so the evening took yet another interesting twist. It was a wonderful way to welcome the new Canadian immigrants into a friendly society.

Mr. Ney went out of his way to make new citizens feel welcome. He also made them feel important and part of this city.

Marina Whiting
Central Vancouver Island Multicultural Society

There were a lot of parties in those days. These community events were certainly visible and available to everyone. For his good work Frank received a life membership in the sente of the international Jaycees, the highest honour that can be bestowed on a member.

The strength of his involvement with community groups provided him with a platform to publicly air his concerns. One day he saw a group of hunters passing through the golf course where children were playing cowboys and indians. The idea of men with loaded guns looking for something to shoot so close to kids playing didn't sit very well with Frank. He was aware that people were within their legal rights to shoot anywhere outside of the outskirts of the city. Since the city's boundaries were very narrow at the time, all anyone had to do was visit an outlying district such as Departure Bay and shoot away. There was no stopping people who wanted to use Frank's subdivisions as target ranges. Frank believed, however,that B.C.'s shooting laws were completely outdated. He outlined what inadequacies he saw and made the politicians and populace aware of what had to be done. He was determined to bring the west coast up to modern world standards.

Mr. Ney and his Jaycees worked hard to make their projects resounding successes. He spent hours on the phone instructing people and many more scribbling words to the papers in his file. The efforts of the committee did not go unnoticed. Frank soon had more than enough press clippings to fill a scrapbook. This book soon fell apart and the pages gradually shuffled into a huge pile of clippings that collected over a period of 50 years.

Polar Bear Swim

NANAIMO B.C. IS SITUATED NORTH of the 49th parallel of latutude. This positioning on the globe makes for some nice ocean swimming in sheltered spots during the summer. The simple fact is that anyone would have to be crazy to swim in the ocean in the winter. It's freezing in there! Not many people would take a casual winter dip; that is until Frank got the idea to make it extra fun!

The famous Mississippi Gambler suit. Coaxing people into freezing water helped sell real estate.

Frank is credited as being the originator of the Boxing Day Polar Bear Swim. Vancouver had long before hosted a New Year's Day Swim and the madness managed to sweep across to the chilly winter waters of Nanaimo. There were no big prizes offered, no incentive or carrot waived in the public's face at all. Frank just announced that at a certain time anyone who felt so inclined could jump into the ocean. These people had been living by the sea for a long time before Frank ever came along and told them to jump in it. It takes a master to pull that one off. The funny thing is that nobody who ever participated ever regretted the experience!

In 1957, Departure Bay was the setting for the big icy splash. It was a great source of annual publicity for Nanaimo Realty ,which put the event together. Besides all that, Frank suggested that it was a good way to "clear any cobwebs from Christmas."

Everyone was invited to join in on the fun. All that was required of a participant was the willingness to show up with bathing attire and register. For some it was easy to run with the mob into the chilly Pacific waves. Some ran out of the water faster that they ran in, while others managed to endure the coldness of it all.

Frank, dressed in his old-fashioned Mississippi Gambler outfit with the top hat, kindly advised the participants not to throw any snowballs at the killer whales. There was no equal warning issued about the Hawaiian dancers tossing bananas into the crowd. These dancing girls had survived a crash course with the Bea Mcleod School of Dance as the initial swim was organized. That was before Marie and Ann Gogo were born into the world of Gogo dancing and became another fixture of the event. The rest is hula history.

Frank just loved it when the bands and bagpipes and everything was going at the same time. The more the better! He would drag out the opening ceremony stuff so long that the swimmers would be so cold as they waited that the water seemed warm by the time thay hit it!

Brad O'Neil

The one person who never did enter the chuck was the host himself. Frank was far too busy to be out there freezing in the ocean. He stood on the platform and handed out straw hats or other souvenirs for each swimmer to take home. In the later years he plunked one or two silver dollars into each shivering hand. There is no doubt that Frank handed out and tossed thousands of pounds of bananas to people over the years. Nor is there any calculating how many silver dollars he awarded to people over his lifetime.

The swim was, and still is an exciting and unusual sight for the spectators to behold, as they munch on complimentary hot dogs and sip on cocoa. A huge bonfire would burn as white flanneled cricketers played a match nearby. A flatbed trailer served as band stand, podium and a grand base for imitation palm trees.

I put on the fireworks in the harbor for years. Frank put together the Polar Bear Swim and asked me, "Fred, how about you looking after a big bonfire down there." So we did that. I would gather up wood from all over hell. It had to be dry so you could get it going. We went out to the lumber yard and everywhere else. We'd get a good truck load. Can't have the ice freeze them you know!

Fred Dorman

People as young as babies and as old as their 70's and 80's have made the mad dash into the chilly chuck. The odd daring swimmer would stay in for half an hour until Frank seriously urged otherwise over his trusty megaphone. Frank would count the number of swimmers and the newspaper reporters would print that figure, occasionally suggesting that it could be divided by 8 or 9. It is true that two or three hundred people would go for the dip but Frank enjoyed the bigger numbers. It was all for fun anyway.

These chilly swims became a winter tradition and were always organized the moment before they happened. Frank would spend a private Christmas Day at home with his family and then get on the phone and let his friends know what they had to do. It is remarkable how these events flew together with so little fuss. Everyone had fun. After a couple hours wear on his megaphone, Frank would then head off for the ski hill. The odd lucky year he would get snowed in on Green Mountain, where the old logging road with its 28 per cent grades and switchback turns were not navigable in all weather conditions. That's when Frank would get on the radiophone and tell the press what wonderful skiing was taking place.

The Post-War Boom Continues

HOT WEATHER ALSO BROUGHT OPPORTUNITIES for publicity stunts. Frank started to play a private game with himself by seeing how often he could get in the newspaper. One summer day he tried for 20 minutes to fry an egg on the sidewalk. He loved to make public statements about the tropical weather, but no luck faced him as the egg sat on the pavement. No omelet was to be had, but newspaper articles rewarded his efforts.

All of this press was great for Frank's business. He had firmly established himself as a well-known personality around town. Nanaimo had not grown very much as a city during the coal mining era. From 1890 to 1950 there was not a major change in residential housing. But now for the first time in years, growth was predicted and a real estate boom was beginning to be felt.

One of the fastest growing industries at that time was one which endeavored to predict how the economy was shaping up. Thousands of Canadian firms were specializing in economic forecast. The newspapers were full of this stuff and Frank thought it was all quite funny. His sense of humour was not at all lost on such dry topics. He liked to confuse the issue by submitting his own economic forecast for publication:

"The commerce department reports sales and income figures show an easing up of the rate at which business is easing off, which is taken as proof of the government's contention that there is a slowing up of the slowdown. A slowing up of the slowdown is not as good as an upturn in the downturn, but is good deal better than either a speedup of the slowdown or a deepening of the downturn and does suggest the climate is about right for an adjustment to the readjustment.

Turning to unemployment, we find a definite decrease in the rate of increase, which clearly shows there is a letting up of the letdown. Of course, if the slowdown should speed up, the decrease on the rate of increase of unemployment would turn into an increase in the rate of decrease of employment. In other words, the deceleration would be accelerated.

But the indicators suggest rather a levelling off, followed by a gentle pickup, rather than a faster pick up, a slowdown of the pickup, and finally, a levelling off again of the pickup."

People were spending more money. They had just come out of a major depression and a major war and were now buying fancier cars, washing machines and better homes. There was more disposable income, more income in general. Nanaimo was experiencing large-scale buying. Frank had predicted this wave and had set up his business well to deal with it.

By banding local merchants and land owners together, Frank was attempting to solve parking problems in the downtown area as new cars filled the old streets. Nanaimo had experienced unprecedented real estate sales of $5,000,000 in 1955 and the numbers were rising still. With eight subdivisions totaling 600 to 700 lots in town, Frank commented, "The town is going ahead and nothing can stop it."

Bank loans had been increasing until it got to the point where the banks had little or no margin over their statutory reserve requirements with which to make loans. The banks were simply running out of money to lend people. The Bank of Canada had increased its money supply from time to time but was unwilling to do so during the summer of 1959. Frank understood that a tightening up of credit from time to time offset the danger of runaway inflation, but was unhappy with the drastic curbs on loans. People certainly couldn't buy Frank's houses without bank loans. He told the press that the curbs were "so drastic that they could easily have a most damaging effect on the economy of this country." He continued:

"The unfortunate part of it is that the little man will be much harder hit than the big outfits that are in a better position to stand the financial drought.

Closing down on credit to this extent, I feel is wrong, in view of steadily increasing population whose monetary needs are expanding day to day. I feel there should be more middle of the road thinking. If the men who call the shots on monetary policy were affected in the same way that the small contractor or businessmen is, I wonder if they would make the same decisions."

Even the local thieves noticed the economic boom. Some even made a boom of their own with detonator caps dipped in nitroglycerine. Nanaimo Realty's 500 pound safe was blown open one night and $1655 in cash and cheques were taken. Frank normally did 95% of his office business by cheque and had only $518 cash in the office. He had left everything in the safe this night because of office delays that kept him out of the bank. The skilled safecrackers were strong enough to carry the safe away and respectable enough to spare the office records and legal documents. Frank offered a $200 reward for the return of the safe.

It wasn't too long until Frank got an anonymous phone call from a person who explained directions to the location of the safe. The safe was resting safely by a turkey farm. Frank was happy to have it back even though it was empty and gave his reward money to the Salvation Army and a Children's Hospital.

Frank was an unfortunate guy to have in on a deal closing because he usually gave away half the commission. If you had a 5% commission and the guy wouldn't close the deal, Frank would close the deal by throwing away part of the commission to make it work. He was trying to please everybody, and consequently he ended up with a lot of friends.

Anonymous Salesman

The fact that Frank was seeing money coming in from his efforts made it possible for him to be that much more generous. While out making money, he never lost sight of the fact that many others weren't doing as well. He never liked to see anyone looking down in the dumps and often asked people what was bothering them. One man had a serious answer for him involving his roof which was leaking on a house full of children. He and his wife were broke, and he was in school trying to make a better go at it all. Meanwhile, he had no part time job. Frank took the man out for coffee to talk things over.

After hearing the man's story, Frank said his bit about the upside of the situation. Having some cash on him, he handed the man $100 and told him to fix the roof. He encouraged the man to be thankful for his wife. He said, "Buy her some flowers and some candy!" There was no hurry for the man to pay the money back, but Frank mentioned that he was free to do so when he was ready. $100 was a considerable amount of money during the 1950's. Frank was not trying to build a reputation for himself by doing this type of thing. It was only because the wife with the flowers mentioned it years later that anyone heard of the incident.

The stories of his benevolence were often forgotten as soon as they appeared. Frank loved to help people, but the recipients of his kindness generally preferred to forget about their problems once they had been solved. Frank appreciated this fact and didn't speak of these things with people who were not directly involved.

The Major Frank Alfonso Ney's integrity had a great impact on his son's life. Frank was always proud of his dad. He had the greatest respect for the old fellow, who was quite ill during his last few years. Every day at 5:30 or 6:00 in the morning Frank would drive to his dad's house and pick him up for work. Frank left him alone on the main floor while he went downstairs to light and stoke the coal heater they had bought at Eaton's for twelve dollars. The father and son would then go to a cafe for breakfast and return to the warm office when the staff showed up. Although the Major was still on a pension from the First World War, Frank felt that it was good for him to go to work so that he could be around people.

The real estate man was still finding the time to respond to the needs of the community. By 1958 he had been the campaign chairman of the Salvation Army's Red Shield drive for five years. He was forever sympathetic and encouraging to the people in need, using his public image to its fullest to raise money to carry out the Salvation

Army's welfare work in the city. While actively involved in raising the required $8500 for the organization, he explained, "The services which the Salvation Army performs for those in need and trouble are such that they could not be performed better by any other group or social agency. Once this is realized I am sure all the support required will be forthcoming." The monetary goals were set and reached. Frank spearheaded a fund drive in 1959 that raised an all time record high of $8800.

Not only was the local work of the organization being maintained but also a substantial contribution to the national work was made. This was a project that Frank took on a number of times, with the help of 400 canvassers. Each year the required amount grew larger but the donations also rose accordingly.

I started working with Frank again in 1955, this time at Nanaimo Realty. The company had an interesting incentive program that I became involved in. If a salesman netted $2000 or more in commissions by the end of the month, he was awarded a new suit.

These were $100 suits. Sometimes you would add $25 or $30 to that and get a pretty darn good suit at that time. I won quite a large number of suits over the years and wound up having to pay income tax on them. I had never given too much thought about them being taxable.

Bob Grey, Retired

Incentives offered to salesmen were an effective way for Frank to keep the ball rolling. He felt that prizes also made the work place a lot more fun. The top salesman every month was awarded a $25 sports jacket, an excellent item for the period. There was always something other than straight commissions for the guys to work towards.

Real estate was an almost exclusively male dominated business during the post-war boom. There was only one woman in town who was out selling properties. Mini Facer was slightly ahead of her time. She was an excellent golfer and real estate agent. When Frank announced his intention to hire her, he was met with some opposition from his staff. He had worked hard to keep the boys happy and working more like a team. Now he had to face the fact that certain chauvinistic attitudes would disrupt what he had going. None of this affected her career. She was happily employed at Newcastle Realty while all the fuss was being made about her in other offices.

Summer became the best time for Frank and his buddies. He and about five other men bought power cruisers and started heading off together to explore the surrounding islands. When this private convoy of boats hit upon Friday Harbor across the U.S. border, the gang walked their sealegs into the tavern.

This pub wasn't much different from other pubs except for the conversation piece that majestically graced its interior. A great big bell was hanging there just waiting for someone to ask what it was all about. The bartender would reply, "Well, you can ring it if you like, but you will have to deal with the consequences." After hearing that, most people changed the subject. Frank triumphantly gave the bell a good ringing. This set off a series of about twenty-five bells all ringing at once. The consequence? The bell ringer had to buy a round of drinks for the house. The bell was so loud that people could hear it outside and so had the option of joining in on the drinking. Frank instantly made a good deal of new drinking buddies. Eight bells and all's well indeed!

There was also a store in that town that was of special interest to Frank. He browsed through a selection of pirate style clothing and bought his first pirate hat.

Every July we went on a cruise with our boats. We went down to Friday Harbor the very first year. That's when he got his whole pirate thing started. He said, "Yes! We're going to go up there and ring that bell!" That's where it all started! He saw all the pirate costumes there and started the whole thing off!

We went every July for ten years. He said, "Well, we've got to go down and ring the bell at Friday Harbor." That was the most important thing right there. We would have to go and ring that bell. Next he started with a pirate hat and a little old haywire black sword. He'd be on the bow of his boat waving his sword when we were coming in. He'd jump off onto the dock and run up and ring the bell!

Fred Dorman

Gabriola Island sits peacefully in the harbour, as it has for a long, long time. Large stretches of its waterfront had been gracefully waiting to be subdivided into residential lots for people to enjoy. This is what Frank noticed upon his visit to this most northern of all Gulf Islands. It wasn't long before Frank had another official title. The head of the Gabriola Sands Development Company was on a mission.

A great area of land was purchased from the McConvey estate. It is completely to the credit of Frank and Bill Ney that the famed Malaspina Galleries sits undisturbed as a protected area. The "galleries", a natural phenomenon cut from a rock ledge by winter winds and storms, overlooks the Strait and roughly faces Nanaimo. The recess in the sandstone are so deep that a visitor can walk quite a distance underneath a complete rock overhang. It is cut into the edge of a beautifully treed strip of land, which juts out to sea at the end of a public road through the adjoining subdivision.

The company did a remarkable job of turning this estate into about 100 private lots. These properties all sold well for $550, at $7 down and $7 per month each. These were very reasonably priced lots, even from a 1950's perspective. Frank liked the idea of people buying and enjoying them rather than holding out for the top dollar. There were many other deals he could move onto from there.

The lots were laid out in a manner which created the effect of each house being hidden away from the others. This project, which showed a great respect for the natural beauty of the area, was titled Malaspina Resort. Hundreds of visiting boaters as well as tourists on foot stop by the Galleries every year to marvel at its magnificence. Local swimmers reported numerous Frank Ney sightings off shore over the years.

Frank Ney A Canadian Legend

I spent most of my teenage years at my parents' house beside the Malaspina Galleries. It is really an amazing area. I would join my friends in jumping off the galleries for summer swims. We used to see Frank pull up with the huge Blue Girl *full of people. They would drop anchor and dive in.*

We were sitting there drinking beer one day and I said, "Hi" to Frank. He hollered, "Howdy boys! Great place hey! This isn't even a park really, it's in perpetuity..." He talked for quite a while. Of course I knew of him as mayor, and I was also aware of his involvement with the initial development of our neighborhood.

Extravaganzo, Graphic Artist

As Nanaimo Realty developed Gabriola Sands, Frank dreamed of new ways to have some fun and create publicity at the same time. Frank, being an athlete himself, often tended to lean towards physical sporting events at such times. He organized and sponsored a 3.5 mile swim from Nanaimo to Gabriola. Every contestant would receive a cash prize in addition to the honour of being guest at the Gala Gabriola Turkey Bar-b-que. Gabriola was famous for its turkeys in the 1950's and it was a real honest treat to get a slice off the grill.

The bar-b-que was scheduled to coincide with the start of the aquatic sports and foot races at 3 p.m. and to continue until 8 p.m. That is a lot of turkey. Guests were free to bring their plates to the water's edge for a good vantage point in viewing the water ski tournament. A dance at the North End Hall was planned to follow the dinner activities. Frank made sure that his company would provide transportation to everyone who wanted to share in the fun.

Twenty-six eager contestants dove into the ocean on August 8, 1958, and a very athletic Miss Meta Torney set the first ever record as she clocked in at 3 hours and 50 minutes. The entire mass swim lasted a total of four hours. The party was a great success with everyone having a good time. The food and entertainment was all top notch, but the swim itself took so long that it was hard to sustain the entire crowd from start to end. That slight problem was not one likely to surface again during Frank's next 30 years of promotions!

By 1958 he had 102 partnerships, joint ventures and other segments operating. He actually had trouble keeping track of them since he wasn't a bookkeeper himself and didn't really have qualified people looking after the finances. His notes were written on a little piece of paper in his shirt pocket and problems were developing with that system. People started to suggest that he get some qualified help. Jim Goodwin, who had earned his accounting degree recently got Frank's phone call and started with Nanaimo Realty in 1958. It worked out that Frank would create interest; then Jim would raise the money and manage the resulting finances.

Some of the smaller real estate companies were being bought up by Frank for the purpose of expanding his insurance business. He even started another real estate company called Nanaimo Properties and went into competition with himself. His real estate signs were everywhere. As a result it was getting difficult for other companies to impress their clients and keep them out of Frank's office.

The typical work day for Bill, Frank and Jim started at 9 a.m and very often continued after the staff went home. Frank would get out his vacuum cleaner and Bill would also help clean the place up. Frank insisted that the front of the office be tidy. This late afternoon clean-up was usually followed by more paperwork until 7 or 8 p.m. It was during these hours that Jim and the Neys would discuss what there wasn't time to talk about earlier.

Communications among the staff was of the upmost importance to the directors of the company. Every month without fail they hosted a breakfast meeting for all to attend. The cook at the Shack Cafe next door woke up extra early to prepare and set out the morning feast in the church hall next door. Frank would bring in motivational speakers to bring the skills and morale of the staff up that one extra notch. It was difficult for a salesman to come up with an excuse not to attend these meetings. What could conflict with their schedule at 6 a.m.? Eventually the cook got tired of the arrangement and Frank had to delay the breakfast meetings until 7 a.m. when the first restaurant in town opened.

I was acting as M.C. at a Knights of Columbus luncheon to raise money for charity. At the close of the day, Frank, who had only just arrived, sat next to me and said, "I've been watching you Kenny and I want you to come and work with us." Heck, I was a bulldozer operator, what did I know about selling houses? He would not take "no" for an answer and insisted I come into the office the next day. As soon as I arrived he sat me down with Maude Atkinson and instructed her to help me fill out my application forms for the U.B.C. real estate course. He even paid my $100 application fee. I took the course by correspondence and a year later I bought a couple of white shirts and some dress up duds and joined the firm.

Ken Gogo

During the years of expansion, Frank kept an eye on many of the local people with the idea of future employees in mind. He was certain to have one salesman from each of the popular local religious groups. This was not just an exercise in religious tolerance but an extremely effective way of getting clients from all corners of society. Each new salesperson who was added to the team got a standard 50/50 split on commissions with all expenses paid, except for transportation costs. A starting salary of $200 per month in charge of rentals could be followed up with the announcement, "It's time for the bird to leave its nest," and another salesman was created.

Frank liked to hire people with a sense of humour. There were always jokes and gags in the office. Society was a lot more conservative back then and Frank was surprised when a salesman told him that one of the employees was gay. With respect to the gay man's privacy, the salesman offered to whisper his name in Frank's ear. The whole staff was watching as they knew beforehand that the gag consisted of planting a big wet kiss on Frank's ear. Some people say that Frank never got embarrassed. There was no other way to account for the shade of red that his face went.

The Sizzle Speech

Everyone wanted to know how this man from London could step into a sleeping town and make everything suddenly start to sell. His successes were simply a combination of hard work, charisma and very good timing. People wanted to hear about it.

Every year saw an increased demand for Frank as a public speaker. Most often he was invited to functions and asked to simply speak on any topic. He was considered to be insightful, entertaining and very funny. Frank was always advising someone about something over his many careers. He decided to sit down one day and write a speech that would become a basis for his improvised monologues. The Sizzle Speech, as it became known, outlined a complete philosophy of life itself.

Jim went to Vancouver with Frank many times to support the delivery of this work. Frank, who was becoming known as a motivational speaker, was often invited to sell the idea of salesmanship. He would show up in his best dark suit and wait until his name was announced to a hall filled with strangers. He stepped onto the podium and waited calmly as the applause faded. The eyes of hundreds of salesmen connected with his as he placed his notes on the stand. He stood tall, breathed deep and soon was filling the silence with ideas, inspirations and concepts intended to uplift any potential listener. One can only honestly advise based on experience. Frank Ney was by no means shy of this criteria.

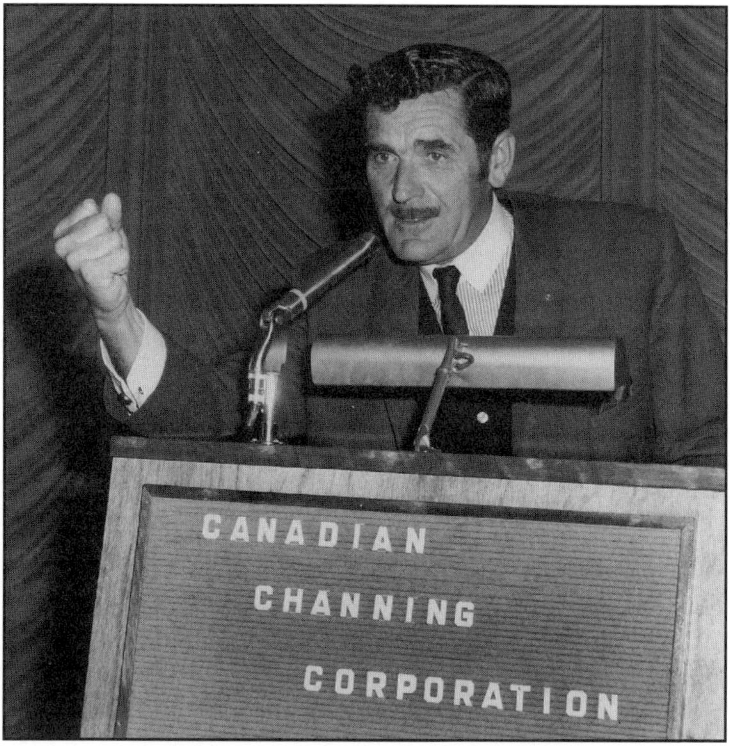

Selling sales to salespeople. Not bad for having had no training!

"Selling Sizzles in a Competitive Market"

Speech by Frank Ney.

opening — two or three jokes (all clean)

The knowledge of the world has doubled in the last five years. The world is full of ever-increasing wonder. And yet with all our tremendous advancements, our most important resources are people. A very important part of this category are the salesman.

The Post-War Boom Continues

What makes people buy? What makes people like you? It's the sizzle. It's always been the sizzle. I think the first sizzle was about the time of the Roman Empire when the merchant, in trying to sell his men customers fancy togas, would simply say, "It'll make you look like a senator." And in those days people didn't mind looking like a senator.

I was in Eaton's store the other day, and an old farmer walked in. He was looking at the long red flannel underwear. And that's when the salesman delivered his sizzler. He simply said, "They don't itch." And if any of you here have ever worn long-handled red flannel underwear, you know that salesman didn't have to say another thing. It's the emotions or sizzles that sell people, and nothing else. Why? Well, maybe it's because the heart is closer to the pocketbook than the brain.

You know, it's not the cow that sells the steak, it's the sizzle. You never saw a cow come into a restaurant selling left shanks. The waiter comes in with the tray. First of all you hear the sizzle, then you see the sizzle, and then you smell the sizzle! Then your emotions are triple impelled, and it's three to one that if you've got the money you'll buy the three dollar steak that's hot and sizzling and forget about that thirty cent salad that's just cold and fizzling.

Sizzles are things like the tang in the cheese, the crunch in the cracker, the whiff in the coffee, or the pucker in the pickle. People don't buy pickles because they're green, yellow, pink, or mauve. They buy them because they pucker. Sizzles are things like the foam in beer, the bubbles in the champagne, and the tinkle of ice in the long, cool glass of lemonade.

Go down to Woolworth's store. The girl holds the beads up like they're ten cents worth. And then go to the exclusive jeweler's store just down the street and they put those same beads on a piece of rich black velvet with a white fluorescent light shining down, and those same beads look priceless.

The Chinese in Hong Kong know the sizzle. You sit down in the chair for a fifty-cent haircut and they put a pair of clippers over the top of your head that are so loud that you think a power mower is going over you. At the same time two girls, not one, are giving you a manicure and down below two boys are giving you a shoeshine. And when they're finished, those two girls are giving you a pedicure, and then they put a tall, cool drink in one hand and a long cigar in the other, and you sit there, king of all you survey. And then they give you a massage over the top of your neck so you think another Tong War just broke out. And when you get up, you have had a Hong Kong fifty cent haircut. In selling, say it with flowers!

Which or what? Phone your wife tomorrow night at five o'clock and tell her you won't be home for supper and you'll think the Third World War just broke out. Timing — but phone up the night before and say, "Darling, what night would it be most convenient for you to have me miss supper, Tuesday or Wednesday?" and the little wife will make the big decision with the feeling that she's the most important person in the home. And don't think you can fool your wife, because when she wants to go to the picture show, she'll simply say to you, "Darling, where would you like to go tonight, the Horticultural Show or Elizabeth Taylor?" and the master of the house will make the big decision and the little wife will go to the picture show.

Timing — Little Wilbur wanted some candy and it was a hot, sunny Sunday afternoon and his Dad was reading the paper. He knew if he asked him for the money his Dad would say, "It'll ruin your teeth and your supper." So he said, "Dad, I wonder if you'd take my bicycle down the steps of the verandah. Mom says if I get lots of exercise and sunshine I'll grow up to be a big strong boy." When they got the bicycle down to the sidewalk, little Wilbur looked up at his Dad and said, "Pop, it's a lovely sunny afternoon. Why don't we walk down to the Drug Store and buy a nice big cigar for you to have after supper?" And his Dad thought that was a pretty good idea. Just as the clerk was giving his Dad the cigar, little Wilbur looked up and said, "Dad, can I have a candy?"

That was good timing. Just like the lawyer who doesn't ask for his bill to be paid on the day his client's going to be hung.

Perseverance. People must have a willingness to risk failure to be successful. Abraham Lincoln — willingness to risk failure:

31 - Failed in business

32 - Defeated for legislature

33 - Again failed in business

34 - Elected to legislature

35 - Sweetheart died

36 - Had nervous breakdown

38 - Defeated for Speaker

40 - Defeated for Elector

43 - Defeated for Congress

46 - Elected to Congress

48 - Defeated for Congress

55 - Defeated for Senate

56 - Defeated for Vice President

58 - Defeated for Senate

60 - Elected President

I always remember the story about the Remington Rand salesman. The sales manager was ready to fire him. He was the worst salesman they had ever had. He knew nothing of the product, and was not a self-starter. The sales manager thought he would make an example of this salesman instead. He instructed him to go into every office in the great Woolworth's building in New York, starting on the bottom floor and simply say at each office, "I am a Remington Rand salesman. Would you like to buy a typewriter?" And if anyone asked him questions about the typewriter, he was told to write down the question and tell them that he would bring back the answer later. By the time he got through the building, he had sold two typewriters. And they carried on with this procedure in the other big buildings in New York City. At the end of the second month this salesman was the top salesman that Remington Rand had in New York State.

I noticed today that the big utility companies are persevering as developers in trying to sell electric heat, and this is as it should be. For developers of electricity — it's cheaper to install, it's cleaner, easier to maintain, and more dependable. The biggest problem developers find is that the financing of electric heat is not as competitive as the financing of oil heat. You know, the car industry would be nothing if you weren't able to buy cars for $75 down and $75 a month. We appreciate that the big utilities are in a difficult position as a public corporation and attempting to go into the financing business, but it does seem to me that with the great investment they have, the great financial resources, and the great powers of electric heat could be reached. My opinion is that the sale of electric heat could be tripled if the public were given easier financing terms.

Thomas Edison made experiment after experiment in search of a new source of natural rubber in plant matter. After the fifty thousandth failure, a discouraged assistant said to him, "Mr. Edison, we have made fifty thousand experiments and no results." "Results," exclaimed the great inventor with enthusiasm, "we have wonderful results. We have wonderful results. We now know fifty thousand things that won't work!" So I say, continue to persevere, and you will come out on top.

The secret to power-packed healthy living is a healthy body and a healthy mind. Schopenhauer, the great philosopher, said, "With good health everything is a pleasure, without good health, nothing is a pleasure." Therefore, it is the greatest of folly to sacrifice your health for any type of happiness, no matter what it be. The road to good health is not a road paved with good intentions. It is a road paved with a strict regime of proper diet, proper rest, and proper exercise. A prematurely sick man is a failure. So begin enjoying your life now instead of having stresses, anxieties, frustrations, tensions like a coiled up spring, pressure from the top down, pressure from the bottom up, harbouring of resentment, bickering in the home, marital shambles, tensions at work. These tensions at work and home only poison your body. Try to adapt to life graciously. avoid undue fatigue, laugh more.

Cheerfulness — Cheerfulness reaches deep down into our whole economic, social, and political scheme of things. An internationally known industrialist once said, "I would give a million dollars to have Charlie Schwab's smile." Schwab himself attributed no small part of his success in developing a picayune business into a gigantic organization to his sunshiny attitude toward everyone is his company.

He never believed in "bawling out" executives or workers. His unfailing habit was to praise good work. Time and again men are picked for important positions, not because of unequaled ability, but because they "know everybody in the trade", because they have a wealth of friends who would like to do business with them: How are friendships won? Invariably by cheerfulness — yes, there is money in cheerfulness.

Self pity, jealousy, and revenge only hurt you. Courage, loyalty, and love bring rich happiness. Don't expect to get your way all the time. Take defeat gracefully. Use recreational time usefully. If you're an excessive drinker, there is only one way to go — become a moderate drinker. You may think that before lunch three martini's, six fingers of rye, and a couple of beers give you a good appetite. But if you do you're on the precipice of disaster in gambling with your job and your family. If you are overworking, get more sleep, buy a new bed. Empires have been won in the bedroom. An investment here can be a good investment.

Never hesitate to see your doctor. Watch your heart. This is the biggest killer. It can burst like an atom bomb and blow you to eternity. The average North American has twenty teaspoons of fat in his blood. The average Chinese, two teaspoons. You have nine lives:

1. High blood pressure

2. High levels of cholesterol

3. Overweight

4. Excessive eaters

5. Too little exercise

6. Diabetes

7. Cigarette smoking

8. Tensions

9. Heredity

The odds are one in twenty you will die of a heart attack.

They are one in fifty if you are okay in all the departments I have just mentioned, but the odds are one in two that you will die of a heart attack if you have two or three of these characteristics. So eliminate these characteristics and the odds for a long life will be increased immensely.

Make up your mind. Indecision means tension and frustration, and if you add office to home tensions you've got a back-breaking load. Learn to say sorry, please, and thank you. Volume of voice doesn't solve a problem. Never make public your problems. Never leave your home or go to bed mad, or tousle to see who is the boss. Don't try to live up to the Jones'. You only live once. Take that trip now. Buy those books now. Take up a new hobby. Get a new mattress. Get that new TV. If you change your job you may get into something worse. Don't downgrade short vacations. If you haven't got your health, you'll lose your creativity, your initiative is stifled, and your ingenuity never even gets off the ground. Keep well, be happy, live longer.

The most important thing we have to offer is service. Why do we lose customers?:

1% lost through death

3% move to another area

5% leave to buy from friend or relative

9% leave to buy at lower price

14% leave to buy elsewhere because of unsatisfied complaints

68% leave because of indifference and lack of interest of seller

I love to get a complaint because that's when we really start to make money. The complaint looked after is not just the beginning of more business, but also new business. For customers well looked after will refer the customers to you. Watch your telephone manners, be kind and courteous to older people. How do you smile, like a mule or a Cheshire cat? Or do you smile with your lips and your eyes and your heart and your whole personality? The roots of success are buried in a smile and the desire to make someone happy.

The first fundamental in success is to take the initiative in liking people. Have you learned the secret of the twinkle? People are instinctively lonely and a little hesitant to make friends. Walk into a room of strangers and then beam in with a twinkle on the first person you see. In no time you will be friends with everyone. It's so simple to be happy and helpful.

Friendship is the world's greatest salesman. It may sound corny, but your Grandmother was right. The Golden Rule and the Ten Commandments are still the strongest force in our daily lives. The friendly fellow going by these rules with a smile in his manner and a warm eagerness in his handshake nine out of ten times makes a favorable first impression. More deals have been made at high corporate and international level just because Joe was a nicer guy than you have ever dreamed of.

"I" or "my," the most overworked words in our country, "my home," "my car," "my trip to California." You know, I don't really care about your trip to California, but come on over to my house tonight and I'll tell you about my trip to California.

Learn to be a good listener first. Forget about your dear little Wilbur, and listen about their little Christopher.

Now these are just a few sizzlers and it's not enough just to write them down or memorize them. You've got to pick them up and fire them like bullets from a gun into the hearts of people so that they remember you forever. and if you do, you'll have greater social success, more financial benefits, and greater happiness than you have ever dreamed of. The Bon Vivants and the Entrepreneurs who have been so successful in the fields of commerce and happy living are only people who have learned the secret of the sizzle.

We are heading for great frontiers and opportunities. The population of the world will nearly double in the next twenty years. There have been more people born in the last hundred years than since the beginning of time. In our lifetime there have been more changes than in hundreds of previous generations. In the Congo there has been as much change in this generation as the previous five thousand years. Fifty percent of the people industrially employed are making a living out of jobs that didn't exist fifty years ago. This world will never again be what we knew it to be when we went to school. Half the people in America will be under twenty-five by 1970, preceding new and even greater family formations in potential purchasers. By 1980, the population of the Western States in North America will equal that of Peru, Canada, Switzerland, and Austria combined.

Will we be ready for this tremendous growth? Will we be ready for opportunities unlimited? Let's sharpen our blades and go into battle selling the sizzle every day of our lives. For people like people who like people. Sell that sizzle in the market-place. It will be the greatest action on earth.

The End

The sizzle speech usually resulted in either an umbrella or a bottle of pop being sold and thrown at the crowd. The shock of throwing a tangible item always made people jump. This high energy performance won Frank the B.C. Toastmasters speaking contest over six other contestants at the Hotel Vancouver before more than 200 members from 39 clubs. He added a trip to compete at the zone conference at Walla, Washington to his already busy schedule. It was not only with trophies and public praise that Frank was rewarded. His words brought on many words from others.

In 1961 I was a woods foreman on the northern end of Vancouver Island. I was a part of a group of six or seven companies that all got together every year. Every year a different company would host what we called the Englewood safety conference. That year it was being held at Kokish, by Beaver Cove, and it was really going to be a first class conference. A lot of ground work had been done, the whole thing was prepared but they were having trouble coming up with a keynote speaker.

I was a committee member so I suggested a very good speaker in Nanaimo who was prone to going around and giving speeches. His name is Frank Ney and he is quite capable of getting people enthusiastic about things. Everyone was saying, "What does he know about logging?", but we prevailed and got Frank up there.

Frank was really a driving force in that conference. He told the crowd of 200 delegates, "Look, I don't know anything about logging, but I do know about sales. A lot of things are easy to sell if they're tangible, like if you want a new car, or if you want a boat that you can blow up and had a couple of paddles, you can sell that like crazy. But the things that are hard to sell in this life are the things that are not tangible. You've got to sell enthusiasm, and that's one of the toughest things that you can ever sell."

He said that he had been a good salesman himself and the secret to the thing was a thing called a "sizzle." He got everyone there all worked up on this sizzle thing. He said that if you're going to get people enthusiastic to buy safety, and it's not a tangible thing, you've got to have a sizzle.

He went on to tell a short story about Cleopatra when she was travelling down the Nile river. She had used an umbrella on her barge to shield her back and shoulders from the hot sun. He whipped out a black business man's umbrella, held it up and said "This is that very umbrella! I've got a dollar, who's got two..." He went into an auctioneer's routine of selling this thing, broke off halfway into the action and said "Sold!"

He threw the umbrella into the audience and somebody caught it, luckily, and people were really excited about the whole thing. He said "Now that's the sizzle! We got you interested, we gave you something that you could get enthusiastic about, and with safety that's what you have got to do!" He could go on for a long time talking about this sizzle thing. He got a standing ovation for this speech, and he doesn't know a choker from a hole in the ground, you know.

Mike Severn, Semi-Retired

The original sizzle speech was written in the 1950's and twenty years later he was still wowing crowds with it. He fine-tuned it over the years and slanted it in the direction of the particular audience that he was addressing. He was live bait in a sea of salesmen. Who could ask for a more energetic potential partner or investor? Being approached with offers became a daily routine for Frank.

I first met Frank at Toastmasters 20 years ago. His famous speech was on selling the sizzle but not the steak. That was pretty well his life philosophy. He could sell the positive points of anything.

Frank Graves

The delegates attending the 1959 B.C. Government Trade Conference at U.B.C. were galvanized as the young dark-haired panelist from Nanaimo swung into action. Frank flashed a card that represented him as a real estate salesman, but was later referred to as "The Billy Graham of Vancouver Island." He hyped this crowd for fifteen minutes with reasons for bringing industrial estates to small cities. "Which comes first, industry or population? When the big man calls to look at your community, he is likely to go away if you haven't plans to show him how and where he can locate. When he goes, you may have lost a chance for ten years or more." This advice was always backed up with facts that could only point to the Island's beauty and inevitable popularity.

This fellow is tremendous! When we went to look at his industrial estate for the construction of a steel warehouse, we had not been with him for half an hour before we began to wonder if we were not making a mistake in not moving our whole operation to Nanaimo. His enthusiasm is infectious.

John Wallace, General Manager, Yarrows Ltd.

There were more facts to back up Frank's hype. In twelve years he had developed 2000 home sites and had 2500 more in different stages of development. His staff had grown to 37 , with 24 salesmen pushing the Hub City for all they were worth. Nanaimo Realty was the fourth largest land developer in B.C. and Frank Ney was a household word in his home town.

All the big money people were wanting to spend time talking about investments and opportunities with Frank. Mr. A. B. Cleveland was no exception. He had owned a large tire recapping business and publishing concern in California in the 1940's. By the end of that decade he had sold it all and moved up to Qualicum Beach. By 1957 this 60-year old millionaire had a proposal for the city of Nanaimo. There were not many millionaires around back then and they made big news whenever they wanted to. This one had been out looking for things to buy and decided to move on the one thing every man wants. He wanted to buy Newcastle Island for $200,000.

Newcastle Island is only a stone's throw from Nanaimo's shore. It had recently been acquired by the City of Nanaimo after having been used as a resort destination by the Canadian Steamship Company. It was not yet decided what the city would do with this treasure. A letter was drafted on Nanaimo Realty stationary and presented to the City Council. Cleveland was offering to leave the present picnic park, improvements, beaches and main park area with room to expand. All the rest of island would be developed as a high class residential area. All this could be possible if the city built a bridge for him. He also suggested that the city could dedicate their portion of the island to the provincial government in return for the province sharing half of the cost of building a bridge. The bridge would require a clearance of 80 or 125 feet. If the city agreed to go ahead with these plans, Cleveland would immediately pay the purchase price in cash.

Mayor Pete Maffeo remarked, "Suggestions for the island's development are coming in with a vengeance!" It was decided that the council would meet with Frank Ney and Mr. Cleveland to discuss the matter further.

It is unfair to view this situation from a modern standpoint. Nanaimo was a much smaller town then and the idea that untouched waterfront would be endangered was a long way off. To some people it looked as if perhaps the town was endangered and development was the key to the community's survival. Frank pushed for Mr. Cleveland to assist the city in every way possible to develop an adequate yacht basin which would make Nanaimo the hub of Vancouver Island's tourist industry. "Up island residents who cannot find suitable anchorage for their yachts and power cruisers would be attracted to Nanaimo and Newcastle Island to live." Frank also pointed out that development of the island would add hundreds of thousands of dollars annually to the city's revenue.

Mr. Cleveland was not available for comment after the meeting as he had slipped off to Seattle aboard his yacht Zodiac II. He faded into history as the city of Nanaimo rejected his proposal along with the many others.

It didn't take Frank very long to find another use for Newcastle Island. Over the following decade he repeatedly called for development of the Island as a Provincial Park, with a proper ferry service. He envisioned reclamation of an old mine shaft and quarry as well as the installation of a $30,000 children's playground. A little train could circle the entire Island, making a stop at a model Native village. It would be "the biggest playground in the country."

The decision of what to do with this 760-acre island didn't come quickly. When all the paperwork was stacked up, the Provincial Government came out as the winner. Newcastle Island now sits proudly as a marine park. The future generations that will enjoy this masterpiece of nature undisturbed will no doubt applaud this final notion. The ferry service is reliable, the quarry is rather interesting, and the playground is a lot of fun. Frank managed to get all his final wishes except three. The old mine shaft is now buried, and the model Indian village remained an idea in a file somewhere. The little train around the island was simply not meant to be. Newcastle Island still does remain, however, an excellent playground.

Boating, islands and real estate. Nanaimo has plenty and Frank had a lot of it on his mind. If Newcastle was not to be had, one only had to wait until low tide to walk onto the next undeveloped island.

Protection Island

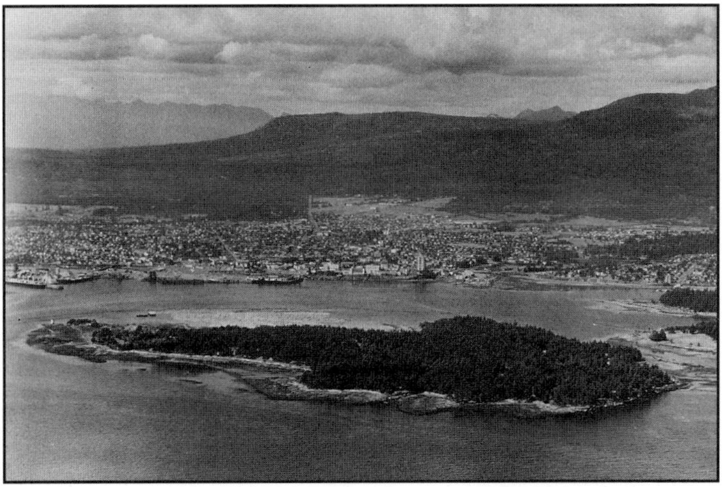

Undeveloped Douglas Island

BY THE TIME THE CALENDAR HAD FLIPPED over to 1959 the Nanaimo Realty boys had settled into a solid working schedule. A day was somehow not complete until the office door was locked and they had a chance to walk across the street to the old Plaza Hotel, (which has now evolved as the Dorchester). The gang would unwind and discuss the day while the 5 o'clock beer was served.

The Plaza Hotel had huge picture windows which afforded a wonderful view of the harbour. The realtors would sit and gaze at the lovely little islands that grace the waterfront. Newcastle Island is joined at the hip by an equally quaint and charming one known as Protection island. Tucked away on the right behind Duke's Point is the larger Gabriola. These Islands created an almost unbroken wall of trees, rock and sand between Nanaimo and the Mainland.

Protection Island

Protection Island is shown on maps and charts as Douglas Island. Good Point, on its western tip measures 5 ½ cables from Nanaimo's Maffeo Sutton park. Some folks may prefer to think of this as being 1 ½ nautical miles, 3300' or 1 kilometer.

As this lovely array of trees, boats and houses stands between Nanaimo and the Strait of Georgia it shelters the harbour from occasional choppy waters. This makes for calm, worry-free anchoring. This island didn't however provide a very safe haven from the warlike Haidas who used to travel 500 miles in huge canoes pillaging the coast for women and slaves. As a result, not many people were living on the Island when Spanish explorers showed up in two 50' schooners on June 15, 1792. Captains Galiano and Valdez spent three days in the Strait before they named a few islands and went away. Not many explorers dropped by again until 1849. Not only had gold been discovered in California that year, but also coal in the area that was to become Nanaimo. This started a 100 year, 50,000,000 ton coal binge.

In 1853 when two native men were suspected of killing a Victoria man, a chase up island ensued. Nanaimo's district of Chase River was named after this manhunt. Once captured, the suspects were tried upon the Hudson's Bay Company ship, the *Beaver*, and subsequently hanged at a point on Protection Island, thus earning it the infamous name "Gallows Point." It was the first time that kind of atrocity happened in the area. Today Gallows Point is proudly crowned with a lighthouse.

Even after the explorers began settling and developing Nanaimo, the Hiada continued their raids. One day 80 canoes with 1000 Haida warriors arrived with the intent of giving the Nanaimo band a bad time. These fellows were deterred by the new settlers who had built a Bastion and had previously used the deserted Protection Island for target practice. Colvilleton was renamed Nanaimo and a battery of naval guns was set up and maintained on Gallows Point. This helped to give the island the nickname "Protection."

A coal seam was struck at 822 feet below the surface of Protection island in 1892. That year the first Protection Island coal was loaded on the barque *Wilna*, which set off for San Francisco. The mine exploded three years later and two men died. There was more bad news on the island later when the *SS Henrietta* went aground. And then the *SS Oscar* caught fire while unloading explosives onto the island.

Since the coal seam on Protection extended to the No. 1 mine in Nanaimo, the miners who worked at the pithead on the island soon didn't have to take the ferry to work anymore. They just walked through the mine shaft that went under the ocean floor. The men that stayed in the shaft could tell the time by the sound of the C.P.R. boat propellors on way to Vancouver.

Tragedy struck again in 1918. The cable that held a mine cage carrying 16 men snapped, plunging 880 feet. During the coal mine era unnecessary death and maimings due to incompetent management were far too commonplace.

By 1938 the mine had caved in. After employing about 300 men over 46 years, the last ton of coal was hoisted up, and an all night party brought the operation to an end.

The 85' high pithead of the mine was set ablaze as a Victory Torch in 1945 during a party that celebrated post-WWII victory. Blackout restrictions had banned such blazes during the war and the first official bonfire was determined to be a good one. The giant old first-growth timbers shot flames high into the sky. The coal slag piles which towered high inside the opening of the shaft became part of the gigantic inferno. The heat and flames also shot downward into the mine and ignited what coal was left in the old shaft. Occasional outbursts of smoke from that coal mine were to be seen for several years afterwards as the red hot mineral under the ocean floor burned on. The long-lasting effects were quite spooky.

Protection Island's stunning beauty and charm was enjoyed by people who would go there for picnics. Frank Ney and Jim Goodwin were always fond of the Island and were amongst the few that would explore and picnic there during the 1950's. Frank made regular trips to a variety of islands on his cabin cruiser with friends, celebrities, and of course investors. Destination was not always the concern. These fellows even had fun barbequing on the completely bald rock named Snake Island. The only investment opportunity there was in feeding the birds.

Protection Island

Jim and Frank were always tossing ideas around. Their work days were certainly busy enough and it was only over a beer after work or during an outing that they really had a chance to relax and detail things out. Late one summer afternoon they were sitting at the Plaza Hotel with some of the sales team talking about waterfront properties. Protection Island was staring them in the face as they chatted away. Frank overheard one of his staff remark, "We should buy that island."

Frank quickly responded, "Well, let's make them an offer." The individuals involved with the company didn't consider themselves to be even remotely affluent and everyone could see that an undertaking of this magnitude was almost out of reach. Frank being Frank quickly sold them on the idea. "If we each put up $100 we will get $1000 as our deposit money. If it goes through everyone gets $200 back." Ten people went for the double or nothing deal.

Nanaimo Realty made a purchase offer of $130,000 to the Canadian Collieries (Dunsmuir) Ltd. which were a subsidiary of the Western Fuel company. That was a horrendous sum of money in those days. The terms that the huge old coal company accepted included the $1000 down and full payment of the outstanding balance in thirty days. The race was on to raise the money. A total of ninety people invested, including the Nanaimo Realty staff. Not only did they hit their target, but they raised enough to develop the island as well.

The first planning sessions brought out ideas that never came to light but would have had immense impact if they had materialized. Frank envisioned swimming pools, playgrounds and stores. "Protection Island at low tide is almost connected with Newcastle Island. We propose to build a causeway that will join these islands at all tides." He suggested that Nanaimo could be connected by a bridge to Newcastle Island. A Protection Island resident could then drive to town. The decision to scrap that concept has proved to be a wise one since both islands continue to retain their unique character.

While Frank oversaw the planning and subdivision he was also masterminding a massive sales campaign. Through a variety of print ads and events the beautiful island was promoted as "the ideal spot for your own cottage." The few people that were squatting on the island had mostly built their homes on stilts by the water. These folks were given first choice to buy the lot that they were on. Since the island was not yet on city services, the promotional materials emphasized the 'summer cottage' angle as well as pointing out the obviously amazing investment opportunity that was to be had. It is safe to assume that everyone who bought at the original prices found a higher resale opportunity at a later date.

"$8 down - $8 per month for a parkside lot. Frank saw a mountain of cheques each month."

In keeping with the theme of the promotion, the entire staff, including salespeople and notary, were dressed for several weeks in full pirate regalia. Frank had rented some very colourful outfits and insisted they be worn at all times. The first day the costumes arrived, Frank was ecstatic as he had the staff in the basement trying on their new duds. As soon as about ten people were dressed and had swords buckled on, he said, "Come on boys, let's go over to the Royal Bank and show our outfits to the manager."

The pirate crew tromped off to the bank obscured by eye patches and funny hats. They burst through the doors with pistols and swords drawn shouting, "This is a robbery! Down on the ground, you swabs!" The pirates didn't intend the bank employees to take them so seriously, but yes, the tellers did hit the floor and there were screams and general pandemonium. It is possible that Frank may not have been aware of the real panic his pirates had caused, as his next suggestion was to try a few more businesses on the main street.

Frank was making his first public appearances as a pirate. He had two grand pirate suits, both red, which he wore for the remainder of the 1950's and well into the 1960's as well. It wasn't until the early 1970's that he commissioned the tailor-made orange velour suit that helped bring him international attention.

By the eve of the grand opening of the new subdivision, Frank had assembled 29 fully-clad pirates. The entire crew was now quite accustomed to going about their daily routines in full ancient naval splendour. The entourage finally congregated downtown and paraded through the business section. A long line of these outlaws of the seven seas went in one door and out the same one right down the main drag. The women were most attractive in full length colourful dresses. The men, with eye patches and weapons to match, did not have the same appeal.

The day Protection Island sales opened, customers ran in all directions toward their choice lots. Frank had big fun with the opening of the Island. Once again he had organized a mass swim and on that scorching summer Sunday, August 7, 1960, 137 swimmers jammed together on the Malaspina Hotel float. At 2 p.m. a pirate-clad Gib Stephens shot off the starting gun and they all hit the water heading for Protection Island. An even one hundred swimmers made it to the island within a little over an hour. The winner of the swim was a husky 30 year old, Norman John, son of the famous totem pole carver, Jimmy John. Norman stroked his way to victory in 28 minutes followed by Mike Palatti, three minutes later.

A fifteen-year old Morey Morrison was a close third at 32 minutes while seventeen year old Uta Allers was fourth at 32:25. David Jones and Barry Finch both came in fifth with 34 minutes. Mayor Pete Maffeo presented cash prizes to the first five. The winner received $50, and the others $25, $20, $15, and $10 respectively. The other ninety-five who finished the race each picked up a $5 prize the next day. Judge Ted Morrison, a well-known swimming expert, described the swim as being the largest mass swim he had seen and possibly the largest in Canada, certainly in western Canada.

Six ferries shuttled a crowd of between 4000 and 5000 people to the shores of Protection Island to welcome the victors as they came ashore. This same crowd made the rest of the party a huge amount of fun. A treasure hunt was launched and youngsters picked up 100 silver dollars hidden in chests throughout the island. Free ice-cream was devoured by the gallon and thousands of bottles of pop were handed out.

Families picnicked while Frank and his gang of pirates kept the action rolling. Frank drove into a field with the Mayor in a buckboard behind two white stallions which later took young sightseers on a tour of the island. He introduced a quintet of striking beauties headed by 1960's Miss Nanaimo, Sandra McMinn. The others, including Miss Protection Island Jean Bennett, were all runners up in that contest. It was a hot day and the heat caused a number of people to faint. They were looked after by Alf Topping, Chuck Mayhill and Osino Grando of the St. John Ambulance brigade.

The Nanaimo Outboard Club members handled the positions of communications assistants and life guard patrol. Gerry Hill, the visionary who created the amazing Yellow Point Lodge, brought along a group of expert water skiers who thrilled the crowd with a spectacular exhibition.

Frank used this celebration as an opportunity to explain a point to the press. He said that the island development would go a long way toward keeping the money of vacationing Nanaimoites at home. Figuring at $300 vacation expenses per family, this could mean an average additional income to the area of $100,000, the equivalent of a substantial new industry.

Arnold Smith, head of the Nanaimo local of the Carpenters' Union, enthused that several hundred summer homes would eventually be constructed, making the development a valuable contribution to employment in the area. The Chamber President Don Cunliffe said that it would provide a splendid resort for residents and visitors alike.

Mayor Pete Maffeo spoke to the crowd in praise of Frank, Nanaimo Realty and Nanaimo Properties Limited for their foresight and faith in Nanaimo and its future in initiating such a venture. He came up with the quote of the day when he said, "This is the biggest thing Nanaimo has seen for many a day!"

These were the days when a developer would stand by his product full-heartedly. Whenever possible, Frank avoided the large scale clear-cut, moonscaped subdivisions so common today. He was very concerned about the ecology of the island and promoted practices that would ensure that many generations could escape to its God-given splendour. This subdivision had a total of eleven parks. Gallows Point wasn't included in the original plan because the mine pithead had been there and it wasn't as attractive as the rest of the island at that time.

One hundred and ninety-eight lots were sold on the first day. The first eight days saw almost three hundred lots sold. When the salesmen would come into the office at 3 o'clock in the morning with papers to be signed, Frank was there to ask Jim, "Has this lot been sold yet?" If the lot in question was still available, Frank would complete the sale by signing it as the "President of Protection Island Resorts." There were salespeople selling lots in the middle of the night and rowing back to have the papers signed. One of these lots was bought by a child who had his friends help collect and cash in pop bottles when he had a rough time making his payment. Thanks to the easy terms and minimal credit criteria this man has a house on the Island today.

Each new land owner was given a full owner's manuel for their new lot. Frank explained some reasonable building conditions. He expressed concern for propor garbage disposal and fire prevention. He strictly enforced a no firearms regulation. "Not only are firearms dangerous on an island such as this, but furthermore the few deer that are there are quite tame and it would be most unsporting of anyone to come on to the Island and destroy the beautiful creatures which the children and tourists enjoy so much."

Three days after the giant party, Nanaimo Realty placed an almost full page advertisement thanking their customers. The entire first days of sales were only open to the Nanaimo market in order that the local residents have first opportunity to invest in the "greatest summer playground in Western Canada." The ad reminded potential buyers that in five days the balance of unsold properties would be advertised in Vancouver where they would sell immediately. The pressure was on for the locals to raise the $8 down payment. To own such a gorgeous property on an island of warm water, sand, good soil and privacy is an unattainable dream for most people today. Almost every lot bordered on either park or ocean, and on that day anyone could have bought one for less than the price of a pack of cigarettes a day.

Five months after the opening day pre-cut cedar house kits were advertised that could withstand 100 m.p.h. winds. These do-it-yourself A-frames could be erected in 1.5 days. At $2 a square foot the prices went as low as $250. If anyone invents a time machine, the author of this book would very much appreciate a short charter.

Frank Ney left a mark on this island that will amuse people indefinitely. A stroll around the island will bring you down to "Pirates Lane," "Captain Kidd's Terrace," "Captain Morgan's Boulevard" and "Treasure Trail." You may wish to visit "Captain Hook's Park" or "Billy Bones Bay." His dream that the roads never be paved is still in effect and the deer still run through the gardens. There are a number of land owners that vacation there only in the summer, but the majority of residents are now full-time ones.

There wasn't time to organize the gruelling Gabriola marathon swim during the summers of 1960 and '61. Frank and the gang were busy with more subdivisions, including a large one on Gabriola Island. Once again the Ney brothers made another massive display of public generosity with the presentation of a lovely provincial park - five acres of picnic and playing fields. This large picturesque meadow sits in between two sandy beaches. People who travel the road through the field are treated with the splendour of beaches on both sides. In true west coast style, arbutus trees skirt the shore of the deep bay graced with anchored sailboats. This park was officially named Gabriola Sands Provincial Park yet it is known by the locals as the Twin Beaches. It is undeniably one of the more spectacular of all the B.C. parks. Could anyone imagine Gabriola Island without the Malaspina Galleries and the Twin Beaches available to the public?

The presentation of such prime real estate by a developer is indeed a rare occurrence. Frank would have been well within his legal rights to fence off, build on or keep his parks as holding properties had he chosen to do so. By dedicating waterfront parks he increased the value of inside lots and made the whole subdivision a more pleasing place for the residents. These were not the only reasons for bestowing such valuable gifts on the public, as the adjoining waterfront lots only fetched $1800 each for the company. Frank was the person who predicted a massive increase in our population and knew very well that God had created only so much waterfront property. His vision always exceeded his personal lifespan. He loved the idea of children playing in the tides for centuries to come. He knew that he was writing history.

Frank's dedication of parkland received very little mention in the media at that time, and has somehow been lost and forgotten by the thousands of people who frequent these spots throughout a number of islands. Despite this, many people appreciated the act at the time and the Gabriola Agricultural Society managed to feed 200 people a turkey and ham dinner during the presentation of the Twin Beaches.

The Gabriola Sands marathon swim had previously attracted some of the best swimmers on the coast. It was missed by the public during the first couple summers of the new decade and was soon to be brought back by popular demand. When the event was revived, the winner of 1959's swim was there at the Malaspina Hotel float waiting for the starting gun. By then Miss Uta Allers was 19 years old. From start to finish she found herself in a neck and neck battle with a 16 year-old Barry Finch. Both were amazing swimmers and were at the time employed as instructors for the Nanaimo Recreation Commission. Barry switched from his breaststroke to an Australian crawl in the final 50 yards of the course. He hit the shore of Gabriola in a mere 2 hours, 32 minutes, and 5 seconds. He was joined by the former champion Uta Allers 4 seconds later.

Frank was pleased to have such a great show of swimming skill in his competition and presented the Ethel Ney memorial trophy in memory of his mother who had passed away in December of 1961 at 69 years of age. The runner-up was also presented a special trophy for her remarkable effort. The two winners remained good friends throughout the day and together contemplated a duo-swim from Nanaimo to Vancouver the following year.It wasn't long before Nanaimo Realty was sponsoring a number of marathon swims each summer.

August 5, 1962 saw for the second time a mob of swimmers heading towards Protection Island. Norman John's record time was smashed by Wandert Van Appelen's 23-minute victory. Van Appelen's weather conditions were not favourable, however, and his exhausting finish was followed by only 21 other swimmers out of a start of 64. Fifteen of the swimmers had to be attended by St. John's Ambulance who were on hand to supply blankets, hot coffee and first aid.

A greasy coating of vaseline was applied to the limbs of each swimmer as protection from the cold while the Harbor Patrol protected them from speeding boats. Three volunteers cheerfully dished out 1600 ice-cream cones to a crowd of 2000 friendly spectators. The swimmers themselves ranged in age from 13 to 42 years and were awarded prizes of cash and bongo drums. Frank was extremely pleased with the turnout of the event despite the rough waters and ugly weather.

The swim continued to be an annual event. The local swim club was always supportive and became the nucleus of the event. The club had asked Frank to host the event, which he always did aided by his private boat to carry the parents of swimmers to the finish line. Sometimes the swim went to the neighbouring Newcastle Island, and every so often the participants would be serenaded by the Nanaimo Pipe Band. Each year of the 1960's saw well over 100 people competing in the swim. Over the years bags of silver dollars were handed out along with thousands of ice-cream cones. There were over 5000 ice cream cones given out to the spectators of the 1965 race alone. During his career as a promoter, Frank gave away tens of thousands of ice-cream cones

---

One summer I had a visitor - Kath Oakley from Oromocto, New Brunswick, and as a way of entertaining her I took her down to the waterfront to watch the take-off of the

swim Frank used to sponsor to Protection Island. It was a lovely day - warm and sunny, and there were mobs of people there watching. Frank happened to stop near us for a minute, so I said to him, "This lady is from New Brunswick." He immediately replied,"Would you like to see the end of the swim, if so, go and get on Blue Girl and I'll take you over." "That would be fine," I replied, " but we have to be back in time to get to Janet Norby's place for dinner at five." Now Frank did not know who I was, knew by sight as he did hundreds of others, I would be an 'old lady' to him. He assured us that he would have us back in time so off we went and really enjoyed seeing the swimmers scramble out of the water, run up the beach and gong the bell! After all the excitement, Frank got on his bull horn and hollered, "Will the two ladies that have to get back please board Blue Girl." We did and back we came. And Kath said, "And this fellow is the Mayor of Nanaimo!"

Kay Woolfson

My girlfriend and I went on our first date during August 1991. We were waiting for the Newcastle Island Ferry and noticed that Frank's boat was tied to the warf and surrounded by people. I asked the pirate what was up and he said that he was off to Newcastle. I asked if he had room for two extra passengers. He asked "Do you have kids in race?" I said no, and realized that he was hosting a swim contest. I had been out of town for a few years and forgot about some local traditions. I wished him a good day and got out of his way.

Five minutes later Black Frank walked across the warf towards us and with a worried look on his face said, "Gee, I'm really sorry about this." I was shocked that he was so considerate, after all it would not be a big deal if I took the ferry as originally intended. I just thought it would have been more fun to go with Frank. He went on to say, "I feel really bad about this." I told him thanks, and not to worry about it. This guy just couldn't do enough for people.

> *Later that night we missed the last ferry back and had a hard time bumming a lift back. I kept thinking that some of these people could share a little of Frank's attitude.*
>
> Paul Gogo, On Holidays

> *I swam in the 1982 Protection Island swim. Normally Frank Ney gave a silver dollar to participants but because it was so cold and miserable that day he gave everyone two each.*
>
> *I was invited aboard his boat along with all those who completed the race. When I stepped onto the boat I stepped into an absolutely raging party! It was great. At one point someone said, "We're out of booze!." The person next to him repeated, "We're out of booze!" The next person did likewise and down the line until it was Frank's turn to say, "We're NOT out of booze." He walked over to a little hatch and opened it. I looked down into the bilge and saw what must have been a million Gala-Kegs (wine in boxes) down there! It was like some kind of ballast. Frank grabbed a couple and the party continued.*
>
> Craig Evans, Agriculturist

These promotions always proved to be a great way to meet people, and Frank made plenty of new friends through his work on Protection Island.

Clarence Entwhistle owned a string of Movie houses in San Fransisco. He heard about this summer paradise and had a waterfront A-fame built to face Nanaimo. He had both money and a willingness to work with it. More often than not, people with those qualities loved to spend time with Frank. Clarence got involved in local developments and like many others his name became immortalized on a street sign post.

On with Business

SINCE THE LARGE AMOUNT OF BUYING AND SELLING of land Frank oversaw was becoming almost unmanageable, he came up with the idea of creating a public company. Being prepared to listen to advice, in 1962 he suggested, "We'll have to get somebody who is an expert at public companies." Frank and Jim went to Vancouver and spent one whole evening with a lawyer.

They came back and started negociating with an investor from Boston named Dr. Cosgrove. He looked the part of a perfectly respectable gentleman with his white suit, white hair, bowtie and spectacles. One day he invited Frank, Jim, and two salesmen out to coffee. When coffee was served, the millionaire doctor pointed at Frank and Jim and said, "I'm paying for theirs." The salesmen had to fork over a dime each.

Dr. Cosgrove quickly earned a reputation as a miserly sort. It turned out that the doctor didn't like the idea of a public company and so bought up all the shares. This really stymied them as a public company.

When those guys built the Westward Ho Motel on the Island Highway Frank wanted to call it the "Gunsmoke" after the popular T.V. show of the time. Jim and Bill jumped on him over that one. They thought that it might give people the wrong impression!

Anonymous

Jim and Frank were feeling quite confident in the industry and by the subsequent year they were ready to start another company. By word of mouth around town they had 500 subscribers before they knew it. This was the beginning of the Great National Land and

Investment Company. Shares were fifty cents apiece. There were no free shares. Everyone was treated equally and even Frank and Jim paid for their own shares. The fact that it was still a private company, created problems for them, so with the help of a lawyer, they put the whole thing into gear as a public company. They became involved with a well respected conservative brokerage house in Vancouver called Odlum Brown and started to sell shares. These people handled the underwriting mainly because they liked Frank.

To some degree Great National Land rode on the coattails of Block Brothers who were a couple of years ahead and had already floated a very successful business. Someone in the east soon noticed that another company in B.C. went public and Great National's shares shot up as as high as $3.20. This turn of events was credited to Frank's enthusiasm, ability to create confidence in investors and his ability to achieve publicity. Although there had been slight dips in the market, his track record didn't include many failures. Frank Ney's personal image was very strong.

People who promote public companies generally receive some form of cheap shares, free shares or options. Frank was unique that he never loaded his ventures with management fees and he always put his money in equally with his investors. His philosophy was that his clients were his friends.

Frank was forced to sell Nanaimo Realty to Great National Land because the brokers felt that there was a conflict between the two. Nanaimo Realty shares were sold at market value but Frank decided to do something different with his. He openly gave all of his shares to his staff for free. His belief was that the more people who were involved, the better the company would be. Although Frank was the boss, he acted more like a partner. He had a real knack for making the other person involved feel as though it was his idea. There was a special leadership quality that made everyone feel needed and worthwhile.

Sometimes a person would get into a hassle with him but find it entirely impossible to win an argument. Frank was often very elusive with his speech. If you were arguing one point he would attack you with another point. He'd listen for a while and then he'd say something totally off track and attack you with it. This was how most arguments ended. You just couldn't win.

At Frank's house the fridge and bar were always open to you. You were always welcome. If it was the middle of the afternoon and he walks in while you are eating a sandwich, he wouldn't even bat an eye, he'd just say hi.

Anonymous

Frank Ney was said to be a fitness fanatic. He indulged in weights lifting, running, swimming, skating, ballroom dancing and dominoes. Perhaps this was what inspired him to dream up a diet contest in 1960 as one of the inner-office activities. This particular contest became a good source of extra pin money for a couple of employees. As with many of Frank's stunts, this one earned, or rather landed on international press during the early 1960's.

The firm paid $25 for the first 10 pounds of overweight dopped, and $2.50 for each additional pound worked or fasted off. Frank claimed to have paid out $325 to his staff over a period of one year. Six of the twenty-seven salesmen slimmed by more than ten pounds. Of the eleven women employees, only three tried to reduce and only one dropped the requisite 10 pounds.

One reporter asked Frank, "Why?." He responded: "Because it makes for greater efficiency all round. Our sales have gone up 15% since my staff began reducing and the over-all efficiency of the office has increased by at least 20%. The whole scheme has been a tremendous success. I have recovered what I paid through the increased efficiency of my staff, and it has also given us favourable publicity. Why, do you know I've just been handed a letter from the Australian

Real Estate Board. They heard of my scene and they want to know all about it."

Frank had first hit on the idea in 1959 when he noticed that a number of men were dying of heart attacks in their 40's and 50's. "In most cases, overweight is the primary cause, and I know from personal experience how it can impair a man's efficiency. I used to feel too heavy to work after lunch, and my staff say the same. They are happier and a whole lot more efficient since they cut down on their lunches and on fatty foods generally. When I look around I'm amazed that more people don't get rid of their surplus weight. They just don't know what they're missing. Weight reduction is the key to a happier, fuller life."

The contest was based on a philosophy in which Frank personally believed. He felt that most men owe it to their families to stay alive as long as they can, or at least until their children have grown up. Frank entered his own contest and dropped his weight from 210 to 170 pounds and felt "100% better for it."

Ken Gogo recalls when the secretary informed him that a reporter from Maclean's Magazine was on the phone asking details of how he won the diet contest. Ken mistook this call as a prank from co-worker Gib Stevens. Ken took the call and proceeded to boast of how he lost "60 pounds in 60 days by eating only hard boiled eggs." The voice on the phone remarked what an interesting office that must be to work in. Ken's reply was that working for Frank is like working for a circus, and if a reporter wanted some good stories, one had only to leave one's comfortable office in Ottawa and come out here in person rather than wasting a busy man's time on the phone!

A couple of weeks later, the reporter came into the office looking for Ken. He was flabbergasted, and turned the reporter over to Frank. The reporter was quite impressed with the number of people coming and going along with the constant paging on the office intercom. The office was abuzz with activity as people had become aware of the reporter. The reporter asked Frank how many people were working in the office. Not even trying to be funny, Frank replied, "Oh, about half of them." The diet contest was news in Europe as well as Canada.

I spent years working with Frank and Bill. I was always treated well and given help and encouragement along the way. The Ney brothers were especially thoughtful of my wife Dodie. There was always a plant or a bunch of flowers for her at Christmas, Easter and for the birth of each of our children. We were nothing special as they treated all their co-workers the same. Into my sixth successful year I suffered a lengthy health problem and upon the advice of my doctors I took a leave of absence for one year. Frank phoned me every day at the Victoria hospital where I had spent a long stint. The morning after I arrived back home, Frank had arranged for me to go back to running a bulldozer for the late Harold Hayes. This turned out very well and I managed to buy the company. I never went back to my desk, and twenty years later Nanaimo Realty still welcomes me to their social events and treats me as though I had never left the company.

Ken Gogo

Most of the work Ken's new bulldozing company did was through Nanaimo Realty because they were building so much. Ken brought the first fire truck as well as one of the first bulldozers to Protection Island. Amongst other things, he unearthed a broken cable and two massive pit-head cable wheels while reworking Gallows point. He brought these relics back to Nanaimo and couldn't find anyone who was interested in having them for reasons historical or otherwise. They went off to the recyclers. Ken also recycled himself every year for decades as Nanaimo Realty's Santa Clause.

You know Gallows point was not included in the original subdivision of Protection Island. That was because the fire in the coal mine had been burning there for so many years that the whole area was comprised of ashes. It was quite messy. We were cleaning the area up and creating a nice slope towards the water with some heavy equipment we had barged over. One very cold day my partner and I built a bonfire and parked the bulldozer with the bucket facing it.

Frank Ney A Canadian Legend

> *We sat inside the bucket, sheltered from the wind and directly in front of the fire.*
>
> *As we enjoyed some warmth my buddy said "Let's get some oysters and cook 'em up in the fire!" Naturally I agreed. Later, as we sat in the bucket he said, "What do you think Frank would say if he walked over and saw us eating his oysters on his company time?"*
>
> *I had a little portable radio so I turned it on. I heard Frank's voice come out of the little speaker. He was doing a live radio phone in show in town. I told my friend, "Well, we have until this program is over until we see him again!"*
>
> Anonymous

The spring of 1963 provided a fun opportunity for Frank to get out of town for awhile. The provincial government was sponsoring a tour of the Canadian prairies and Frank was asked to join representatives from various B.C. towns in making the trip. He was singled out as being a confirmed tourism booster, orator and banana benefactor. It was asked that he speak of beautiful weather, amazing scenery, and the supreme enjoyment of a trip to B.C. Frank was, of course, well versed on these topics and had a marvelous time shaking hands across Alberta, Saskatchewan and Manitoba.

After the tour had ended in Winnipeg, all of Frank's travelling companions scattered back to their regular lives. He continued on to Montreal. There was a SRN 2 hovercraft in service on the St. Lawrence River and Frank simply had to see it.

When Frank arrived on the St. Lawrence he did more than look at the hovercraft. He boarded the 75 passenger craft and travelled at 70 miles per hour. It slowed enough to safely ride over a three foot high wall that supported its landing ramp. Frank was extremely impressed and met with the people who represented the product. They told him that this vessel, which rides above water on a cushion of air, would be ideal for the Strait of Georgia because it can glide over floating logs and other debris.

The smile was still on his face when he returned to the west coast and presented a photo of the vessel to the newspapers. "There was absolutely no vibrations at 70 miles per hour and no need for seat belts. The hovercraft would be ideal for pedestrian traffic between Nanaimo and Vancouver." He made immediate arrangements for a team of engineers to carry out an economic report on downtown service. Frank told reporters that if the economic reports were favourable, he would immediately form a company to operate the service.

One of Frank's companies owned an ideal spot for a hovercraft depot on the Nanaimo side, and the Bayshore Inn would be an ideal destination on the other side of the Strait. The trip would only take twenty minutes. Besides the vessel Frank had fallen in love with, there was also a 40-car, 350-passenger model also available. The team of engineers could determine which model to go with. The huge crafts looked like giant, inflated, rounded off 1950's cars-of-the-sea, complete with overhead wind propellers. The impressive looking beasts fit the missing piece of Frank's vision for the west coast. He was crazy about these hovercrafts and became known as one of the most knowledgeable men in the country on the subject.

The project was shelved once the feasibility study came in. "Cost of operation and limitations in times of adverse weather conditions indicate that the service would not be economically feasible." The craft used so much fuel and required such a large staff to operate that one would do better investing in conventional aircraft. The idea of a fast crossing of the Strait of Georgia was so exciting to Frank that he never gave up on the notion. For the time being, however, he had to bury his thoughts in other matters and hope that technological advances may some day provide solutions.

One day in the early 1960's Frank gave $100 to the late Monsignor Baker. A hundred bucks was a lot of money back then...a whole lot. I asked him, "Frank, are you Catholic?" He laughed,"Why do you ask that?" I responded, "Well, you just *gave $100 to our church." He then told me that he gave that to every church.*

Janice Hubbard, Digby, Nova Scotia

Figure skating was another lifelong passion for Frank. He decided to take on the position of President of the Nanaimo Figure Skating Club. There were about fifty people involved in this organization. Amongst the directors, advisory council and other titles sat many of Frank's good friends. They all worked together to put on some wonderful shows for the town.

Over 100 people were included in the gigantic cast of the 1963 Ice Carnival. "Silver Cycles" was presented as "Western Canada's Foremost Ice Show." This performance was designed to delight both young and old. The music of Gershwin, acts from Walt Disney, and every type of championship filled the bill. This warranted a full-page newspaper advertisement to let everyone know what was in store. Frank wasn't about to let his own kids miss out on such a big show and had three of them included in the cast.

Figure skating became a bigger attraction in town than it had been previously. These were the days before people sat at home and watched movies. It was remarkable to get crowds of 2000 people from such a small town paying to see an ice show. Frank would round up corporate sponsors for the show so as to keep ticket prices down. All in all, it was good, solid, clean family entertainment, and the shows were always fun for the audiences. The technical skating was as much a delight as the multicultural dancing. Frank had nothing to gain by putting his time into this type of thing other than the fun of doing it. He always got his reward.

The first time that I met Frank Ney was when I was walking with my son and he tripped on us.
He apologized deeply.

Jenny Bently

On with Business

It was on to the next island for the developer. Three hundred lots were subdivided on Mudge Island, which Frank renamed "Driftwood Island," but the name didn't stick very long. Once again the company was financing $1200 waterfront lots at $15 down and $15 per month. The inside lots were a bargain at $450. Terms were easy at $5 down and $5 per month. Frank explained that he could afford to continually provide property bargains because he applies "supermarket techniques" to his land development business. He was offering hundreds of waterfront lots on a number of islands.

The other subdivisions didn't see large promotions in their honour. The Protection Island party was fun to attend, but the cost in terms of time and cash was considerable. Frank loved to put on big bashes but didn't need to go that route to promote new developments. The word was already out and the prices were certainly low enough. Everything sold, party or no party.

An eager salesman had sold a house to a women three days previously, and she had come into the office of Nanaimo Realty and was really concerned that she had overbought, and she wanted to back out of the deal. The salesman had said OK, but you will have to pay the commission I would have earned if the deal had gone through. This amounted to quite a sum, and the woman was quite agitated.

Apparently Frank overheard this conversation, and immediately joined in and said NO WAY and cancelled the deal and gave the lady her money back.

Pat Leahy

The real estate company kept growing and more salespeople were being added to the team. As the1960's rolled along the Neys and their staff were feeling quite crowded in their office building. They had already moved once since the conception of the company. Trapped between a church on one side of them and a bank on the other, there was no room to expand. It was once again time to move to a bigger office.

The bank next door was a huge pillared landmark building of architectural respectability. It proudly occupied the corner lot at the junction of Church, Chapel and Commercial Streets. Thanks to the Neys, it still stands there and most likely always will. Frank had walked by this great outstanding corner lot building hundreds of times. Located within one block of every office that he had occupied since moving to Nanaimo, it gave Frank had plenty of opportunity to put his thoughts and dreams together about its future use.

The building that Frank liked so much had been erected in the heart of Nanaimo in 1912, and in the 60's the bank that owned it could neither rent nor sell it. The building had been considered by members of the community for use as a branch library or a businessmen's club but every idea was found to be impractical.

Dr. Cosgrove and his sister Grace Cosgrove financed the $30,000 purchase of the building and in turn sold it to Nanaimo Realty. Frank had for quite some time advised these millionaires where to invest money and guided them through this deal.

I got the listing from the Bank Of Commerce. Frank was excited about getting the building. He was excited about everything he bought. I never knew him when he wasn't.

His company already owned the property next door. The nature of the building interested Frank. The history of the building interested him, as well as the idea that they would be renovating it.

Bob Fawdry, Nanaimo Realty

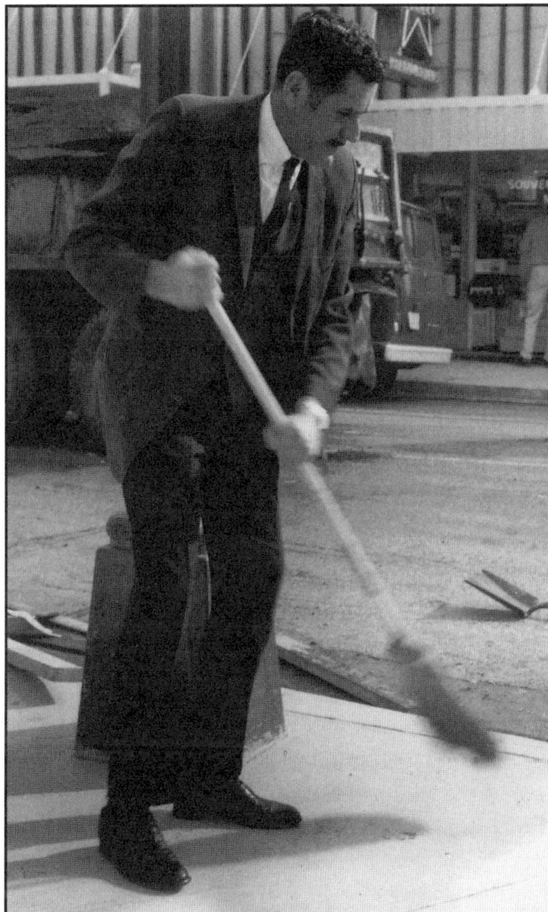

A customer's first impression is valuable.
The construction of Frank's new office building left debis on the sidewalk.

Frank explained,"We feel this building adds a touch of class. It gives a fragrance - is that the word - a business stability. And that's very difficult to project in most media."

"The Frontier building is now protected by the Heritage Act. It cannot be demolished or altered in any way without permission of city council. If anything happens to us, we know the building is going to stand for another 100 years. We're a big company and no one knows what can happen in the corporate world tomorrow morning."

The idea was to make the building a financial institution. Frank, Bill and Jim planned a long range expansion plan for Nanaimo Realty and Nanaimo Properties. These plans included further land development and the availability of financial facilities for the whole of Northern Vancouver Island. The purpose was to assist home owners, farmers, small businesses and individuals requiring money for expansion. The company was also planning to finance and erect commercial and industrial buildings for lease. Frank reported, "When the new expansion program is under way within a few months, it will mean that borrowers who formerly had to go to Vancouver to seek capital for sound business undertakings will no longer have to do so. This will make Nanaimo the financial center of the Middle and Upper Island."

The company spent thousands renovating the old building with a special concern not to upset the old style decor. One consultant wanted to have the old counters pulled out, but to no avail. The new building was indeed very impressive. It was time to put it to work.

When the renovations were completed, the staff rolled their furniture in and kept on working. They found that this old building was similar to the previous one in that it also had a coal-fired furnace. Every Monday morning when the salespeople came in, a line-up was organized to carry the cans of ash out to the back to be picked up. The sales staff were never too excited about this extra perk and Frank would go looking through the cafes trying to round them up. One of the main investors was not particularly well-loved by members of the staff, and so the thought of doing little extras to benefit him brought down morale on occasion.

Frank had a large iron ring implanted in front of his newly acquired office building. On one of his several daily walks he was stopped by some tourists who recognized him. They complimented him on the building and asked him what the big iron ring was for. Frank told them that it was not too long ago when these streets were traveled by people in horse-drawn wagons. If one of them were to show up again, there was a good ring for them to tie on to. The tourists were impressed that the city would prepare for such an eventuality. Frank accepted the compliment and led them a few feet down the street and pointed out a second ring. He explained, "This one is here to show that Nanaimo is not a one-horse town."

Frank was always, not openly, picking people's brains for ideas. He always wanted to know other person's ideas on certain projects that he might have in mind.

Frank had a tremendous amount of energy. The reason that he was able to go the way that he did was that he would cat-nap every opportunity that he had. When he was in the developing of acreage for a subdivision he would often say to me, "Come on Bob, let's go and see how it's coming along." He would get in the back seat and immediately go to sleep as soon as the motor was started.

He would sleep on the way to wherever it was that we were going and then the same thing coming back. He would be sound asleep. I feel that this is why he had the amount of energy that he had. He took every opportunity that he could get to recharge his batteries.

Bob Fawdry

Frank wondered if anyone could swim all the way across the Georgia Strait. He just loved to get people out swimming and posted a $100 reward for anyone who could make the 17-mile distance from Nanaimo to Sechelt. Barry Finch had the chance to live out his dream of swimming the strait and so entered yet another of Frank's contests.

Barry had been a winner at both the Protection Island and the Gabriola Sands marathon swims and was spending his days studying English and Phys-Ed at Victoria College. Ernie Yacub was working his way through the same courses at U.B.C. when the two decided to make an heroic attempt at the crossing. These fellows had a history of ending up as swimming partners. They had both tied for first place amongst the 170 entrants after they spent 32 minutes in that year's Protection Island swim.

This time the duo was disappointed. After 55 minutes and 9.1 miles, they decided they were not trained sufficiently to continue. Not the least bit discouraged, they enthused about the idea of entering the swim the next year, as it was planned to become an annual event.

More than 350 people attended a completely different type of evening at the Tally-Ho during August, 1966. A local businessman, ex-longshoreman and Master Mariner named Captain Mike Murray was in the running to represent the Social Credit political party in Nanaimo.

This well-known figure was a strong contender for the job. Unfortunately for him there was a newcomer to politics there that evening who ended up walking away with the nomination. It was a spellbinding night with speeches by both men who made the event the largest of its kind to date. Frank raved about the progress the area was making and said, "The working man is the most important cog in the machinery. Are we going to be the oil for the squeak in the wheels of progress?"

Frank Ney was quickly featured in bold headlines as the new Social Credit representative. The 48-year old realtor was stepping into a field that would eventually consume much of his energy over a number of years.

Frank lost his first race for the legislature against Dave Stupich by a little bit.

Prior to the polling, Doctors Howey, McKerricher and their wives were at our house for dinner and we were discussing how we might help Frank's campaign. We came up with some catchy slogans which were humorous too. I was selected to get these printed on some cards to be handed out and in a couple of days I had a good supply. They were distributed to our operatives. The following afternoon, Frank phoned me and said that someone in his campaign organization had gotten one of the cards at the hospital and his campaign group suggested that further distribution of the cards should be halted. He said, "I kind of like them myself, Dick, but our advisers think they might backfire." He asked me if I knew who was distributing them and I said I had a good idea. He asked me if I could stop them and I said I thought so.

That was the end of my campaign effort.

Dick Bond

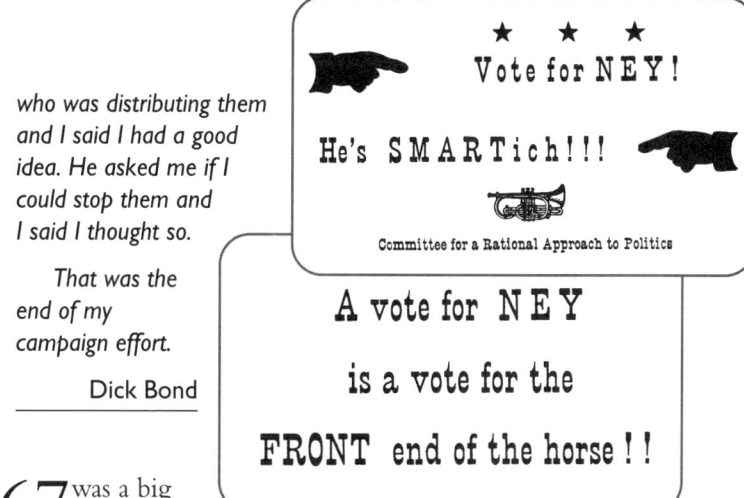

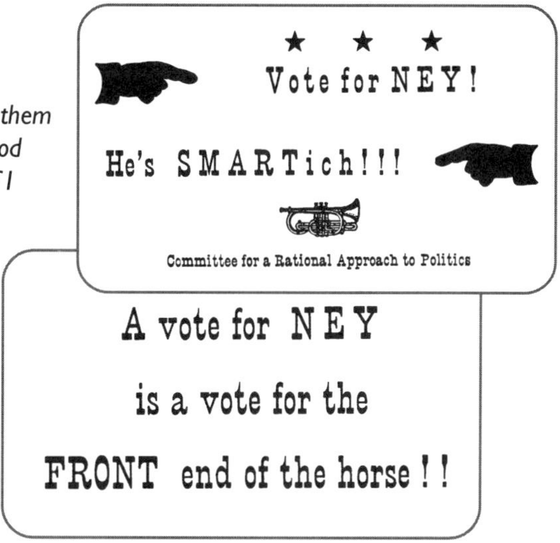
★ ★ ★
Vote for NEY!
He's SMARTich!!!
Committee for a Rational Approach to Politics
A vote for NEY
is a vote for the
FRONT end of the horse!!

1967 was a big year for Mr. Ney. Nanaimo was going through a massive building boom and Nanaimo Realty seemed to be spearheading the whole thing. He was appearing in newspapers much more often for reasons both functional and social. He was even shown in his Mississippi Gambler attire attending the biggest New Year's Eve party of the year. His very presence was becoming news.

The list of accomplishments by Great National Land was looking very impressive. The developments included industrial as well as residential properties and carried names like Lynburn, Country Club, Forest Park, Long Lake Park, Departure Bay Highlands, and the 220 lot Cilaire. This $6,000,000 waterfront subdivision included all of the modern services and received plenty of flack from residents who objected to the unusally large number of trees that had to be removed to accommodate the project. However, it proved to be one of B.C.'s finest developments.

Two of the largest planters in Canada sit alongside the entrance to Cilaire. Some people were curious and went as far as asking Frank how he knew for sure that these decorative planters were really the biggest in the country. He in turn invited all who wonder to find evidence of larger ones. No one ever took up the challenge and Frank won by default.

The development itself was designed around a large circular road which ran through the entire project. In the same traditon of some of

Frank's other projects,it had its own elementary school.This subdivision earned a reputation of being the more up-scale part of town.The sight of the immaculately landscaped yards around the stylish waterfront homes could create no other impression. It is refreshing to see how much public access green space was drawn into planning these neighbourhoods. Frank always left areas for the kids to play, despite the high market value of the pieces left undisturbed.

The company also owned and managed numerous properties and quality apartment buildings. Frank was open to the idea of building apartments as a private investor as well as forming partnerships with any well-intentioned developer. He was providing housing for every income level from low income to the ritzy set.

It was much more common in those days for the average working person to own recreational properties as well as their secure home. Frank was still actively filling this market for summer cottage lots whenever he could find suitable locations to develop them.They were usually waterfront, or close to it, and time has now proven that they provided the easiest and best real estate investment opportunity available to the postwar generation.

There was a huge list of resort developments available.A buyer had a mind-boggling selection from choice sections of Hornby Island, Decourcey Island,Whalebone Beach and a host of other intriguing places. Frank was kept busy naming beaches on a number of these islands.

Frank was also the one who always named the streets in his company's subdivisions. People quickly noticed that this man had a penchant for unusual street names. He also let one of his children name a street as a toddler, and now Dingle Bingle Hill Terrace is recorded as numerous people's official residence.

Twiggly Wiggly Road was named in honour of a character in a children's book Frank read to his kids. He took inspiration from honourable historic sources as well. Bergen-Op-Zoom Drive sounds like another wacky street name but is actually a dedication to a town in Holland where over one thousand Canadian boys died and were buried as a result of a big battle that was fought during World War ll.

On with Business

Arnhem Terrace and Amsterdam Crescent grace a subdivision developed by Old Dutch Farms. Gabriola Island's Moby Dick Way, Pequod Crescent, Queequeg Turnabout, Captain Ahab's Terrace, as well as Bluewhale, Killerwhale, and Spermwhale Lookouts are also etched into Frank's folklore.

Residents have differing viewpoints about living on streets with remarkable names. Most folks find this to be a good conversation piece and get a chuckle out of people's reactions to their address. Others find it irritating to have humour built into their I.D. cards and wish for a change. Overall the vote goes in favour of people enjoying a little spice on the local map.

Sometimes Frank would honour developers or employees such as sales manager Carnduff Scott with Carnduff Place. Neil Drive was named for listings manager Jack Neil. Housebuilder Tom Bracewell inspired Tom's Turnaround; and Dawkins Lane was for salesman Cyril Dawkins. Goodwin Road was rightfully named after Jim Goodwin.

In 1966 the Barkerville Caravan came into town. Frank was busy as always organizing things. There was a replica of the SS Beaver in the harbor and I, as the president of St. Peter's Players, was having a play put together. We were reenacting the story of the first jury trial on the west coast where two men were convicted and hung at Gallows Point.

The local Natives were not very happy about the play. They felt that there shouldn't be such a big emphasis about the fact that the two men were Natives. Frank did a wonderful job of smoothing the situation out for everyone. He was very good at turning contentious situations around.

He would phone me up with suggestions of what could be done with the events being planned. He was organizing everyone. An incredible P.R. man really. I would ask him a question like "How am I to get that done?" He would answer with "Oh, I don't know, but you can figure it out." He was forever getting people to do things. He was always "up." Very positive and energetic.

Geraldine McKinnon

Nanaimo Realty was sponsoring all kinds of events around town. There were trophies awarded and parades attended. The Empire Day preparations alone were costing Frank hundreds of dollars personally each year. There was no expense spared when Frank's fun machine was in action. The newspapers across the country were eating it up.

Nanaimo Realty was building so many new houses that they could offer a service called the Nanaimo Mutual Trade-In Exchange. Anyone could trade in their old home on one of the deluxe new ones with over 600 plans to choose from. The boom was booming!

At his plush Beach Drive waterfront home, Frank estimated he had handled the sale of a quarter million acres of land during his first twenty years on Vancouver Island. He had bought vast areas of waterfront property from Duncan to Courtenay and his total land bank was already at 2000 acres of prime properties. He had worked hard, his timing was nothing short of magic, and it was all starting to pay off. For years people had been suggesting to Frank that he run for mayor. Frank always told them that he did not want to run against the popular Mayor Pete Maffeo. Pete was especially popular with the local children, who came by his ice-cream plant to be treated to nut freezes and milk shakes. He and Frank had become friends. They would go on fishing trips together and have lots of fun. Pete always wore a big cowboy hat and Frank always wore a big smile.

The year 1967 became famous everywhere as a year of great social changes. Nanaimo was changing along with the rest of the world. Canada had survived its first 100 years as a nation and it was time to party!

The World Championship Bathtub Race

Canada's Centennial Year

CANADA WAS ABOUT TO CELEBRATE its centennial year. The federal government invited and encouraged every town in the nation to form its own committee dedicated to celebrating the big year. Pete Maffeo, being Nanaimo's Mayor in 1967, had the responsibility of making it a special and memorable year for the residents of his city. He needed ideas. Big Pete was a regular guest on Frank's boat and was very familiar with Frank's 20 years of very successful promotions in Nanaimo.He was an obvious choice for the task of guiding the town into the festivities. Pete asked Frank to come up with a few good ideas to help celebrate Canada's centennial year.

Frank loved the idea of promoting fun for Canada and agreed to serve as the chairman of the Centennial Committee. He was already wrapped up in his real estate work, but figured that centennials only happen every hundred years, so why not seize the moment! There were ten men and three women appointed to Frank's team. The whole idea was to have a lot of fun coming up with ideas for events as well as attending and supporting the numerous ones that were already planned. Frank was already very well-known and well-liked by everyone he ran into. It was time for his notoriety to take the next step.

One of Frank's first ideas was based on a familiar theme. He walked into the newspaper offices announcing the Nanaimo Weight Reduction Contest. He had already secured approval from the Nanaimo Pharmacist Association and arranged scrolls and centennial medallions as prizes for the unsuspecting public. The challenge was set out for anyone who was willing to lose 100 ounces or six and one quarter pounds, whichever came first, in 100 days. Anyone could enter providing they were serious enough to lay down the 25 cent entry fee.

Listening to a cyclist's heartbeat. Almost all of Frank's early promotional efforts were concentrated on physical fitness.

At the official weigh-in, Frank, who looked as slim as anyone would want to be, was amazed to discover that he was a few pounds overweight. He pulled a quarter from his pocket and entered his own contest. He explained, "I didn't know I was overweight until I weighed myself. A hundred ounces is not a harsh challenge. Harsh blitzkrieg programs usually result in the weight going up again. Heart disease is a big killer. According to my information there is one chance in eighty for the average person to suffer a heart ailment, but one chance in five for people who are overweight. Besides, you feel better and work better if you're not overweight." Less than thirty people signed up in the first few hours.

There were plenty of other events around town that year, including art shows, symphonies, and arrivals of traveling historic caravans. There was also a fashion show where Frank revealed his latest bathing attire complete with top hat, umbrella, cold drink and colourful Mexican-style poncho. All delivered with his now famous smile. People claimed that he looked like a mixture of Charlie Chaplin and Red Skelton as he raised funds for the YMCA and YWCA.

This was a year dedicated to promotions. When a camera or microphone appeared in front of an obviously publicity happy Frank he would push and push tourism to the hilt. At a Rotary Club luncheon at the Malaspina Hotel he explained some little known local history, "Sir Francis Drake was the first to see Vancouver Island in 1579, long before Captain James Cook and others arrived. Aboard Drake's ship was a junior officer who was later to gain fame and fortune - Lt. William Bligh, whose command of the Bounty was to go down in the annals of the sea."

History states that coal was discovered at Nanaimo in 1852. Frank said, "Not so. The Hudson's Bay Company knew of coal here in 1836, but kept it a secret, pending the settlement of the Canada - United States border dispute."

"We anticipate over 1,000,000 tourists to this beautiful Island in 1967. Tourism has increased 81 per cent in the last five years. We should push tourism!"

The moustache was a trademark of Frank's personal image. Only once did he publicly flaunt a beard. He joined two other bearded men in welcoming Rt. Honourable John Diefenbaker at the Cassidy airport. This Prime Minister of Canada was approached by the grizzly looking trio and fined $1 for being found in British Columbia during the centennial year without a beard. Frank then issued him a permit to roam at large throughout the province without a beard. Mr. Diefenbaker was heartily amused and commented, "This is a most unusual way to extend a welcome." Frank was well aware that "Prime Minister Fined" would make hilarious national headlines.

These teenage girls got a kick out of Frank joining them in curling. There were stacks of paper waiting for him back at the office.

This year really did boost Frank's public image. As the chairman of the Centennial Committee, he was invited to speak at numerous events where he was often introduced as Nanaimo's "most dynamic personality." He continued to speak on themes based on his personal philosophy, advising everyone to "think big." He told the delegates at the annual conference of the International Northwest Parks and Recreation Association that one must "go out and sell" to get better recreational facilities in a community. He entertained with a non-stop "One must accept life graciously. To make everyone around you happy is the great secret in life. But if you are not thinking big, then you are not going to do the job you should be doing for your community."

"The big thing is to think big and think big and think big."

"Enthusiasm is the most contagious disease in the world!"

A handshake for the winner. Frank almost forced enthusiasm on people as he moved around in his new centennial jacket.

Thirty-five people ran 100 miles that year. Frank convinced 65 people to pay a $2 fee into the idea of running 100 miles in one year. The running had to occur at an appropriate course with units of one mile. No more than three miles per day was allowed to be entered onto the score card. The whole thing was done on the honour system and became yet another annual event for Mr. Ney. "Here is an opportunity for those wishing to keep physically fit. Make up your own group, run on your own time or challenge another group in being first to complete the 100 miles by the end of 1967." The first record was set as Ross Valliere completed his 100 miles in 34 days.

Frank was pushing physical fitness again as the Nanaimo Centennial Committee jointly sponsored a marathon swim with the Sechelt Centennial Committee. Most every town in Canada did form a committee that year. This particular swimming event was similar to others in that anyone could join, but different because nobody had ever finished the course. This was a race for serious athletes. Once the race was announced, Frank would watch the competitors train when he took his kids for a swim at Departure Bay.

The 16.1-mile race between the two coastal towns started at Neck Point, just north of Nanaimo. Six shivering people stood in the 6 a.m. gloom on the shore above a sea that was replete with little grey caps and foam. There was no pirate suit on Frank at this hour. His voice was amplified through his megaphone and lost to the wind and surf. The few people that were there couldn't hear a word he was saying, but the swimmers all understood that the time had come for them to get into the water. They looked at each other, waded in and pushed off.

The cloudy day brightened up, and the mist that hit the shores finally gave way to rocks and sand. The 25-year-old Mike Powley won the competition in 9 hours 23 minutes. This water safety instructor survived the race by eating a piece of bread with honey at sea. He grabbed a beer on the shore and recognized the one other remaining competitor as a spot on the horizon. Mike got into a dingy and rowed the last bit along-side the swimmer, saying, "Why so slow? You're holding up the reception dinner!" Less kind words were returned to him from a disorientated Ernie Yacub when he hit the shore after 11 hours 13 minutes in the water.

The unkind words were all in fun. The two winners had trained together for weeks to become the first people in recorded history to ever swim across the Georgia Strait.

Frank had backed this event wholeheartedly. He was always on hand as he accompanied the swimmers on his private boat for the entire duration of the crossing. The winner received a $100 cash prize and the Cochrene-Johnston trophy. Frank said, "We hadn't planned on a second prize because we didn't know if one, let alone two, would finish." He arranged for the one other successful swimmer to have a cash prize as well. "We're really delighted with the result. They are both fine people."

At this point it dawns on us - as to how we are going to get back, and on the way to the reception we suddenly also realize we have no clothes either just a T shirt each, what a way to go to a reception! Frank Ney comes to the rescue with

> *some libation on the boat and it is on our way back that we learn that half of Frank's family and crew had been throwing up all over the place during the first half of the day, so we all have a big yuk about that too.*
>
> *EVERYBODY SLEPT WELL THAT NIGHT !*
>
> Mike Powley

It had been ten years since Frank's first run at promoting a swimming event. The incredible athletic feats were still recognized in the local media, but this approach to publicity was becoming too standardized for the public to really stand up and take notice in a big way. Frank needed another idea.

The Great Race

IT JUST SO HAPPENED that at some point in the fabulous 1960's, a gathering of students from the University of British Columbia raced some bathtubs in Vancouver as a gag. The concept of a bathtub race was for a short time just a minor flash on the local news and one that was destined to obscurity. Another fellow had made headlines when he tried unsuccessfully to row a tub across the English Channel to France. Bathtub fever was beginning to surface.

Frank gathered together a small group of citizens in Nanaimo to brainstorm some more new ideas to make the Canadian Centennial a really memorable one. Amongst other wacky notions, Glen Galloway, a salesman at Nanaimo Realty at the time, suggested the idea of having some bathtubs floating with the swimmers in the Protection Island annual swim. Frank told him that it couldn't be done. Glen was a good salesman and kept on at Frank about the idea. Frank finally told him that if he could make one float he had himself a deal. Little did Frank know that he was one day to be described by the Nanaimo Indian Band Chief as the "Chief of many tubs."

If the truth be known, the very first idea of a bathtub race started about 30 years ago, when I was reading a comic strip called Chilly Willy and Wally Walrus. It seemed that poor Chilly, a penguin, was always cold, wore a wool toque and scarf and wished to go south as often as possible. One day he found a bathtub in an old house and decided it would make a fine boat. When he put it in the Arctic Ocean the water shot up from the plug hole. Chilly's solution was to plug the shower pipe into the hole and turn the shower out of the back of the tub. This caused the tub to go forward toward the warm South Seas.

Then came the 1967 Centennial celebrations. "Do something unique and zany as your contribution," said the T.V. ads. Then came the first thoughts - go to Vancouver in a bathtub - get free publicity - get off the Island! Better yet, get two or three others so I could beat them - even better publicity. How to pay for it? Another great idea - ask Frank Ney, my boss to pay. He was always a great guy and never one to dampen youthful enthusiasm.

Frank greeted the idea with cautious excitement and offered a budget of up to $500 for me to prove that a bathtub would float. Stabilization, not flotation, was the question, I explained, but by then Frank was talking to someone else about the price of tea.

The late Sandy Miller offered a galvanized bathtub for the first trials. It was very small and round bottomed. Suddenly flotation was a problem. Clearly a large porcelain roll top tub would displace the volume of water we needed, but they weighed about 250 pounds. Eventually we had Ken Spence of Lantzville form a tub, using a real one as a mould. A new era had arrived.

The first tub had a 20-foot pole out one side amidships, with three bleach bottles half full of water. They wouldn't sink and they didn't lift out of the water either.

The great public unveiling was on Boxing Day, 1966 and was an unqualified success. Powered by a 3 h.p. Johnson and no flotation, it ploughed along at a safe and sane speed of 2 knots. No further development was necessary for a bathtub race, except possibly to correct the tendency to turn right.

The rest is history and the race that Frank Ney spear-headed in 1967 was beyond anyone's vision.

Glen Galloway

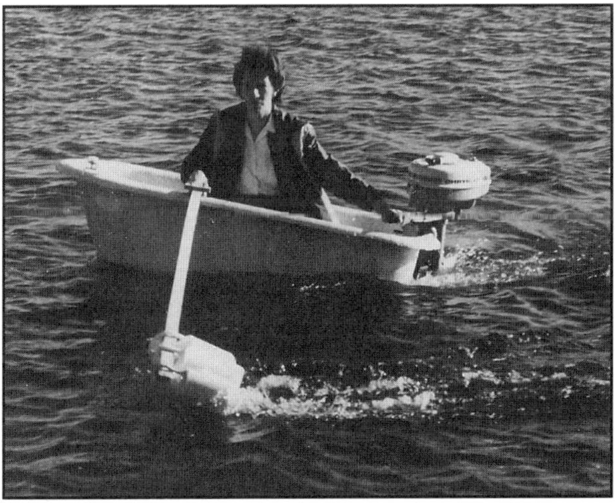

The first prototype floating bathtub. Heavy, slow and hard to manoeuvre despite the protruding bleach bottles. Bathtubbing has come a long way in just a few decades!

The very first prototype racing tub was put to the test in a fish pond behind the Nanaimo Realty office. Frank was very pleased when he saw a floating bathtub. His first thought on the subject was to have more built and announce a race to Vancouver. The whole thing would merely be a gag because only the pilots of the tubs would know that they were only to go around an outlying Island and come back to town for the big surprise finish.

A fiberglass version of the original heavy porcelain monster was soon assembled. To everyone's delight it survived its maiden voyage at sea during the Boxing Day Polar Bear swim at Departure Bay. Glen Galloway performed the honours of being the captain of the tub. It didn't go very fast, but it did stay afloat.

It was agreed by all the friends involved that a committee and a race be organized. Frank, being the Centennial Committee Chairman, was already responsible to the city council headed by Mayor Pete Maffeo. Frank brought the new idea before the City council, and they approved the event, believing that it was to be a simple race to Gabriola Island.

Frank immediately started running with the idea of a bathtub race. Every media and corporate connection in town had already been his for years and all he had to do was show enthusiasm towards an idea and it would spread. There was no way to predict or outline the entire project so the guidelines rested around the basic criteria of fun and zaniness.

Everyone's Going to
The Great Centennial Bathtubbers Ball

SATURDAY, DEC. 9th - Branch 10 Canadian Legion - 9 p.m.

COME FOR ½ HOUR....COME FOR 4 HOURS....COME AS LONG AS YOU WANT....WHEN YOU WANT....WITH WHOM YOU WANT....OR COME ON YOUR OWN AND MEET NEW FRIENDS. IT WILL BE A MAGNIFICENT EPIC AND SAGA IN TRUE BATHTUB BUCCANEERING REVELRY.

***LIMITED DANCING * UNLIMITED INFORMALITY * NO TABLES - MEET NEW FRIENDS * NO LIFEBELTS NECES-**

SARY * DRESS (AS CRAZY AS POSSIBLE) * UNLIMITED REFRESHMENTS * LIMITED FORMALITY * CHAIRS AVAILABLE FOR THOSE WHO GET TIRED OF TALKING * FREE JOLLY ROGER HAT TO FIRST 500 PEOPLE * 1 FREE CAKE OF SOAP and 1 FREE MUG OF CLAM CHOWDER TO ALL * GO-GO GIRLS IN A CAGE * DANCING 9 'TILL ?

Tickets $1.50 per person

3 BATHTUBS ON DISPLAY
Unlimited supply of bathtub salts, exotic soaps and toilet plungers. SEE 1000 Cartons of soap hanging from the ceiling.

COME ALONE OR
Bring All Your Friends Boyfriends or Girlfriends

Yes there were prizes! Twenty-four trophies were to be awarded in eleven classifications. The winner of the race was to receive a beautiful wrist watch. To keep costs down for the participants, each tub was issued free paint and free gas for the outboard engine.

If by chance the race was found to be a little monotonous by the halfway point, the tubber could enjoy intermission music in the middle of the strait in the form of the Silver Coronet Band playing "Singing in the Bathtub." There was of course absolutely no guarantee that a bathtub could make it all the way to Vancouver. The idea was unfounded and completely silly. Somehow it struck a nerve that excited the spirit of the times.

The first tub to register for the race was a huge contraption made bouyant with the help of 40-gallon barrels. The very first floating bathtubs were quite funny to look at. There was no precedent, so why not have a 6' keel or stick wings with styrofoam? The inventiveness and spirit of fun was quite commendable.

Frank continued to push every event in town.
He congratulated these ladies on their bowling championship.

As public enthusiasm grew, more issues had to be dealt with. How can a person or business from another town assemble a tub and transport it to Nanaimo? Frank answered that question by commissioning Ken Spence to manufacture fiberglass racing tubs to order. These tubs were lightweight in the shape of an old cast-iron tub and available for $32 plus $1.60 tax. Frank wrote memos to all inquiring tubbers and sold slightly over fifty of these custom racing tubs by mail order.

A few hundred inquiries were sent to Frank in the mail and he somehow managed to find the time to respond to everyone's questions. "Is it true that only one man can ride in the tub?" asked one or two enthusiastic potential tubbers. What hotel do you recommend? What is the maximum horsepower allowed for a tub? Frank kept a file of all of this correspondence as a personal souvenir of the summer of '67.

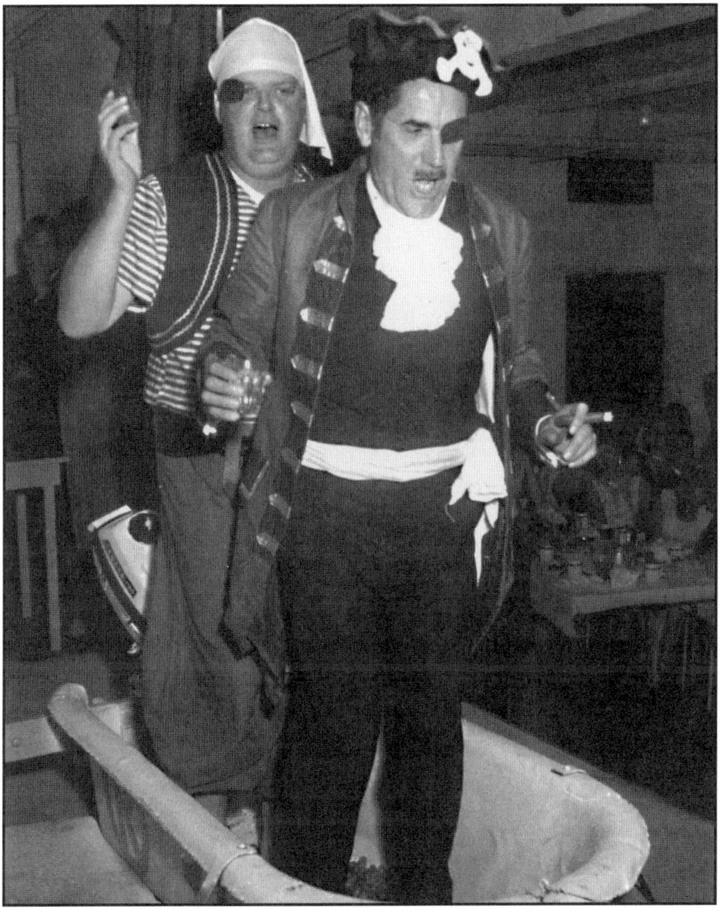

Frank arrived driving a motorized bathtub. The grapes in this bathtub were crushed with bare feet and Frank appeared to enjoy drinking some.

Frank had an up-and-down relationship with the Royal Bank of Canada that spanned his decades in Nanaimo. Everything was smooth sailing in '67 and even this bank got in the spirit of things and published some "Helpful Hints for Travelling Tubbers." The bank had literature printed that advised tubbers to take along suntan lotion laughable in '67, sun glasses, gravol pills and insect repellants. The list continued with aspirin, games, credit cards, styrofoam walking shoes, traveller's cheques and one 32-mile extension cord with a 60-watt bulb. The bank also distributed a "travellers currency guide" for those who stray off course.

As news of the race spread, a shroud of secrecy prevailed in one corner of the festivities. Never before had so many people spent so much time altering the design of a tub for non-bathing purposes. Designers from a variety of professions were busy in the garages and backyards of Bathtub City. Construction on hydrofoil-pontoon and sea-sled hulls ran rampant. As designs and approaches varied, one common ideal threaded all the bathtubbers together. Nobody wanted to let the public see their creation before the race.

The curious public read newspaper articles without the satisfaction of actually seeing a photograph. The pre-race practice tryout brought out the defects and virtues in design, as well as the flash of many patient cameramen.

The most remarkable celebration of sea worship on record was in the making. No fewer than 221 men, women and children were preparing to put out to sea in a bizarre array of hot-rodded bathtubs, supported by various types of flotation devices and powered by common 6-hp outboard motors. Frank had decided that for the actual race itself each tub was to have an escort boat for the purpose of affording protection. The hundreds of escort boat captains had to be extra cautious in waters filled with speeding bathtubs.

When the full extent of the event was realized by the city council, they threatened to call it off as being far too dangerous. The potential for disaster was enormous. With so many possibilities anything could go wrong. There is a lot of deep water between Nanaimo and Vancouver. The mayor was very nervous about the race, and was not shy about letting his feelings be known. Frank was too busy promoting the idea to let that bother him too much. He was already doing everything that he could to make it a safe event.

The Great Race

Getting chaufffeured around in style. This great little car drove easily on land and water.

Bathtub fever was running high. Tub-lieutenants of the zaniest navy on earth studied weather forcasts, tide and current tables, and sniffed the breeze for a storm. The race was to prove to be one of the most spectacular events, if not THE most spectacular event of Canada's centennial year. One thing for sure, it was certainly given greater publicity than any other event, even Expo 67 in Montreal.

The CBS flew in a crew of seven from Los Angeles to cover the race from both sea and sky. Their film was scheduled to be flown to New York to be aired on American national television. A crew from Amsterdam arrived to make a movie about the race. The British Broadcasting Corporation was also in town to film the event and assembled it into a documentary. Here in Canada the CBC was on hand to make a 1 ½ hour film. They had also entered a tub in the race and suitably christened her "Miss Sea B. Sea".

Princess Margrete had just married Prince Hendrik in Denmark. The beautiful wedding was filmed and televised by Laterna Films, a top-notch Danish film crew. These three photographers were in for an extra treat that summer as they quickly boarded a plane to Canada. They checked into a hotel and joined the pre-race festivities.

Life magazine was in town to cover the event. All totalled, an army of 40 to 50 newspaper and radio reporters from all points of Canada, USA, and Australia were ready to take notes. It was the first time in history that the city had received so much international publicity. People in New York were soon to read about the wacky race in Time Magazine. The word was out. "I didn't know that the media were just aching for news," Frank later recalled, "I thought goodness me I'm just doing this as a joke and these people are serious!"

Reverend Thomas K. Palmer wasn't very happy about the fact that the race was to be held on a Sunday.

If, as Rev. Palmer states, the stagers of the bathtub race are responsible for contributing to juvenile delinquency, vice (of all things), and other crimes, thus "aiding and abetting in the disintegration and destruction of mankind," then the world is truly in much worse shape than most of us were aware of.

Attitudes like Rev. Palmer's, I feel, are doing more to turn young people against the church than any other factor.

I am certain that anyone who had any spiritual roots to hold on to, did not lose them for missing one church service to attend the bathtub races.

Miss Lee Wilson, A visiting U.S. College Student, 1967

It turned out that every World Championship Bathtub Race held during the 20th century was held on a Sunday. It is simply the one day when the least number of people have to work all day. This started a tradition of some services being postponed or rescheduled. Everyone managed to work things out.

The pre-race activities ranged from the silly to the sublime. One of the more inspiring moments came during a potlatch and salmon barbecue on Newcastle Island. Native dancer Leslie John performed a special movement to seek cooperation from the spirits. "Mr. John is one of the best of the Native dancers and we are fortunate to have obtained his agreement to dance for us." There is no question that the intention of the dance was realized. There were so many people on Newcastle Island that a waiting period was required when taking the ferry back. Frank is credited in creating some of the first ferry overloads in the Vancouver Islands.

The Bathtub Capital of the World was all abuzz the night before the race. Everyone was completely bathtub-happy. People were swaying all over town singing sea shanties to their heart's delight. All the hotels and motels were full of these bathtub crazy guests. Frank was busy making four appearances on television that night.

There was confusion around town about the actual starting time of the race. Frank explained, "What we mean is this: the bathtubs are to be there at 9 am, but the race will not actually begin until 10. We want them there early so that we can have a grand sail-past, so that the public can see the boats before they start out on the race."

Mayor Pete Maffeo was still very nervous about the whole thing. Twenty minutes before the race was scheduled to begin, he hurried down to the water front. After squeezing his way through the crowd he caught sight of Frank. The mayor pleaded with him, "We've got to stop this! These people think they are going to Vancouver, there will be suicides!" Frank diplomatically explained that the whole thing was now too big to stop. This didn't make the mayor any less nervous, but it did convince him of the legitimacy of the old phrase "the tubs must go on."

Race day commenced on July 30 at 10:30 a.m. A squadron of sea planes filled the sky, and on that day two hundred and thirty two tubs graced the starting line. Rev. Trevor Williams was on hand to recite the prayer for the tubbers while the mob of excited bathtub spectators bowed their heads in praise. Pete Maffeo had by then conceded to the game and accepted the honor of firing the starting gun. These two official blessings were followed by the shrill whistles from the tugs and Navy ships. The harbour was one big wet panic.

No one knows how Frank ever calculated the number, but in the first twelve minutes one hundred and eighteen tubs sank. Included in this number was the tub containing Glen Galloway about five miles east of Newcastle Island. One after another shivering bathtubber started to drop out of the race despite the encouraging cheers from the escort boats and a floating rock 'n roll band complete with a gaggle of go-go girls.

More than 20,000 people made it out that morning to witness the funniest race in the nation. Vancouver's upper level highway made a good vantage point for motorists and was the scene of an instant traffic jam.

There were representatives from two navies in the Nanaimo harbour watching over the twenty-five hundred yachts and tubs from England, Denmark and the U.S.A. The International Establishment of Gentleman Bathers and Cricket Players from Vancouver entered a tub, as did the venerable Burnaby Drinking Team. Not to be outdone, two politicians put forward the 'S.S. Socred' in honour of their political party. The Turkish bathtub was in the running, as was the elaborate steam tub. Not only did the radio and television stations report the event, they sponsored their own tubs!

Thirty-two miles away at Fisherman's Cove in West Vancouver a $100 prize was waiting beside an additional gold watch. Twenty-three handsome mounted trophies were put up by the Centennial Committee. Three and a half hours after the start of the race, the winner was in sight. Vancouver's Rusty Harrison could hardly acknowledge the cheers of the 15,000 Vancouver bathtub fans as his 6 hp motor pushed him ashore. The 22-year-old draughtsman was so cold that he could only manage to say, "I wouldn't go through that again for all the money in the world." He got the chance later to explain: "The waves were about 6' tall and I sort of surfed all the way from Nanaimo."

In this modern age of $7000 naval-architect racing-tubs it is funny to remember that some pioneer bathtubbers actually crossed the 32 miles in heavy cast-iron bathtubs. Rusty covered the course in 3 1/2 hours in a tub he had assembled the night before the race. It had a simple but effective flat bottomed hull attached to an unpainted white tub by six short angle support rods. The bow consisted of a slightly raised triangular chine.

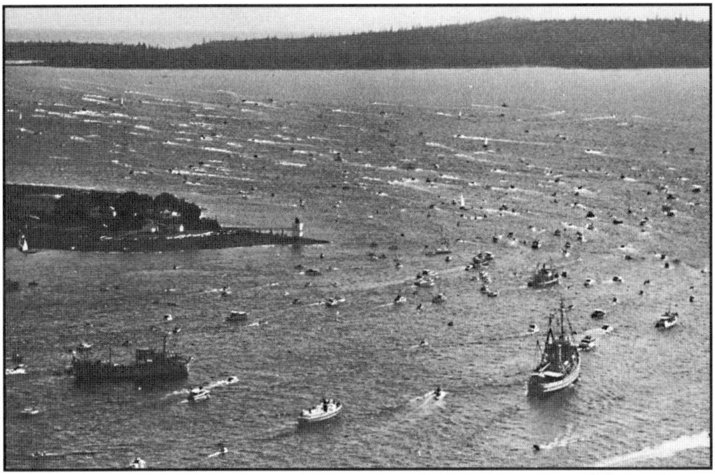

Bathtubs fill the harbour as a testiment to the unique spirit of Canada.

Forty-one tubs made it to the finish line the first year. The remainder of the tubs were either towed to shore by their escort boats or dragged down towards the lost underwater washroom of Atlantis.

There was no indication at this point that it would ever happen again. The cameras were pointed towards Frank, the impeccably dressed Mississippi Gambler, as he proposed, "Let's do it again in another 200 years." His well-worn outfit of tails, topper, gold-tipped cane was soon to give way to a more suitably maritime outfit for such events. Both the gold watch and cigar survived the transitions from one costume to the next.

As the race officially ended on the mainland, the purest epic and saga of raw courage and true bathtub seamanship was just beginning. The initial bathtub race sported many unique crafts, ranging from the paddle-wheeler to the sporty power tub. The most amazing effort in bathtub history came from the collective minds of a creative crew from Gabriola Island. A group of teenagers wanted to join in the fun and displayed an incredible spirit never to be matched. The eight enthusiasts converted a 50-year old riveted tin sheep-watering tub into a Spanish Galleon, complete with poop-deck and styrofoam pontoons. *The Gabriola* was the world's only sailing tub.

When the designing, building and decorating was completed, the crew dressed as go-go dancers and started the race with all the other tubs. Their enthusiasm hadn't dampened by sunset when they finally made it out of the harbour. They sailed off into the night under the watchful eyes of Clyde and Amy Coates who stood guard on Henry Silva's fishing/escort boat. The cabin cruiser *Charade* was also on hand for the adventure.

The sailors took turns piloting the slow-moving tub as the darkness set in. As they reached the halfway point, another boat appeared. Frank and his crew were heading back to Nanaimo and met up with the sleepless sailors. Frank was both astonished and deeply impressed by what he saw. He was mostly concerned for their safety and tried to convince them to abandon the mission and come back to town with him. It was quite apparent that they had not won the race. The hearty young sailors were not to be dissuaded. The sailing tub and the centennial chairman were simply two ships that pass in the night, but not before Frank presented everyone with silver bathtub plugs.

We had a great bathtub race! There was a few guests aboard Frank's boat as we chased the tubs off to Vancouver. On the return trip, which was about one o'clock in the morning he had invited so many people aboard his boat that it was almost overloaded. We cruised at about seven or eight knots and it took about three hours for the crossing.

At one point he stopped the ship and took a swim. Several other people joined him right in the middle of the salt chuck, which was quite dangerous, I thought, but that was Frank!

Frank Graves

There were rough seas and contrary winds for the crossing of the strait and the crew of *The Gabriola* had forgotten to bring any food with them. They basically survived on pop for the 36 hours it took them to complete the race. One of the girls had fallen overboard in the rough water that swamped the tub and almost foundered the escort boats. The girl's immediate rescue was followed by a fire aboard the *Charade*. This in turn was dealt with and the race continued.

When the tired teens arrived on the shore they were greeted by sea gulls and shellfish. They spent several hours wandering around the empty beach hoping that someone would show up and officially acknowledge their finish. The race had been over for quite some time. There was no press, no bell to ring, no ice-cream cones. It looked as though there would be no mention in the record books of this epic crossing.

When the gang arrived back at Gabriola Island's Silva Bay their parents had a much deserved fanfare waiting for them. A crowd of about 300 blasted flares, rockets and fireworks into the sky to the accompaniment of car horns, shouts and cheers. The young crew was too tired to enjoy the festive dinner set out for them. Meanwhile, Frank could not stop thinking about the show of commitment he had witnessed out in the Strait. He would not let the story fade away so quickly.

Our parents weren't too sure about letting us go through with this, especially with Clyde Coats as our escort boat. We were all much younger then. They got another escort boat for us and away we went. We went to Woolworth's and costumed ourselves as go-go girls [boys excluded]. There was no wind at all. It took us 'til dusk to get out of the Nanaimo harbour and all night the boys took turns rowing the sail tub. To make matters worse, despite all our preparing no one brought any food. All we had was some pepsi I had brought. Frank Ney's boat met us on its way home. Frank tried very hard to persuade us to come back but we would not give up. When we got to the other side no one was there and we wandered around for quite some time hoping someone would show up and record our arrival.

When we returned to Gabriola our parents had arranged a celebration dinner. We were much to tired to eat.

Judy (Heddle) Preston

The week after the race proved to be just as hectic for Frank as the previous one. He had a pile of miscellaneous bills to sort out and hundreds of letters to answer. He also had his usual dozens of real estate deals on his mind. Business waits for no man. It was also a good idea at this point for Frank to catch up on some missing hours of sleep.

One week after the race, Frank arranged for the Canadian Navy to "capture" Gabriola Island and bring fanfare to all prisoners. The HMCS *Porte Quebec* left her berth in Nanaimo with a full crew that included officers and one prominent civilian named Ney. They cruised around the north end of the Island and just at dusk slipped through the Flat Tops into Silva Bay. It was the first navy vessel to enter the harbour. A 10-gun salute from a turnip-firing gun on the forecastle blasted perfectly innocent turnips into the harbour without resulting in any casualties. The ship was tied to the wharf and the officers and crews marched ashore. The Island fell to the navy, lock, stock and barrel.

It was one big happy time. The Islanders loved it. The navy was having a great time participating in such an historic mission. Frank had convinced the newspaper, radio and television reporters to be at Silva Bay for the occasion. The sailing tub with its blue and white sail was picked up and paraded around the space in front of a makeshift grandstand. Frank publicly praised the tubbers with what he called "the raw courage they showed in a 30-hour struggle with wind and wave across the gulf. It was a magnificent bit of bathtubmanship."

Lieutenant Peter Stow presented the "Centennial Bathtub Race Endurance Trophy" to the crew of *The Gabriola* while announcing, "I have the greatest admiration for anyone who would attempt to cross the Gulf in such a craft." He also presented a plaque to Clyde Coates. Frank was awarded a new megaphone; his usual one went overboard as the waves tossed him around on race day.

There was another festive dinner hosted by the crew's parents where more speeches, thank you's, and awards were tossed around. The bathtub heros and heroines were Ann Coates, 24, Judy Heddle, 16, Jenny Brown, 14, and Vicki Cross, Wendy Meyer, Dan Brown, Norman Kebblewhite, John Gillen, all 17 years old. As the cameras flashed the reporters talked amongst themselves of the fact that Frank had been in the newspapers too much already. It was decided that the articles would mention but not show him. This was not to be. The next day a smiling Frank was shown standing aboard a Navy ship in all the papers.

A 30' cedar log raft manned by a crew of 5 had also made it out for the race that year. Like *The Gabriola* saga, there was only a breeze to greet them upon their late arrival in Vancouver. This "breeze" blew them 15 miles back to sea in the direction they had come. Frank had the centennial committee give them a royal welcome back in Nanaimo, but alas, there was no tub on board and therefore little media attention. The crew of the *Centurian* raft were of the unanimous opinion that the "highlight of our adventure was meeting Frank Ney. No one but Frank shared our enthusiasm quite so well or did so much to foster a true spirit for the centennial idea."

Jim Cathcart had this to say, "He is, without a doubt, *THE* Mr. Canada and a man to watch. He has written all over him: Get off your hands Canada, and do something. The city of Nanaimo must be very proud to have such a man in charge."

Most people were quite pleased with the raving success of the first international Bathtub Race, but there is no pleasing everyone. Frank's phone rang a couple days after the race with an irate retired navy chap on the other end. The fellow was in West Vancouver and wished to share his dilemma with the promoter of the race. He complained in a strong British accent, "Because of your tomfool race I put a metal bathtub in my swimming pool and attached a 9-hp motor. It sank. My wife is raising the absolute dickens with me because the dratted thing is plugging up our pool!" Needless to say, Frank was thrilled!

The entire year was a triumph and the centennial Committee had become well-loved and celebrated by the community. The Committee was presented with silver rose bowls. Frank was delighted and called the whole experience "a pleasure and a delight." Frank was recognized by Secretary of State in Ottawa and received a confederation medal offered for "valuable service to the nation." Frank spoke out, "I have received this honour not for what I did alone. This has come as the result of the work of a good committee I had around me this centennial year. It has come because of the enthusiastic people who together made the year the success it has been." Frank was again invited to speak at numerous outings and often chose "Nanaimo after centennial" as his topic. He publicly expatiated on his visions of beautification.

To the Editor, Re The Great Bathtub Race

Quite some time ago, when the idea of the bathtub race was suggested, the writer, as a professional seaman, was horrified at this project, feeling for sure that there would be much loss of life and injuries to persons etc., etc. Events have proved my thinking wrong.

Mr. Ney has done such a fine job in obtaining publicity for our town, our province and indeed our country, that I sincerely suggest that the citizens of this area show their appreciation to Mr. Ney by prevailing on him to run for Member of Parliament in the next federal election. Our country needs such men of the calibre of Frank Ney to help make it a better place in which to live.

E. B. Murray 1967

It was great year for the Ney family all around. Frank's Uncle Fred (Major Fred J. Ney) was awarded an honourary doctorate by a British university in acknowledgement of outstanding public service. He had dedicated years to international education and was the only holder of a doctorate of laws in town. Meanwhile Frank had been riding the Centennial helicopter with the Mayor.

The annual Protection Island Swim wasn't lost in all of the hoopla. The customs float began to sink with the weight of the 217 swimmers before they jumped, scrambled and fell into the water in a solid mass of bodies. For the first 50 yards the swimmers hardly had room to move their limbs. They looked like a giant school of spawning salmon. This mass swim had become the largest one in the nation.

Frank's *Jolly Tar* was amongst the 217 escort boats. It was recognizable as being the only one with a Scottish piper aboard. Frank joked that the music "scared away the killer whales while valiant swimmers fought riptides and icy waters." Frank appeared to be everywhere at once during this mass swim. The master promoter and showman was in fine form in his pirate suit. The pirate theme had not dominated the events of the year, but was destined to be a major selling point of future promotions. One thing was consistent with Frank's events, his volunteers handed out thousands of free ice-cream cones.

The next step for Frank was a flight to New York and Montreal. He was invited to appear on a popular New York television show called "To Tell the Truth." This early game show was based on a simple and amusing concept. Three guests would be introduced as all being the same person with the same name. A panel of celebrities would in turn ask questions of the guests to determine which one was really who he claimed to be. On this episode three men, all claiming to be "Frank Ney" were introduced, seated and interviewed.

Bud Collyer, who had been famous previously as Superman on the radio, was the gentleman host for this long-running series. He read out the statement that Frank had previously written to explain his identity. Bud recited the story of the bathtub race and got a good laugh out of the audience when he mentioned the tub that had its navigational lights reversed so that other tubbers would think it was going the wrong way. The syrupy violin-based theme music commenced, the studio audience applauded and the show cut into its first commercial.

After learning what there is to know about Vanish bathroom cleaner the questioning was started by celebrity Orson Bean. "Number Three: now, you have eleven children how have you found time to organize bathtub races, polar bear races or anything?" "Well, it's all lots of fun!" "Well, I like a man who lives life to the hilt!" The audience laughed away. He asked questions of the other two men and landed on serious but inaccurate answers.

Kitty Carlisle was the next celebrity to question the guests. "I knew Canadians were very sensible; it turns out they're as kooky as we are." She spoke very quickly and found out that Frank was wearing a different costume during the race than the one he was sporting for the T.V. show.

Next up was Tom Poston. He asked the two imposters about the cricket matches and the eleven children. He asked "Number three, where do you bathtub your bathtub races?" "Well, we don't have...This is the first time in history that we ever had a bathtub race." As the bell rang Tom repeated "Where did you have it?" Frank quickly belted out "Across the Straits of Georgia, thirty-two miles with eight-foot waves!"

Arlene Francis was the last celebrity panelist. She asked each guest what he does for a living to support so many children. Number one said, "I'm in the land developing business". Number two, "Land developing business." Number three, "The real estate business." She then zeroed in on the real Frank and asked him "Who is the Prime Minister of Canada?" Not more than two seconds had passed before he shot back "Lester Pearson." The bell rang and it was off to another commercial.

The celebrity panel marked their ballots without consultation. Tom Poston was first to read his, "I voted for number three. He's just full of spunk and spirit enough to do this kind of thing and enjoy it and he's just rotten enough!" The crowd roared with laughter.

Arlene Francis, "I agree with Tom. I think you have to have a tremendous sense of humour to have eleven children, and also to do ridiculous things like this, having eleven children, you know, and also he looks ridiculous in that costume!"

Orson Bean, "I think the eleven kids come in very handy because if you ever get in a fight with your wife you can get lost in the crowd. I voted for number three, it could have been any of them but I voted for number three because he looks like Pappa Dionne (Father of quintuplets in Ontario).

Kitty Carlisle, "Well, guess what, I voted for number three and I'm not going to give any reasons. Anyway he intimidated me!" The host cut in with "We'll meet the real Frank Ney in just a minute; right now a word from our sponsor."

He confirmed that all four panelists, as well as the audience had all voted unanimously for number three. "Will the real Frank Ney please stand up?" All three men made motions of lifting from their chairs and

Frank finally arose to the applause. The other men were identified, Frank said a few words and accepted his prize of $75 US.

The Ney family was photographed every year for personalized Christmas cards. Frank liked to take advantage of good locations regardless of the season.

The New York style of insulting humour was not adopted into Frank's personality as he left the Big Apple and headed on to Montreal. During his Montreal visit he attended Expo 67 and had a wonderful time. "Every Canadian should see it if he possibly can get there." He raved to the press about the mini-skirts he had seen and encouraged Vancouver Island to participate in the new trend. "Every woman is wearing them - at least all those up to 40 and then some. The mini-skirts are a bit longer than the seven-inch English ones, and are all the rage back in New York and Montreal. It was quite a contrast to get back to western Canada again and see all the girls covered up."

"Hardly anybody in New York has ever heard of British Columbia, but many had heard of the bathtub race. It took the trip back east to make me realize one of our greatest assets in Nanaimo is fresh air. In New York and Montreal I had to close the window of my hotel to keep the bad air out. But the mini-skirts are all sorts of gorgeous crazy colors, all very bright."

It was exciting for the people of Nanaimo to see their number one booster in action. Having made a good name for himself in the community, there came a point in Frank's career when he was ready to assume a position that would enable him to do the most he possibly could for the community he loved so much.

The experiences over the year 1967 transformed him from being an outstanding citizen to Mayor. By the end of the year he stood proudly with a robe on his back and a rose bowl of appreciation in his hand.

Mayor Frank Ney

THERE IS NO DOUBT that Frank loved Nanaimo. He was Mayor of this city from 1968 to 1984 and again from 1987 to 1990. People had suggested that he run in earlier elections but he did not want to run against Pete Maffeo who was Nanaimo's popular Mayor from 1957 to 1967. As Frank told it, his decision to run for Mayor came by accident. "In 1967, Pete Maffeo was the Mayor and he appointed me to become chairman of the Nanaimo Centennial Committee. I got into the campaign, and that was the year I started the bathtub race. Pete fell on the ice while curling that year, and he hurt his head quite badly."

The injury convinced Mr. Maffeo not to run in the election. Frank later declared, "So I thought, by gosh, I'll run! I'd never been in politics and there were aldermen running against me, but I had been pretty active in the community. I had been chairman of the Salvation Army drive for twelve years, and I had ten years with the Empire Days, and was involved in the polar bear swim. It was just one of those things."

When Frank announced to the press his intention to run he was quoted thus: "In Mayor Pete Maffeo's retirement we are losing one of the greatest and most popular mayors the city has ever had. In throwing my hat into the ring I feel I can offer the leadership the city will need in the years ahead. I feel I know what the city needs at this particular time." There followed a long list of his contributions to the community including his role as vice-president of the Nanaimo Swimming Club and president and director of the Nanaimo Figure Skating Club. As president of the Junior Chamber of Commerce he represented Canada amongst four other countries that sponsored participants in the Commonwealth Youth Movement Tour of Great Britain.

He told the town that a corporate mind was needed at City Hall and that he would "rather be defeated by a vitally-interested public than retained by an apathetic one. A well-informed electorate is a happy one."

Frank's platform promised major public works improvements. Urban renewal, public housing, the creation of a friendly climate for resource industries, commerce and tourism were all offered without raising taxes but rather by taking advantage of subsidies offered by both federal and provincial governments.

"Subsidized housing doesn't mean cheap housing but I feel that a good quality subsidized house can be produced in Nanaimo at competitive prices. Public housing does not mean low standard housing. It means, rather, subsidized housing to help a certain section of our community."

He felt that urban renewal would create more jobs for everyone and that young people who were just entering the employment market would have far wider opportunities at home with such a program. He concluded, "It is my hope that if I am elected mayor, we shall be able together to make Nanaimo one of the most exciting and beautiful waterfront cities in this province."

The two other mayoral candidates were very well versed in local politics. Alderman Jack Parker had been on city council for nine years and the recreation commission for six years before that. Both he and Alderman Ted Barsby were well known and presented serious competition for Frank in the election of 1967. The most important thing that these men shared that year was a runner-up position to the new mayor of Nanaimo. Frank cleaned up with 2402 votes against Barsby's 1060 and Parker's 619. Frank was swept into office by the largest majority any Mayor of Nanaimo had ever received.

Pete Maffeo and his wife went out to dinner one evening at the Grotto during the yuletide. It was a special night for them as they were not only celebrating their 44th wedding anniversary, but they were also preparing to leave for a visit back east with their daughter. Frank and his wife had also planned to go to the same restaurant that evening. To everyone's surprise and delight they all ran into each other there. Frank pulled two tables together and ordered some champagne.

The two couples had a wonderful time together. After the Polynesian hot pineapple chunks were served as desert, Frank paid the bill and toasted congratulations, happy journey and a Merry Christmas.

The next stop for the Neys was Yellow Point Lodge, the scene of the annual Nanaimo Realty Christmas party. All of the staff were there, and it was a rousing and enjoyable affair. There was never a shortage of reasons for Frank to celebrate, and Christmas was perfect because the partying was built right into the season. He was the man who gave others an excuse to party at all points of the calendar year.

"We had an incredible 602 swimmers out" estimated a centennially clad mayoral candidate as Christmas Day gave way to the Boxing Day Polar Bear Swim. "One of them was from as far away as the Northwest Territories. But I don't think we had any swimmers from Victoria. Maybe next year the old Victoria Polar Bear Club will send up a team. They will find our waters warmer than Victoria. And if they don't swim, well, they can serve tea during the cricket match. I'm sure they'd be good at that."

All swimmers received two centennial dollars, a Jolly Roger hat and a banana. Frank didn't expect the exceptionally large turnout of swimmers from 4 to 71 years of age. "We went through the original $1000 put aside for the event in the first 45 minutes. After that it got a little embarrassing but people accepted IOU's and they will get their money."

Frank Ney was sworn in as Nanaimo's Mayor right before the calendar turned over to 1968. Pete Maffeo had already returned from his Christmas holidays and was happy to attend the ceremony. Frank once again showed respect for the retired mayor in saying, "He set a great example for those of us who follow." Pete became a "Freeman of the City of Nanaimo," an honour shared with only two other living men. Sadly, Pete Maffeo died soon after his retirement. He had been highly respected by the people because of his interest in children, fair play and sportsmanship.

Howard Nicholson was Frank's good friend as well as being the city controller. He revealed his amazing ability in remembering names as he stood as master of ceremonies at the mayor's banquet that year. Howard, without pause, reeled off name after name of guests present, and the places they occupied in the community. That feat, and the food served were both described as "fantastic." Many people wondered who was paying the bill for the extraordinary meal served that evening. The hall at the Shoreline (now Dorchester) Hotel was filled with guests enjoying a gourmet treat rarely available to local diners. Even those who were a little squeamish about eating frogs' legs were appreciative of Frank for dipping into his own pocket to pay for it all.

Pete Maffeo opened the new Overwaitea store as his last official act as Mayor and Frank sponsored Dave Stupich in a walkathon to raise money for underdeveloped countries as one of his first acts. As soon as Frank was elected, he bought a full page newspaper ad featuring two aerial views of the city, a list of the city's features and a personal message welcoming inquiries from people around the world, signed, "Enthusiastically yours," Frank J. Ney.

On the first working day after his election, Frank showed up at the City Hall one minute before the staff arrived, and started what he thought was his job as the first magistrate of the City of Nanaimo. Senior staff soon acquainted him with the facts of life, so answering the telephone, opening the mail, and perhaps sweeping the floor were not in his job description, but he was sure willing to try! Frank had energy to spare.

Jerome L. Harrison, City Hall Staff, 1955-1990

Nanaimo got its final centennial year newsbreak at the stroke of midnight Sunday, December 31, 1967. The CBC had chosen Nanaimo as the city to host the New Year national radio broadcast. The new mayor sat in front of a microphone with cigar in hand and headphones on head. The CBC announcer was thrilled as the tuxedo clad Ney took to the air. "I am positive that the centennial spirit will carry on. 1967 has been a wonderful year and a wonderful party. We have had our fun and fireworks, and now we have to have our future."

"I have a feeling of nostalgia in my heart for the centennial year." He made the show his own by saying, "British Columbia feels friendship and affection for our brothers and sisters in all the nine provinces." He told the east, "I know you won't be offended when we come out there later this year and bring back the Grey Cup to where it belongs. And even if we don't get it, British Columbia will still be the bathtub and cricket capital of Canada, and Victoria will probably remain the tea-drinking capital too."

The bell at Nanaimo's famous Bastion was heard from coast to coast as the last seconds of the year faded away. After the bell had rung in the new year, Frank explained to all of Canada, "In other days this used to warn of Indian attack, but today we are members of the same family." The year had ended, and a new era born. The city of Nanaimo refers to the next twenty years as "The Frank Ney Era."

I guess it was at the end of the 60's and 70's I saw this name of Frank Ney, Mayor of Nanaimo popping up more frequently when I was living in Vancouver. I wondered could this be the same Frank Ney I used to play hockey with in Scotland? When I saw his picture I knew it was. The older I get, the more I feel that some sort of pre-destination brings people together at intervals.

Don M Ross, Retired Hockey Player

It has been said that two hours with Mayor Ney was like two hours too many in a sauna bath, the end result being complete exhaustion. No one could figure out where the new chief magistrate got all his natural energy. In his real estate office he had typists clatter a steady stream of mortgages and agreements for land sales or transfers. The desks were packed cheek by jowl and the walls thickly festooned with framed press clippings, photographs and certificates. The phones would ring over top a booming public address system.

Chief Bill Wyze and Frank made a terrific media pair.

The cafe next door was an extension of the office activity. When a salesman entered the cafe looking for approval of an apartment sale, Mayor Ney advised, "This $20 000 cash? Try and get it up a little higher. Looks as though you have a deal. Give me two hours for the final decision. Looks good though." A match book representative was next in line. When Frank returned to his office, a constant knock on his door, ring on the telephone and staccato conversation accompanied him.

Amongst the various people who wished to speak with Frank were members of the press. His busy schedule and quick wit drew plenty of attention. When asked about himself, "People tell me I'm egotistical. Well, I am. I figure if anyone wants to know anything about me I'm the best person to tell them." How does he plan to handle pressure groups? "No problem with pressure groups. That sort of stuff has already started. I just listen to them, tell them they have a good point and suggest we talk in the press so that the public can know what they are saying and what they're threatening. Very effective so far. They just back off."

Reporters always went away with great quotes: "There is no room at City Hall for party politics of any kind...I'm going to dedicate myself to being a damn good mayor...With a little teamwork and co-operation the future of this island will be absolutely incredible. This is the jewel of the west. Just fantastic."

"With the tremendous mass of young people coming up we have to think big about education, and then think even bigger. We can't hold back on this one because youth can't wait for us...By the way, here's a coloured photograph of my family and two buccaneer hats. You're now a member. You've just got to stay enthusiastic...By the way, did I tell you that retail space in Nanaimo increased by one-third last year and that the retail product was $38 million, will soon hit $48 million and will be close to $70 million by 1970." In the same spirit of his hockey and piloting careers previously, Frank had set out to be the very best Mayor this town could imagine.

We were at a convention in Moncton for the Federation of Canadian Municipalities. During our free night out Frank asked about a good restaurant, "Do they have cloth tablecloths!"

He checked with a member of council from Vancouver and found out that it was the best place in town.

Anonymous

The aldermen in 1968 thought their new Mayor's enthusiasm had carried him too far and told him so. Frank had been talking publicly when he outlined his picture of the city's future. The council had not had the chance to transform the new ideas into a policy before Frank went off and raved about what was going to happen. It was suggested to Frank that he not do that type of thing. It could not have been too surprising when the next day's newspaper sported a photo of the new Mayor complete with top hat asking, "Do you want a leader, or a boneless wonder? Do you want a puppet?" The next twenty years provided an answer for him.

Two decades later Frank recalled, "One of the first things I'm pretty proud of, and one of the first things I did as Mayor was the work we did on the waterfront. I worked with John Morris of the engineering department and with the assistance of W.A.C. Bennett, we had the promenade started. I wanted to accent and beautify the waterfront."

As an import from Ft. McMurray, Alberta, I arrived here without a job. A teacher since 1966, I couldn't acquire employment with the regular school system here.

When UIC did the "proof of search for jobs" on me, I went down to city hall. Being tax time, there was a huge line-up. I had no time for waiting in line, so knocked on Frank's door. Upon hearing, "Come in," I did just that. We spent quite some time discussing Ft. McMurray, as Frank knew the former mayors. I was so impressed that this man, in an elevated position, could give me the time of day. I left there with his words of wisdom - "You're doing it the right way - banging on doors!" He reinforced my self-esteem.

I left there thinking that Frank Ney was a very 'human' person who would take the time to talk to anyone. I was very impressed.

E. Joy Lillies

There was simply no end for the demand he created for himself as a public speaker. There was a lot of momentum built during the Centennial year and Frank encouraged everyone to keep the wave rolling. He would dazzle audiences with topics usually considered to have limited appeal. He made the man on the street excited about sales, advertising, growth and charity. After his appearance as a guest on the popular television show "To Tell The Truth," he was able to explain the many procedures necessary for its production. He wanted people to understand that the mysterious magic possessed by the people that move and shake the world is simply knowledge put into action. Everyone can prosper. It is up to the individual. Frank offered to be there to help and encourage anyone anytime. It is not surprising that the majority of top realtors and developers in the area all got their start with Mr. Ney.

Commerce was certainly not the only factor that Frank considered important in maintaining a healthy society. He was the first to launch an inquiry into regulations governing the population control of sea lions, hair seals and elephant seals. It appeared to him that there seemed to be less killer whales around in the late 1960's than there was the previous decade. Conservation of marine life was not the social concern during the booming decades as it is today. Frank insisted the issue be dealt with.

Mayor Frank Ney

Nanaimo shared an increasingly large illegal drug situation with the rest of western civilization during this period. Frank was receiving more and more phone calls from parents whose kids were experimenting with drugs. His phone would also ring with calls from people who simply wanted to express their concerns. Frank estimated that for every case reported in the newspapers about people having bad trips on LSD, there were about ten more that only he heard about. He stated, "The drug situation is quite serious here and it has to be a matter of alarm for everyone in the community." His proposed solution was one of educating people. The Mayor talked with the Education Minister and urged him to implement mandatory drug education programs in B.C. schools. Frank's idea of fighting drug abuse through education stands as well today as it ever did.

The generation gap didn't stop the teenagers from the flower-power age from speaking with Mayor Ney. Five high-school students met with Frank and presented him with a plan. The youths explained the need for a Drop-In-Centre. A house could be purchased and renovated to provide a coffee-house type atmosphere. It would be open to all teenagers seven days a week. Frank readily agreed that there was a need for some program. He considered the plan to be very ambitious but also wondered if there may be problems with details not yet outlined. The cost of maintenance and taxes on a privately-owned house could be prohibitive. He wondered if the Civic Properties and Recreation Commission could not be worked with in providing a place. Why not use the present machinery that deals with community activities?

The young people then explained, "Teens feel that if it is something run by the city and organized, that it will turn them off." Frank asked why they would feel that way. They explained that there exists a majority of teens who don't go to anything that is tainted with city or CPRC organization because they feel that the need to conform is too great. It infringes on their informality.

Frank offered the teenagers the use of the old firehall and picked up the phone. He had to retract his offer when he learned that is was in use as a storage shelter. He picked up the phone again and arranged for the teens to meet with the person who supervised programs for the city. As always the mayor had to be someplace else quickly.

A two-story purple Victorian house was eventually acquired and decorated with a variety of couches. The "1927 Drop-In" was a great success until the early 1970's.

Nobody ever had to knock on his door. It was always open. The fridge at his house was the same deal.

Anonymous

The telephone at Frank's house had many hours of use. Before he had gotten into politics he had received his share of business calls at home. But once he had became mayor, there entered a new era of telephone madness in the household. When Frank came home from work in the evening he was usually greeted by his wife, children and telephone. People were never shy about calling the mayor at any hour and telling him what was what. These calls, which ranged from the polite and important to the drunk and abusive, represented a trend that was to last his lifetime.

He read the paper every day, including the obituaries. He went to a whole lot of funerals. He had a tremendous respect for the old timers who had been coal miners in their day. Whenever an old miner passed away he showed up and sat in the back row at the church. It didn't matter what he had to cancel to be there. It was that important to him.

Rhonda Evans, Hairdresser

Meanwhile back at City Hall, the updating and beautification of the town was set into gear. Frank was crazy about coloured sidewalks. He convinced businessmen in 1968 to support a beautification drive which included the installation of new colourful sidewalks. During the 1970's all a person had to do was go for a walk to put some extra color into the day. With the continual widening and repairing of roads,most of our sidewalks have now returned to a pale grey shade. If one is to walk along Chapel Street between the Great National Land building and the Fiesta Bowling Ally, one can admire and marvel at what is one of the original remaining coloured sidewalks in Nanaimo. If that is not enough, check out the one in front of the Dorchester Hotel. A red sidewalk is certainly a curious thing.

There had been no new sidewalks in Nanaimo for thirty years. People wanted some improvements, and they got them. "There is nothing like things you can see to warm the hearts of people... If you want to make a city sizzle, put cosmetics on it...If we sit on the lid of progress it will blow us all to pieces." Frank was a great source of quotes as he occupied the main seat at City Hall.

Previous administrations had already put a major portion of the money aside for Operation Blacktop. Frank stepped into office and put the program into high gear. "They never got around to getting on with the program. The roads, many of them are in disgraceful condition. If we are to keep our own people happy and attract other people to Nanaimo, then we must have good roads and attractive streets."

"It has always been my philosophy, and always will be, to talk only about things that can be done. I think people appreciate this sort of positive thinking. In the past too much time has been wasted discussing the things that can't be done."

By the final city council meeting of 1968, 6,300 feet of sidewalks had been installed, 12.4 miles of blacktop had been laid and 258 new traffic signs installed. As the meeting adjourned, Frank brought down his gavel. Its head flew off and hit the city engineer square in the noggin. Not bad for a year that started with the rescue of a pig from a culvert as first official duty.

The responsibilities had somehow managed to pile up in Frank's life. Managing his large companies, large family and growing city scarcely allowed time for anything else. As more and more work was delegated to others, this problem managed to solve itself. Frank was addicted to the idea of promoting new ideas. If he wasn't in the middle of a promotion he was planning his next one. Some of the older folks around town admired his drive but were becoming ashamed by his antics. The rest of the population wasn't terribly surprised or shaken when the Mayor showed up dressed as a sailor for his own "World Championship Pea Shooting Contest."

A smile and a handshake. Frank's new bicycle draw has a winner!

The aim of the game was to hit a bottle ten times with a supply of twenty peas from a distance of twenty feet. Having accomplished this, an award of 45 cents was granted. About 1,000 youngsters between six and twelve took the challenge. Younger competitors were allowed to stand a little closer. Arnie Miller, who was only two, appeared to be unaware of the rules and had a whale of a time. Ten-year-old Clinton Eccles won with a perfect score and was presented a gold pea shooter by Mayor Ney.

Frank invited five other Mayors from the Island to participate in a separate Mayors' Championship. Two joined the fun, two were too busy, and Victoria's Mayor politely declined the invitation. In keeping with tradition, free pop and ice-cream were distributed to everyone after the game.

The constant stream of promotions turned a lot of heads. The CBC invited him to Vancouver for another half-hour interview. Many people saw only one side of the man that news clips showed whooping up a crowd. Was he a genius or a nut case? The radio and television people felt that it was time to let the man speak for himself. Freelance reporters also often found him to be an interesting topic for mini-essays. A glimpse into his life was revealed one day:

Portrait of Perpetual Motion

The Man Behind the Bathtubs:

It's Tuesday. Just any day of the week Tuesday. Frank Ney is up and running. I'm trailing him around. I want to make a "what makes Frank run" story.

"Well, what do you want to know? Want to look at my press clippings?" He picks up an inner office phone and within seconds two of the staff burst in carrying folders bulging with clippings and photos. The bathtub race. The World's Champion Pea-Shooter contest. The Famous Mayor's Ski Race. The Polar Bear swim. Frank Figure Skating. With His Kids. In his RAF Pilot's uniform. The photos spill out onto his desk.

Help.....where do I start? The Bathtub Race seems the most obvious.

"Do you know why it was so successful? Because 10,000 people were part of that show. Every guy who went out on his boat to follow the tubs was part of it. Remember all those motors starting up in the bay at the beginning of the race? I guess that was the greatest moment for me."

I try to keep the interview going but it's hopeless. The phone buzzes endlessly. Staff pop in with papers to sign. City Hall wants his opinion on a project. He keeps disappearing down a labyrinth of hallways. I do find out that amongst other things he is now the director of the Neurological and Cerebral Palsy Association.

Despite the bedlam he's cool. Never seems to change his pace. Handles every problem right off the top of his head. What's the secret?

"I make the decision right now. I don't carry it around with me. If I lose money, so what. At least I've made the decision. Look, I plan most projects four to five years ahead. It's so easy because at the beginning no one else is thinking of it. By the time they see what's happening I've already got it tied up.

Is Nanaimo Realty really the second biggest real estate company in B.C? "Well, no one ever said it wasn't. Better say it's reputed to be."

Where does he get the energy to keep up the pace? "I drink two quarts of buttermilk a day. Perhaps that's it. Don't you think buttermilk's good for you?" He asks in such a disarming small-boy way that even if I disagreed I wouldn't have the heart to tell him that buttermilk's a lousy drink. "My father was a businessman, conservative type. Perhaps I got it from my mother. She was sparkling."

I ask to see his children. Frank Ney has 11 kids, all born in the last 13 years. He phones home to check with his wife Joc (Joss). "There's a reporter here from an up-Island paper. She wants to see the kids." He covers the mouth piece. "She says she doesn't want publicity." "Look sweetheart, she wants to see the kids. No really, don't dress them up, just the way they are." No dice. He looks disappointed.

We dash for lunch at the Kiwanis Club. He's a past director. Les Corfield is giving a talk on the work the Shriners do for crippled children. When he's finished, the Chairman asks Frank to say a few words. "Sorry I didn't win the World Champion Pea-shooter Contest. I'm pretty sure it was rigged. If I hadn't twisted my ankle the day before I probably would have won."

Mayor Frank Ney

Lots of applause and good natured laughter. Nanaimo's favourite son. Its favourite booster. Next he's scheduled at an elementary school where 10-year-old Christine Denton has won a plaque for her "No Smoking" poster.

Les Corfield says he'll drive us and on the way up Frank puts his speech together. Puffing a cigar, laughing about the time he won the B.C. Toastmasters' speaking contest.

On the way to the school he sees a sea of bikes. "My God, Les, look at all those bikes. Let's do something with them, there must be a thousand." Les says there's 200. "At least 300. Think big, Les." He kicks around the idea for a safety program. Pop and prizes. All the kids in town involved.

Later we stop at his Cilaire residential development. Expensive homes under construction with a beautiful view of the harbour. We've got twenty of these developments plus the Nanaimo Industrial Park. See that planter up there by the gates. Biggest one in Canada." How did he know? "Well, no one's ever challenged me."

We switch over to his white convertible and go up to City Hall. The car radio blasts me out of the seat.

Doesn't he feel pressure? "Look, I surround myself with good men. Delegate the work, give them the responsibility. I've never had to fire a man. I can tell what he's like by looking into his eyes. No, I never feel pressure. Never let my mind get that involved in anything."

At City Hall he puts on his robes for a photo then promptly forgets I'm there. The door opens and Civil Defence committeemen pour in. Didn't I want to stay for the meeting? I beg off.

Later as I walk along the street with him people continually call out, "Hey, Frank!" Even the youngsters." When the kids all call me Frank I know I'm doing O.K."

He decides to take me up to his house despite Joc's stand on publicity. He mixes big tumblers of rum and pepsi. The kids hang around him, baby Monique in his lap. "Not one of them looks like me except Russel and he's adopted." Plump little Russel, a two year-old Indian beams from his high-chair.

Joc has softened. She's in the kitchen peeling potatoes, talking about psycho-cybernetics, keeping her eye on the clock as she is due in sculpture class at 7:30.

As I leave he's talking about going swimming that week-end with the kids. Last week he took 17 of them over to his summer place. Frank's doing O.K. He's great.

Morgan MacGregor, Summer 1968

This was the era when politicians used to shake hands, slap backs and even kiss babies, when appropriate. Frank was no exception to the norms of the day. It so happened that one couple in town had a very tame pet monkey that they brought around with them. This couple was standing at the wicket in City Hall one day waiting to pay a bill. Their monkey was dressed in a pretty pink snow suit and looked like a little girl from a distance.

In walked Frank. He looked around and spotted the two voters with a baby in their arms. He walked over to shake hands and give the baby a kiss. With his arms out stretched, he got within about a foot of a kiss, recoiled and started laughing. Two little beady brown eyes were staring at him from that little furry face. "I kiss babies, but only those who can vote." Of course everyone had been watching and joined in on the laughter.

The phone in Frank's office was always a well-used one. One of the principals from Pacific Hovercraft called up the progressive mayor and set up a meeting with him. This firm from Richmond was proposing to run a SRN6 hovercraft between Nanaimo and the mainland. Reporters were asking Frank about the 35 passenger, 50 mile-an-hour possibility before he had a chance to find out the details himself. It had been five years since he decided not to go ahead with the project. "This is an exciting possibility. I am looking forward to talking to these people. Perhaps some new factors in hovercraft transportation have come up. If Pacific Hovercraft find it possible to run such a service, that's fine. It will be a great thing for the Island."

Frank met with the people and gave their application a go-ahead. They had a modern looking vessel that had been a hit at Expo 67 in Montreal. A crowd of spectators stood by the water behind the Malaspina Hotel as it pulled into town. All the civic dignitaries, reporters, businessmen and other curious people braced themselves for a surge of wind they all predicted would come from the craft. They were surprised by a slight breeze as the crew tied the lines while the rubber skirts deflated until the hull rested in the water.

Mayor Frank Ney and the press were invited aboard for a spin in the harbour. As the craft rose on its cushion of air, it gained speed and headed towards Newcastle Island. It skimmed over a slightly submerged reef and a deadhead without a tremor. The trip went very smoothly. Frank was having an absolute ball and asked the reporters to please be supportive of this venture. He had no personal financial ties to the project other than a share in the prosperity it could bring to the local business community. "This is only the beginning. If the company can make this financially successful, I think we'll be seeing a new means of transportation, possibly with a different type of hovercraft."

I remember going to Vancouver on the hovercraft. It was so rough out that day that we had to travel between a bunch of the Islands rather than go straight across. It was still very rough, even in the sheltered spots. When we got to Vancouver I could see a barge standing about 4' above the water. This was the landing barge. The captain blasted the engine and we flopped on top of it. The wind pushed us half way off again and we were stuck on a sharp angle supported by our seat belts. Imagine a huge room full of people hanging by their seatbelts!

The captain said all the "Don't worry" stuff until a tug boat arrived a pulled us off. Once again the engine roared, this time to a successful landing. I found it unnerving and decided to take the regular ferry back home later that day. It

> *turned out to be an obvious choice because the rest of the runs that day were cancelled due to the weather.*
>
> Anonymous

Unfortunately the hovercraft was not be be a lasting addition to the Island's seascape. The same problems that were outlined five years previously in Frank's report still held true. Frank was not too happy to learn of this but was too tied up in other things to dwell on it for too long.

Frank took great pride in working to draw people to live on any of the Islands. His idea was to continue to publicize the area in a positive direction. People could visit and participate in the festivities or just enjoy the natural splendour. The combination of a breathtaking landscape and a well-serviced community was enough bait to transform visitors into house buyers and tax payers. It was not simply the financial rewards that Frank was after with expansion. He was proud to show off his town and loved the people who came to appreciate it. The more people the better as far as he was concerned.

Presenting the Eaton's Cup. Many of Frank's best friends were reporters.

He used every opportunity available to promote Nanaimo as not just a great place to live but as a complete lifestyle in itself. He created and promoted Nanaimo as "The Sunporch of Canada" and when he couldn't go to the media he made reasons for cameras to come to him. Frank promoted Nanaimo as an industrial and retirement haven and made sure that the facilities were in place for both to be successful. This vision was becoming a reality before the very eyes of the man who moved into the crumbling company town as an unemployed veteran.

The author still has the silver dollars that Jim Goodwin is shown giving to him at this early Polar Bear Swim.

N-A-N-A-I-M-O that's how you spell NANAIMO
And our mayor is Frank Ney
He lives in Departure Bay
We are famous for our tubs, and our good old English pubs.

Children's song to the tune of Twinkle Twinkle little star

From day one there was no question in his mind that the city was going to grow and develop. The media would normally have no reason to take notice of a municipal Mayor boasting about the magnificence of his town. Frank made them notice. Not only did he dress and act like a pirate, more often, he created a complete personality around the theme. "Black Frank" was achieving an amazing amount of free publicity for Nanaimo and British Columbia in general. He was creating events, opportunities and careers for people. The raving pirate was becoming more than a gimmick. "Black Frank" was becoming a respected national personality.

Despite opposition allegations that he couldn't handle two political jobs at one time, the Mayor decided to run for Member of the Legislative Assembly (MLA) one more time.

The Premier of British Columbia in the late 1960's was a fellow named W.A.C. Bennett. Much like other premiers, he was somewhat controversial. He was addressing some loggers with facts from a book once, only to meet with disbelief. He tossed the book to a logger in the audience and told him that he could see for himself. The press picked this up as "Bennett throwing the book at loggers."

Bennett was scheduled to appear at the "Capitol Theatre" in Nanaimo, where the parkade on the end of the Bastion Street Bridge is now. Six large loggers were waiting for him in the front row wearing hardhats in anticipation of hardcovers being tossed their way. On that evening in July 1969, Bennett was escorted to the stage by an equally large logger. This impromptu bodyguard warned the Premier of the loggers and of one in particular named "Tiny" who was in possession of a hand held martial arts weapon. Bennet laughed, "I love this kind of stuff!"

Premier Bennet hit the stage, and he hit loggers with quotes rather than books. He ranted, "Guys with heads as hard as yours shouldn't need helmets." When Tiny began to rattle his weapon Bennet exclaimed, "Did somebody bring their baby?" He then looked into the crowd, saw the giant man and hollered, "WOW! Some baby! 400 pounds!" The embarrassed giant logger walked out.

Bennett continued the program with some serious Frank Ney election hype. Frank had been nominated to represent the Social Credit Party in the upcoming provincial election and his platform included building a seawall at Departure Bay Beach. Premier Bennett chanted at the crowd, "Give me Frank! I want Frank! Elect Frank and you've got your seawall!"

Premier Bennett and Frank spent considerable quality time together during the election of 1969. Frank had arranged for the Premier to give a speech one afternoon at the Nanaimo Indian Reserve in front of a number of delegates. Frank had passed up a personal opportunity to appear before a crowd at the "Moose Lodge" in favour of supporting Bennett's scheduled visit to the reserve.

Mr. Bennett didn't show up at 6 p.m as scheduled, so the event was postponed until 6:45. Back at the Malaspina Hotel, Premier Bennett was taking a nap. One of his campaign organizers reported that he was in no hurry to get up. In hearing this, Frank jumped to his feet and said, "I'm going to wait five minutes more and then I'm going." As officials tried to dissuade him, he let it be known, "I've waited here for an hour already. I have had it." Another member of the waiting party backed him up with "I don't blame you. I feel the same way myself."

In less than five minutes word came that the Premier was dressing. At 7:20 he arrived in the lobby. He and Frank rushed down a flight of stairs to the banquet hall where they thanked people for support. They shook people's hands all the way into the huge waiting cars. The shouts, whistles and general hollers of support could be heard above the car horns from down the road as they finally got the evening off to a start.

Frank and I campaigned against each other provincially in 1966, 1969 and 1972. He won in 1969 and I won the other two.

I was a member of the Chartered Accounting firm that did most of the auditing for Frank's empire of real estate companies. It seemed that every election campaign coincided with the period of heavy activity in his office, particularly for myself.

The telephone system within his office building was a public address system. Whenever I got a phone call, it would be announced over the loud speaker system so that some 60 real estate salesmen, plus staff members and anyone who happened to be in the building for whatever purpose would hear that announcement. Frank never objected that my name was heard much more often in his own office building than was his own, even in the middle of an election campaign.

David D. Stupich, Accountant

Frank loved to invite his opponents out for a beer. He was a leader in the field of keeping party politics out of city council and was known to exclaim, "The leftists are voting right and the rightists are voting left."

> *He would talk to anyone. As soon as a committee meeting was over where people had fought tooth and nail, the conflict was left behind the door.*
>
> Bob Rowledge, Retired Director of Finance

Member of the Legislative Assembly

THE NEWSPAPERS IN VANCOUVER AND VICTORIA zeroed in on Nanaimo's "flamboyant mayor" being elected to the legislature. The Victoria Times took the cake in the quest for the funniest adjectives when they described him as "Nanaimo's Bathtub Hippie Mayor." Frank laughed and laughed when he read that one. "First time I have been called a hippie. Likely a proofreading error. It should have read 'Nanaimo's Bathtub Happy Mayor'." Some people would never have seen it as being a misprint in the light of the social issues facing Frank as he served as MLA for Nanaimo from 1969 to 1972 at the same time he was Mayor.In typical Ney style, the newly elected MLA made sure his grand entrance did not go unnoticed. He hired a piper complete with kilt and marched into the legislature as the bagpipes wailed away. Departure Bay soon had its seawall. No problem.

Member of the Legislative Assembly

I served with Frank in the B.C. Legislature, and he was one of the best liked members of the house. He was very hard-working, and I would marvel at his stamina: the ability to work all day at the legislature, often very late, and then drive back to Nanaimo to be able to chair a meeting the next day - and then back to Victoria.

Grace M. McCarthy, Social Credit Party

Frank Ney was a truly genuine person. His benevolent spirit will never diminish. I was raised on a large farm five miles north of Duncan. We operated a fruit and vegetable stand along the Island Highway. At least once a week, around five pm, in would drive a large Lincoln Continental. A statuesque, well dressed man would enter our store. At first I thought my eyes deceived me, but it really was Frank Ney! In his typical style, he would purchase a large variety of vegetables, mentioning as he left, that he had a large family to feed. Sometimes on weekends Frank and his wife would drop in at the stand. My father, Douglas Griffiths, owner of the store, served him on several occasions. We remembered Frank as a person who supported the small businesses, regardless of his demanding lifestyle.

Geraldine Hearsey

All of the years Frank had spent as a public speaker had prepared him for his new position in government. He had embarked on an entirely new era of speech-making. He wrote and spoke effortlessly on complex issues such as taxation, transportation and the economy in general. He was known to present both problems and solutions. His personal beliefs were ironclad, and they were after all the reasons he had stepped into politics to begin with. Because of this he was not easily swayed and was not afraid to vote against his own government on issues he felt strongly about.

The well-loved MLA upset the legislature one day by taking the floor dressed in deerskins and snowshoes. Frank drove the Island highway to Victoria for the meetings and was very aware of the sad state of that well travelled road. He adopted suitable attire in order to accentuate a point he wished to make about the condition of the highway. Nobody would have benefited from an improved highway as much as Frank. He hastily drove up and down the Island for meetings on a regular basis. "They used to call me the roadrunner."

Everyone wanted to see improvements of the island highway, but as per normal, the big stumbling block was the raising of the cash. His idea was simple; if lottery tickets were printed and sold, post-prize funds could be liberated for the cause. Unfortunately for those who frequented the highway at the time, lotteries were illegal. The powers that be were not willing to overlook that fact. It took a number of years for the highway to begin to see a new facelift, and when the new hardtop went down it was the taxpayers footing the bill. Lotteries, meanwhile, have of course become a mainstay of our society.

Frank didn't stop there. "I have advocated in the House one cent a gallon extra on Vancouver Island in order to accelerate the construction of a four-lane highway, or if this is not politically acceptable, put it across province. Each one cent brings in $ 5,000,000 a year and this money could be spread through the province to get ready for the great growth of the '70's." "It was only a 100 years ago that Nanaimo was a city of mud trails, typhoid wells, people living in wooden shacksand primitive conditions. We are indeed a privileged people to be allowed to play our part in the history of this beautiful Island as we enter the soaring seventies."

On December 26th, 1969 at the time of the Boxing Day swim, after we had had a very warm spell of Fall weather, I noticed that a bush of raspberries in my garden had some plump berries on it. Frank, of course, was always boasting that Nanaimo is the "Sun Porch of Canada." So I went out and cut a branch of the bush and took it down to Frank at the beach in Departure Bay as he was getting the swim underway. He was delighted to show off and, with the C.B.C. filming the scene, I was asked to put a berry in Frank's mouth. That evening on the National News, behold, this scene was played out as an item of the broadcast.

Beryl K. Bennett

A new pancake house is born.
Buildings sprouted up like mushrooms along the highway.

Those were the days when growth, progress and expansion were not questioned as being desirable goals. Frank had decided that he was the man to bring them. Those were also the days when it was a rare luxury to find a passing lane on the Island Highway. He told us, "It's the farmer in the field that makes the farm a success, not the person peering over the fence telling him how to do it."

With growth and progress often comes social problems. Frank was proud to oversee the presentation of a beautifully illustrated sign on the highway that read "Welcome to Nanaimo - Bathtub Capital of the World." It became ever so apparent to him that a new problem was arising when the sign was vandalized to read "Heroin Capital of the World."

Frank rounded up representatives from 28 organizations for a big meeting. He asked each group to give their ideas on what the community needs to fight drug addiction. His approach to the problem was to link the community in a co-operative effort. Frank listened to and sorted through all the information and prepared to bring some solutions to the B.C. Legislature.

It was during a budget debate that Frank called on the government for special assistance to finance his new program. "Let's get on top of the problem now. Let's wage a war on the persons who are supplying our young people with heroin. Let's not wait five years when it will be too late. By this time well-organized criminals will be running the drug rackets. If this happens, we could then have the problem of violence and crime never before known in our city. There were no heroin users here three years ago. Today it has the second highest ratio of heroin users in Canada."

"A trafficker in Nanaimo supposedly clears $3000 a week. This money has to come from somewhere. Stolen articles sell for approximately one-quarter of the regular price. At least 85 per cent of crime in Nanaimo can be attributed to drug use of one kind or another. Traffickers have no regard or concern for the welfare of the addict or user and hence the danger. The user requires more heroin as time progresses to obtain the desired effect. Subsequently, in order to support his habit, the addict has to turn to crime. He or she has to steal, prostitute herself, or go to any end to obtain the necessary amount of money to continue the habit."

He called for four more policemen to combat the dealers. As a preventative step he asked once again that a complete program of anti-drug education be started in the schools throughout B.C. at the grade one level. "Let's make them aware of the dangers of this temptation in their associations with other children. Let's get them the proper insight into what drug abuse is and not have them receive their knowledge from other children. Drugs are a sociological problem in our society. We must get to the root of the problem; are young people doing this as the "in" thing, or a sign of rebellion or just for obtaining kicks, or to fulfill a human need?"

"Drug problems are not new to us. Alcohol and nicotine are reaping their toll amongst our citizens, but at least we've graded and controlled these drugs even if we support them through taxes."

Frank also pressed for provincial funds for the establishment of a methadone clinic where heroin users could be treated. "Testing and supervised treatment could be supplied free of charge to addicts." He outlined the mechanics of such a system, similar to ones in larger cities.

Popular opinion states that the weather and social programs attract transient drug users to the Nanaimo. Everything that Frank ever said in promoting our way of life to the world reads like an invitation to criminals as well as industrialists. The defaced "Welcome to Nanaimo" sign that Frank had adored was eventually removed, but the heroin problem never did go away.

I met Frank on the street passing the time of day and asked him, "Are you busy these days?." He said, "Yes, I'm Mayor of Nanaimo, an MLA, CEO of Great National Land, President of Nanaimo Realty with three secretaries on the go. The only sleep I get these days is in the back of the Lincoln on the way to Victoria."

Murray Barbour

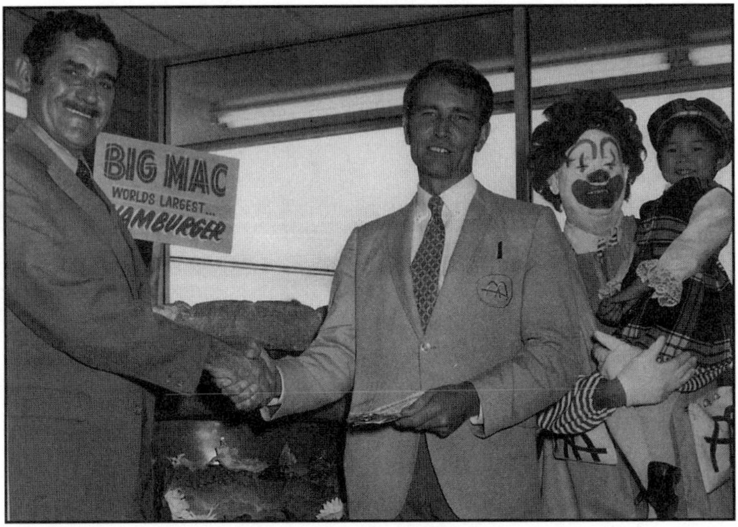

Nanaimo had one of the first McDonalds restaurants. The grand opening featured the world's largest hamburger. The patty and the bun were real, but the tomato was painted steel. The line-up of children understood that it was to be consumed by the animals at the zoo.

Member of the Legislative Assembly

When I was 5 or 6 years old my mom and dad, two sisters and four brothers were going through downtown Vancouver in the family van for a summer cruise. Dad said "There's Frank Ney!" We all looked and saw an amazing pirate with a sword walking down the street. I will always remember how cool he looked!

Paul Gogo

It certainly was not all fun and gimmicks for the new MLA. One of his first areas of attack was the medical system. He demanded a review of expenditures and called for a more sophisticated approach towards giving taxpayers top value for their dollar. "It is a waste of taxpayers' money to have nurses serving meals that could be done by orderlies or nursing aides, to have doctors doing administrative duties that could be done by ward clerks."

The responsibilities were starting to pile up on Frank's shoulders. His careers were starting to overlap. He simply had to find the time somewhere to do all the work that he had brought upon himself. He had for a long time practised the personal habit of waking very early each morning. This in-demand personality was also known to have some late nights. His daily routine included driving his huge car to the service station for a fill-up. While the gas was being pumped, he would find his regular chair by the heater inside the station house. He became a familiar sight snoozing away on his chair. Nobody ever wanted to wake him up and remind him that he was due at the Legislature, but the duty was always done.

The position of MLA gave Frank a chance to bring his beliefs to a higher level of government. A few weeks before Christmas in 1970 Frank had become aware of a complaint from the highways department concerning the handiwork of beavers. The fuzzy creatures had plugged a culvert and built a dam in a stream. Residents were concerned that the backed-up creek would flood out their basements. The conservation officer said, "The beaver have got to go," and hired a trapper to kill them.

Frank's phone rang off the hook with calls from citizens who were outraged and appalled by the slaughter. He also received his share of calls from people complaining that their basements may flood. Loggers were saying that they had been dynamiting beaver dams for years when they got in the way. Nothing had ever been done by the government to stop them.

After hearing both sides of the argument Frank stated, "I'm shocked that this has to go on. People are saying we should save wildlife, except when the animals bother them. I suggested a citizens' committee to clear the dams once a week but they tell me the beaver build them again overnight. It would be such a tragedy if these animals have to be killed."

Jack Turnbull lived in the outlying community of Extension. He described himself as an "over 60 retired trapper" and made national headlines as he held a permit to "remove beavers as a nuisance." He armed himself with a coni-bear trap that kills them instantly and headed out to the colony of an estimated 60 animals.

As the first two beavers were exterminated, Frank drove to the rescue. He prepared his notes as he hit the highway to Victoria where he addressed the Provincial Government. "The beaver is one of the emblems of Canada. It is an animal that stands for industry and ingenuity. It costs a little more money to live-trap them, but in this day and age we just can't slaughter them. I think we're going to have to have a greater respect for animals." The "beaver evacuation" program had began.

The grizzled trapper continued his work until Frank convinced Recreation and Conservation Minister Len Kiernan to issue an order to stop the killing forthwith. Frank proudly announced that special traps that could take the beaver alive were being sent to town. The highways department was to send crews to destroy the existing dams, and the beavers were to be shipped off to live in other areas as the farmers had requested. The trapper removed the last 75-pound dead beaver from his trap and obligingly discontinued his services.

Beavers had a hard time adapting to new areas in the winter. With this in mind Frank proposed to leave them alone until the spring. Letters and phone calls from people wishing to adopt them started to add up. A professor of mathematics with a quarter section of land on the McMurdo bench south of Golden B.C. wished to have a small brook dammed. He was trying to return his property to its wild state. He was willing to drive into town, pick up the beavers and provide food and shelter for them until spring. Frank forwarded such requests to the Fish and Game branch of the Recreation and Conservation department. His work here was done and he was needed elsewhere.

We dealt with him a lot. He was always asking for things for his community he thought were important, like more parkland and an improved ferry service. He had a lot of enthusiasm. He was a great salesman.

In my ten years as premier, Mr. Ney managed to get more things for his community than any mayor I knew. He knew how to knock on doors in government, and when he couldn't get an answer anywhere, he'd knock on my door. He was one of the most effective civic leaders I've ever dealt with in my time as Premier.

Bill Bennett, Former B.C. Premier

Regular monthly radio interviews scheduled Frank as MLA. On top of that, he arranged for more interviews as Mayor. Anyone could sit at home and listen to Frank discuss problems with the transit system, ambulance service or any issue of the day. If you had something to say, the telephone line was wired into the broadcast system and all you had to do was phone in and be heard.

"Communication is the marketplace of ideas. I need ideas from people in order to initiate programs for the benefit of the people." Frank had suggestion boxes installed at City Hall as well as the Court House. Many good ideas were brought to council this way. Frank sent a BC Hydro manager to Lasqueti Island to assess the possibility of those residents getting power lines to their homes. It was worth looking into, even though that island only showed 4 votes in Frank's favour during the election.

Frank Ney was a politician in the best sense of the word. On one occasion he did a favour for a friend of mine who was a very active member of the N.D.P. and would never vote for any other party, at least provincially or federally.

Art Olivier had a meat-cutting business in the residential area of South Nanaimo. It employed him and his son and provided an income for both families. It was evidently non-conforming in that area, and when the City inspector heard about it, he gave Art forty-eight hours to close up shop and get rid of all his supplies and machinery. Art went to Frank Ney's office and Frank told him he would look after it. True to his word, the very next day, Art had a phone call from the License inspector who told him that everything had been straightened out.

It was very close to election day but close in the sense that the election had been held one week prior to that date.

David D. Stupich

"I thank the Lord for the very good health I have. Of all the things that are important in life, I think the most important thing is to take care of your health. With good health, nearly everything is a pleasure. It's foolish to sacrifice your health for any endeavor." He was never embarrassed if people witnessed part of the 15 minutes of air force exercises he did in his office each day. He walked the half-mile from City Hall to Nanaimo Realty at least once a day. The walk took less than fifteen minutes if there was no stopping along the way.

I used to do my business with Frank on the main street of town. My wife never thought this to be proper but it was the only way I could get hold of the guy.

Mr. Thompson

Frank always maintained the body of an athlete and used his physical advantage to enter good-natured competitions whenever possible. He joined 18 representatives from Island municipalities in a bicycle race for the United Appeal Fund. In 1970 he let the media know that the race would "prove conclusively and incontrovertibly that Nanaimo has the healthiest Mayor in B.C." He proved his point by sending out photos of himself "in training." The newspapers once again showed pictures of Frank dancing vigorously with two can-can dancers.

The Edmonton Journal caught Frank at a mayor's convention. He made friends everywhere!

My parents moved from Stony Plain, Alberta in June of 1970. At one point in their journey west they picked up a second car and agreed to meet at an agreed point once they hit Nanaimo. My mother took a wrong turn in Nanaimo and ended up in front of Nanaimo Realty's downtown office. She parked right there and looked for someone to ask of some assistance. Her luck wasn't all bad because the first person she met in town was Frank Ney.

Frank Ney A Canadian Legend

She didn't know who Frank Ney was. He got an earful of her sad story detailing how she had lost my stepfather in traffic. She let him know that she was now lost.

Well, Frank Ney took her hand and led her into his real estate office and poured her a cup of coffee. In a short period of time, Mr. Ney was able to locate my stepfather and to reunite the couple.They in turn became great fans of Mr. Ney (myself included), and my mother always insisted that everyone should vote for him. On top of that, all of their real estate transactions were done through Nanaimo Realty. He sure knew how to make an impression!

Diane E. Ursel

When Frank first entered local politics, Nanaimo was a very small town that consisted of the downtown core as the heart of what is known as the bowl area.This fan-shaped street plan was drafted 100 years earlier by an overseas firm who had never stepped foot in Nanaimo. It's boundaries were Comox and Victoria Road, capped off with Pine street. Outside of these city limits sat districts ten times its size. Harewood, Departure Bay, Northfield, Wellington and Chase River were all without services such as water and sewer in those early years. As a mayor, and a realtor, he had to deal with this issue constantly.

Mayor Ney tried for years to get all the districts to join forces and each time the notion was voted down he would concede with a gem like 1970's, "If we are going to have a marriage, we want it to be a happy one, not a shotgun marriage."

As a politician Frank always reiterated the concept that it doesn't matter what the politicians want; it's important that the people get what they are after. Being both a politician and a developer, there were always people who would doubt his sincerity, regardless of his actions. He made it perfectly clear to the press that an amalgamation of districts was not for the benefit of developers, but was a result of a demand from the people. He explained, "Amalgamation, or metro-government with other districts, is one way to cut duplication of services and assist the taxpayer." He also pointed out how the provincial government would increase financial assistance based on a larger population. The town would also receive benefits from the federal government. Grants were offered to municipalities in lieu of general taxes for federal buildings. This did not apply to unorganized territory. If the whole area united, the highly progressive biological station would immediately qualify for grants.

Mayor Ney called in his inaugural address for the people to start working together. He hosted a seafood dinner at the Shoreline Hotel and explained the benefits of amalgamation to the guests. Chief William Wyze appeared in his full regalia with Frank and puffed peace signals on cigars during dinner. The two leaders had agreed to co-operate on community undertakings. "Next year we'll smoke a peace pipe." Frank was soon to be up for re-election and was confident that he had made enough friends to keep the ball rolling.

Frank had a bizarre sense of humour. He was host to a huge group of delegates coming to town one day. He and a few other guys set up a table and presented a nice picnic lunch for them. When the guests came into town, they were chauffeured to the scenic spot and led to the dining table - right at the city dump. Anything for a laugh.

Anonymous

Many people were brought to Vancouver Island through the publicity Frank generated, and plenty of them moved to the jewel of the west once they became captivated by its natural beauty. The long-time residents were feeling the effects of an expanding population by 1971 as the Island entered its "finest and most prosperous era." Frank set his sights on directing the city's spirit towards greater accomplishments. In the midst of his speeches about ."..the great and powerful economy of Vancouver Island," while at the same time speaking enthusiastically of his vision: "we look forward to horizons unlimited...," he would put a new light on the entire subject. Frank was becoming known as an 'environmentalist' long before the term had become commonplace.

A budget debate speech was scheduled one afternoon for Frank. He saw this as another great opportunity to be heard. As a prelude to the debate he slipped on a fuzzy red hat and marched into the chamber with his snow shoes tucked under his arm. Before he said a word he gave a virtuoso performance of the yodelling he had picked up in the Swiss Alps. The entire house applauded this.

Once he had everyone's attention he explained that he was drawing attention to the plight of the elk and other wildlife in the mountain area of Vancouver Island. "The time has come to give the wildlife their own bill of rights. There are between 2000 and 3000 elk on the Island today. How many will there be in 10 years if we do not preserve and maintain enough forest range?" He was suggesting setting aside a certain percentage of the timber stands in the logging valleys as wildlife preserves. He saw that the acceleration of logging operations, together with the tourist boom, had increased the urgency for action.

Frank declared that Vancouver Island was receiving more tourists than Hawaii. "We should remember that Vancouver Island's great attraction is its natural beauty and its wildlife and fishing. If this goes, tourism goes." Frank believed in the early 1970's that such a program would not interfere with the overall harvest of forestry operations, providing more stringent regulations on harvesting were adopted. Besides all that, it was a great opportunity for one more push in the direction of turning his beloved Green Mountain ski hill into a provincial skiing park.

To the Minister of Forests Frank insisted, "A great number of people on Vancouver Island are concerned because of poor or irresponsible logging practices in the areas surrounding lakes or rivers, the interest of public enjoyment in the future or the preservation of fish and wildlife is prejudiced....Fortunately, many companies, when it is pointed out to them or because of sound management policies, take steps to preserve those areas in the interest of good public relations. But this is a hit and miss method and depends on the logging policy and good faith of the companies concerned. I submit that the time has come that in the interest of fish, wildlife and environment, legislation or a permit system be used to control the danger of irresponsible logging on private lands." He had seen first hand what mistakes had been made in Europe and didn't want B.C. to suffer the same consequences. These complex issues have yet to be settled in British Columbia, and by the winter of 1993, fewer than 450 Roosevelt elk remain on Vancouver Island.

Other speeches went along the lines of "As we enter the new year, it is evident that the environmental issue cannot be dismissed as a fad. All of us must accept our responsibility to work in harmony with nature, the parent of human life."

"Outpouring of noxious waste is overwhelming the biosphere's ability to cleanse itself." He spoke of the "treacherousness of herbicides, oil spills, fish kills, industrial wastes, overcrowding and sewage. Population is the basic cause of pollution and people are concerned."

Frank detailed and did what he could to make people aware of these important issues. He explained the problem of rising costs of fighting pollution on the one hand combined with the need for a strong tax base through attraction of industry and the creation of jobs. He stated that the city council was caught in the middle of this challenging problem. In grand Ney tradition he added that, "In the final analysis, we want a city where people count. If we make this our prime objective, all other objectives will be more easily reached."

The first step in backing up these statements was the unveiling of a plan to build a new sewage treatment plant. He let the taxpayers know that they would feel this one, but would be better off in the long run. "Many municipalities are not undertaking sewage treatment. In the end, their lack of vision will cost their taxpayers more."

The sewage treatment facility was completed in 1971. Frank was very happy that his efforts in that area gave the city an enviable environmental record. As he put it, "We have one of the best sewage treatment facilities in B.C., and one of the cleanest harbours in North America." This achievement alone marked his presence as being very valuable to society. It is amazing to think that it took until then for the city to invest in such a plant. What is even more amazing is the fact that some other, larger cities still haven't taken the initiative to follow. If every city was blessed with such a forward-thinking Mayor, one could safely swim and fish in the waters off every coastal Canadian city.

Another time at the photographic studio Frank came busting in and said, "I have two minutes to take a portrait." I said, "Sorry, I can't take a portrait in two minutes." Thirty minutes later he left. I found him a very easy person to work with and a lot of fun.

Jim Peirson, Photographer

Frank offered many solutions to some of society's problems. No one, however, ever carried these out. His concern about the impact of automobiles on the environment led him to initiate an idea that would mean fun for everyone. He proposed to turn Vancouver Island into a "bicycle paradise." He explained the widespread popularity of this means of transportation in Europe where great importance is given to encouraging participation. "If we are thinking in terms of a growing population, we should be thinking of bicycle paths." The first, and most important path he advocated was a hardtopped one bordering the highway from Victoria to Campbell River. This170-mile (278 km) stretch covered mountains, valleys and shorelines.

It was decided that there was really no room for bikes beside the highway. Frank persisted with "Bermuda has made money out of cyclists and we can do it here." With so many balls in the air at that point Frank could well have dedicated his life to any one of them. Luckily some issues could be dealt with on the spot. When Victoria talked of poisoning the pigeon population, Frank asked if the nuisance called for such drastic action. "They too have tourist value, and besides, they are living creatures!"

On Febuary 6th, 1972, one of ny sons was home from University to celebrate his birthday. And while home he phoned Frank Ney, who was Mayor and M.L.A. at the time, to ask him about a project to earn some money under the Youth Employment Activities Program which the government sponsored for University students. During the phone call Frank suddenly asked to speak to me. When I answered he told me that Dr. Roy McMillan had just resigned from the Board of

Malaspina College. He was a government appointee and Frank had been asked to name a possible replacement so he asked if I would consider the appointment. Political affiliation did not enter into the nomination. Startled as I was to be asked, I retained the position for fifteen years! I think this is an example of how Frank reached into the community in such a personable way to tap resources and stimulate involvement.

Beryl K. Bennet.

Frank always managed to add a few issues to the constant stream he was already dealing with. He brought up buried subjects that many people have to deal with. Mobile home owners with clear title had no way to register their home unless it was set permanently on a separate lot. Frank urged legislation to require the registration of mobile homes on the same basis as automobiles. This would give the owner of the home some proof of title and make it a whole lot easier to sell. Where would Frank get an idea like that?

In 1972 Frank narrowly lost his seat at the legislature to Dave Stupich. He carried on as Nanaimo's Mayor and found that he didn't have to drive to work in Victoria quite as often anymore.

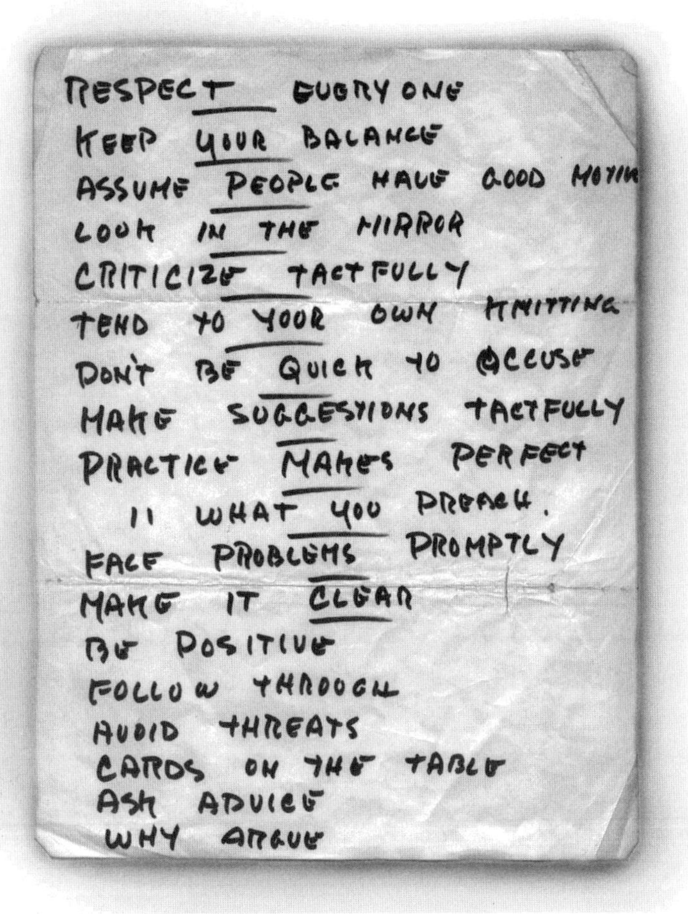
RESPECT EVERYONE
KEEP YOUR BALANCE
ASSUME PEOPLE HAVE GOOD
LOOK IN THE MIRROR
CRITICIZE TACTFULLY
TEND TO YOUR OWN KNITTING
DON'T BE QUICK TO ACCUSE
MAKE SUGGESTIONS TACTFULLY
PRACTICE MAKES PERFECT
" WHAT YOU PREACH.
FACE PROBLEMS PROMPTLY
MAKE IT CLEAR
BE POSITIVE
FOLLOW THROUGH
AVOID THREATS
CARDS ON THE TABLE
ASK ADVICE
WHY ARGUE

Frank's notes triggered his ad-libs.
His speeches were always based on personal philosophies.

Re-elect Frank Ney, Again

My wife, seven-year old son Lee and I applied to emigrate to Canada from England in 1972. I had met Frank in the fifties when I spent four years in Nanaimo. In those days it was not easy to emigrate to Canada and you had to have a sponsor. Frank not only offered to sponsor my family but also offered me a job when I got to Nanaimo.

Very nervously we all set off to London and the Canada High Commission for an interview which was critical in order to be able to emigrate. We sat on the edge of our seats and politely waited for the probing questions from the government agent but he was scanning our application with a smile. He looked up and said, "So Frank Ney is sponsoring you eh? Well whatever is good enough for the Mayor of Nanaimo is good enough for me." He promptly stamped our application, passed.

I have never forgotten that and will always be grateful to Frank and to Nanaimo for our lives here.

L. Jack Patten, Jacqueline and Lee
Aide de Camp to Lt. Governor of B.C.

During his early terms as Mayor, Frank was proud of improving Nanaimo's waterfront and downtown area in general. He pushed for larger ferries to Gabriola and Vancouver Island and dreamed of a natural gas pipeline to Vancouver Island. He saw that as being the most economical and least polluting solution for taking the winter chill out of the people's homes.

Mr. Ney loved to boast about our mild west coast climate "where the waters are as warm as the waters off Hawaii." A favourite oddity for anyone travelling the island highway can be seen opposite the late great Jimmy John's totem pole beside the Pearson Street bridge. There grows our imported Trachycarpis fortunels, better known as windmill palm trees. Frank donated these trees years before he became Mayor. He remarked in 1963, "There is no reason why we should not make

Nanaimo the 'Palm City of Canada'. I hope others will donate palms for this purpose. We only need about one hundred trees to do so."

"I got the idea during the Second World War when I was down at Torquay, Devon, where palms line the waterfront. I planted three in my garden two years ago and they have grown so well I ordered this pair six months ago from California. We have a similar climate and setting here. Our flowers bloom a month earlier than Victoria. We have lower temperatures and no high winds. This is the most temperate climate in Canada."

Frank had imported one hundred pounds of bananas from Costa Rica for the official planting. To this day they are still alive and healthy, thanks to the special treatment they receive from the Parks Board.

Hawaiian dancing has wrinkled some great suits throughout history.

I met Mr. Ney when I was only 4 years old. He always came and handed out the awards for the Nanaimo Realty Majorettes when I was a baton twirler. In the fall of 1972, I told my mother that I was getting worried that the palm trees downtown would die because it was getting cold. She suggested that I call Mayor Ney and let him know I was worried. Since I had already met him from baton, I called his office. When they put me through to him, I told him of my very large concern. He spoke to me for 10 or 15 minutes about the trees and about baton, telling me that he remembered me. He said he was glad that I brought the palm trees to his attention and he would make sure that they would be looked after properly.

When he had finished speaking to me, he talked to my mother, and obtained our address. A few days later, I received a letter in the mail. It was a big thrill for a four year old to receive a letter from the mayor. I have always remembered him as a kind soul and a real people person. He could have hung up the phone and forgotten me, but instead he had someone write to me and also had the palm trees covered within the week.

Mr. Ney made me feel so important. Many times during my years growing up in Nanaimo, I would see Mr. Ney, and he always said hello. He always remembered me by name. I still have the original letter, and I will always keep it. I even have lots of pictures from awards nights with the Nanaimo Realty Majorettes. Every time I see one of the pictures or see anything about Mr. Ney, I always remember 1972 when he was caring enough to write me. He was an incredible man and I hope people remember him that way.

Brande Gilmour

The idea of tropical fruit growing in the Bathtub Capital had an appeal that really captivated Frank. Twenty some-odd years after the initial palm trees hit the dirt he was still importing exotic species to be introduced to the area. The one hundred palm trees Frank had hoped for never quite happened, thus leaving some space for his lemon and grapefruit trees. Frank also had a local species of tree planted along either side of the highway coming into town. There were always stories of Frank using his own personal money to finance a number of his beautification projects. He never made a public outcry about doing so, but there was much public speculation and admiration surrounding such stories. One thing is for sure; lines of trees started to appear!

If he had any fault at all, and it's not a bad one, it's that he used to try to please everybody, and that's impossible without getting yourself into tricky situations. He was a very generous person. For the number of things he did for the community people knew about, there were triple the number that they never knew about. He was always available, always approachable.

Larry Thomas, Reporter and Radio Personality

In 1972 the boxing club was located at the Gyro Youth Centre on Machleary St. under the Parks & Recreation. Our registration was $5 per person for one year. We took in $155. It was to be turned over to the Parks & Recreation for rent and in exchange they would supply us with equipment. Skipping ropes, gloves, etc. As it turned out it was not in their budget to supply us with equipment but we had to turn over the $155 for rent. Well we didn't, we spent it on equipment instead.

The Boxing Club was told to vacate in two weeks or pay the rent. I called our mayor, Frank Ney, and told him of our predicament and he said he would get back to me in two days. Always a man of his word, Frank called and he arranged to have the Rotary Club pick up the tab on the rent for $155.

Frank has been to every one of our boxing events in 21 years. Approximately 50 events. He has always supported amateur boxing in Nanaimo. He was our best fighter.

Les Varro, Nanaimo Amateur Boxing Club Coach

It wasn't an easy job managing a city whose population jumped from 15,000 to 43,000 literally overnight when the citizens of the outlying districts finally voted in favour of amalgamation in 1975. The city then took on responsibilities previously held by 25 different agencies.

"The next decade is going to be the most exciting period in the history of the Island. During that period I am going to create an environment of enthusiasm. We can create our own environment you know, in fact we have to. That's my target for Nanaimo and I'm going to make it!"

I was working at Nanaimo Realty in the early 70's. Frank spent a whole day in a wheelchair and found all the places that were not accessible to people confined to chairs. Shortly after that we had ramps added to the curbs and then of course the back entrance to the city hall with the ramp.

Mrs. F. Silverthorn

Frank was always there to lend a helping hand. He especially took an interest in disabled people, those in wheelchairs. I served on the committee for the elderly and the disabled and I also helped with the planning department ramping sidewalks. Yes, Frank was there when you needed him.

Anonymous

As Frank became more and more of a figurehead and celebrity, he was asked to attend an increasingly large number of events. It was common for someone from out of town to simply want to meet the man. Frank was invited aboard a freighter to meet a captain who had stopped in town. He drove down to the assembly wharf and spent as much time with the fellow as he could. Frank left in his usual hurry. His drive home was one he would always remember.

People who frequent the assembly wharf know the rules of the road. There are huge piles of lumber stacked high, and when you drive to the end of one, you stop and see what is around the corner. Frank's driving isn't always highly touted in the local folklore. Sometimes he went too fast. This time he cornered around a stack of lumber and straight into a massive lumber-carrier. The protruding boards missed Frank's head by inches. He arrived at City Hall that afternoon looking as white as a ghost!

Frank was always on the run, with people chasing him holding papers that needed to be signed. It was not easy to sit him down for a full conversation. Often a person entering City Hall with a question would be directed into the room Frank was in. Frank would stick his head out the door and say to the most available person, "Please come in here; there is someone that you would love to meet!" The staff member would enter the room, be introduced and Frank would excuse himself for "just a moment." The staff would always have a good laugh as nobody expected his immediate return.

The staff made certain allowances for Frank's schedule. Everyone realized that he had to keep up his image of mayor while attending to his other roles. None of the staff begrudged him for the hours he spent away from the office. Many of them still describe him as being fair, thorough, knowledgeable, inspiring, and the best boss they ever had. One staff member also coached two of Frank's kids in minor hockey. He frequently saw the mayor show up at the rink in his pyjamas to drop off two of his sons. These were early mornings after some late nights. People who were aware of his workload became quite sympathetic whenever he arrived late at his next destination.

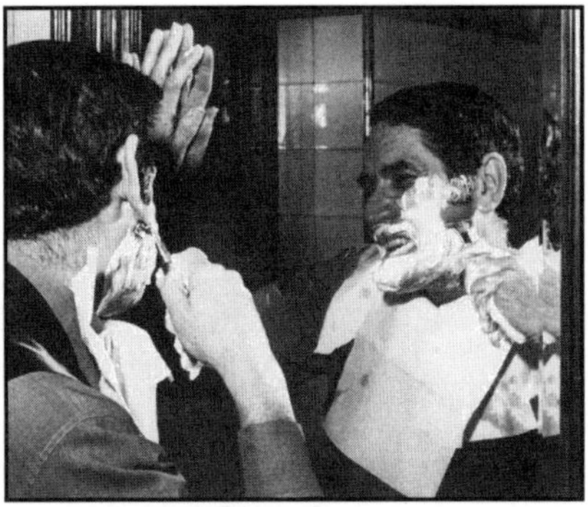

It remains a mystery exactly why Frank kept 8x10" photographs of himself shaving.

Frank was notorious for always being late. He had an appointment with a local chap. Frank was late as usual. His secretary couldn't find him and messages were sent out. The chap was getting annoyed.

Every so often I would go in and say, "I'm sure he'll be in soon." The fellow replied "I've got a mind to give him a poke in the nose when he gets in!" Frank arrived an hour late and gave his usual greeting, "Sorry I'm late," et cetera.

The chap says, "I should poke you in the nose.....no, I will poke you in the nose." So he takes a swing across Frank's desk and misses. I heard this from the next room, came in and said, "No need for all this!" The reply, "I'll poke you in the nose!" Frank slipped out and the guy left.

Anonymous

Mayor Ney refused to respond to a community delegation at one city council meeting. There was a long pause and the city clerk had discovered that Frank had fallen asleep. Without drawing too much attention to the tired chief magistrate he dropped a book loudly on the table that was being slept upon. Frank opened his eyes and casually said, "Next item, please."

Re-elect Frank Ney, Again

When I was about 10 years old I walked downtown with two friends. As we walked by City Hall one boy took a pee in one of the bushes. That was when Mayor Ney walked by. He looked like he had a lot on his mind. The non-peeing boy walked up to the Mayor and said, "Excuse me Mr. Ney..." Frank stopped and gave the boy his full attention. The boy pointed his finger and continued, "He's peeing on City Hall!" Frank was not so amused as he continued into the building to deal with other issues.

Anonymous

He turned out to be the best mayor I ever dealt with.

George Strathdee, Former Chief of the RCMP

One day Frank picked up the phone and found that he was talking to Mrs. McGillicuddy. He immediately started in telling her how much he had enjoyed the "farm fresh eggs" he had gotten from her. He went on, "The yolks were so perfect and yellow! Definitely the finest eggs I have tried. Next time I must get four dozen or more because they were just so delicious..." He went on for about five minutes. Suddenly he puts the phone on his desk, looks at his co-workers and says, "Oh, wrong Mrs. McGillicuddy."

City Hall is often approached by disgruntled people and sometimes these people threaten physical violence.

Frank was confronted by one of these people on the street in downtown Nanaimo. The person threatened to shoot him. Completely unflustered, Frank immediately referred the "attacker" to Jerry Berry, the City Administrator, as the person who dealt with such things for the Mayor. He sent him on his way up to City Hall (hopefully not with a gun).

Gerald Berry, City Administrator

We would be in council half way through the agenda. Frank says, "What item are we on"? The answer was number eight. "Well, I'm looking at number eight." Frank is asked what he has there. "Oh I have such and such."..........Frank, you have last weeks agenda.

You see, he was so busy all the time.

Anonymous

Well, Tara, Gina Gazolla and I went to Duncan on Dad's fourth or Fifth election campaign to pick up something at the auction. Low and behold, we picked up a baby calf for $10 and put her in the back of the truck. The calf was sucking on our hands and faces untill we got back home and put her in the woodshed. Dad called home to see if everything was fine.

One of the kids told him that we had a cow running through the house. Moments later he had a radio interview. Dad was asked, "Frank, how do you feel about winning another election?" All dad could say was that he was a little concerned about this cow running through his house, and that he had to get home to believe his eyes.

Brad Ney, Nanaimo Realty

When I became Chief for the Nanaimo Band, I had known Frank for quite some time before that. He'd call me up and say, "Chief, I'm getting my picture taken today with the Heart Foundation so I'm gonna have my buckskin outfit on. Could you put your regalia on and come on down?" I'd say, "Gee, I'm sorry Frank but I don't have regalia." (He'd say) "Oh, That's too bad Bob, O.K., O.K.."

Two or three days later the phone would be ringing again. He say "Chief, I'm getting my picture taken with the Cancer

Society, could you put your regalia on and come down again?" (I'd say) "I'm sorry Frank I don't have any regalia so I won't do that." (He'd say) "Oh well maybe next time chief."

Next week we'd do the whole procedure again. He'd say, "Bob, we're doing a thing for the Bathtub Society, all the media's gonna be there. Can you put youre regalia on and come down and have your picture taken? I'm gonna have my pirate's outfit on." (I'd say) "Oh Frank I'm sorry I don't have any regalia." "Oh that's too bad, he says."

This went on the whole time he was there and I'll always remember him for that.

Chief Robert Thomas

It was no mystery to anyone that Frank had a large personal interest in the giant local real estate empire. Providing new services and rezoning for outlying areas greatly increased the value of his holdings. Frank had for years offered shares in his ventures to the public, and in this way everyone could share in the wealth. Those who did not wish to purchase shares in Frank's business could rest assured that the man who pays the most taxes is the one most concerned about keeping taxes low. Nonetheless, not everyone was convinced of his good intentions for the city.

Reading with the Bahai people. Frank had a great respect for other's expressions of spirituality. He practiced transcendental meditation and found that it gave him great energy.

An allegation of conflict of interest had been made against Frank in 1974 over a waterfront motel he had an interest in. After an investigation it was found that he was doing nothing illegal. Frank had demonstrated how scrupulous he was about such laws by leaving the council chambers when the deliberations concerned his personal affairs. This was not required by any law but Frank liked to avoid any discussion on the matter at hand. He really didn't need the stress of being suspect.

At three council meetings between February, 1976 and 1977, he left the chair three separate times during each session. One alderman found that he was jumping up and down like a yo-yo to take over Frank's chair everytime he left. During one session, a man who had bought a property from Nanaimo Realty came before the council with a request for a zoning change. He saw Frank stand up, excuse himself and leave the room. Although there was no impropriety in staying, Frank explained "I just felt it could be suspected that maybe I'd provided that if he bought the property I'd get the thing zoned through or something."

He maintained that as a realtor he was no more in conflict of interest than many others. "What about teachers, civil servants, union people; they have special interests that they don't seem to think prevent them from voting on issues which might in some way benefit

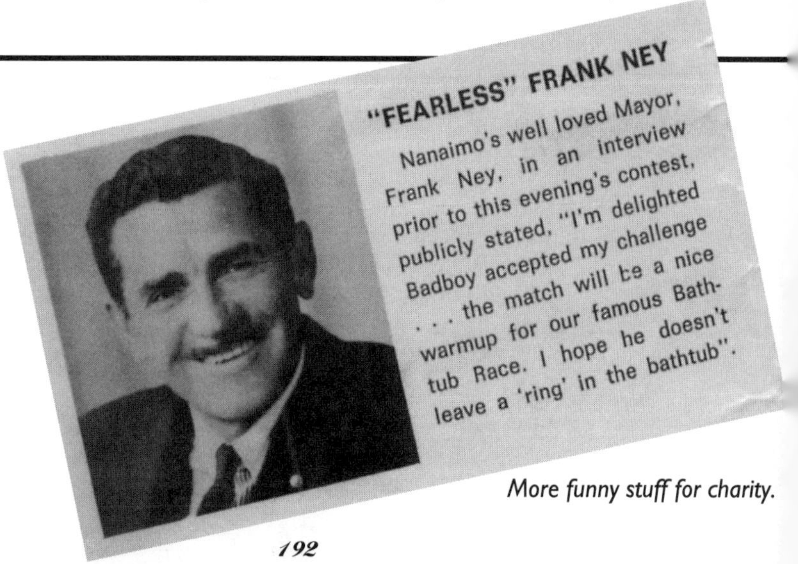
"FEARLESS" FRANK NEY
Nanaimo's well loved Mayor, Frank Ney, in an interview prior to this evening's contest, publicly stated, "I'm delighted Badboy accepted my challenge . . . the match will be a nice warmup for our famous Bath-tub Race. I hope he doesn't leave a 'ring' in the bathtub".

More funny stuff for charity.

them in some roundabout way. The way they are talking, everybody has to have some conflict of interest, but if we start cutting out some aspects of society from politics, then we are eroding democracy. Divide and conquer is a story as old as the ages. Pilate tried it with the Christians, Hitler tried it with the Jews, the Russians tried it with the Mennonites, but it will never catch on in Canada. Take my word for it."

By 1977 the propriety of large landowners holding municipal office became a growing concern in B.C. A municipal affairs department committee had worked during the NDP term on a proposal to ban any land dealings in a municipality by the local politicians while in office. The politicians would still be able to hold land, but they wouldn't be able to buy or sell it. A mayor would have to get council's approval to sell his own house. In effect, a person like Frank would have to suspend all land dealings by his companies. This committee never produced any such legislation, even though it was set to go before cabinet for approval in 1976.

"Pretty soon we're going to say millionaires shouldn't run for city council, or people on welfare shouldn't or the news media shouldn't. Are we going to have a democratic government or are we going to have pressure groups dictating who's going to run?"

"BADBOY" SHIELDS

When hearing of Ney's challenge, Shields is quoted as having said, "I'll meet the bum in the ring or in a bathtub . . . either way he's going to get cleaned up".

Those were times of enormous change for Vancouver Island and Frank had a big hand in bringing them about. He saw the huge growth coming for Nanaimo and took advantage of low-cost federal loans to expand city services. Over considerable opposition, he managed to float a thirty million dollar bond issue for water and sewer. That put Nanaimo second only to Surrey as the city with the biggest debt load.

Nanaimo's survival follows from financing that enabled development to continue throughout the community. Without water and sewer you can't have development.

Howard Nicholson, Retired City Clerk

Another charge against Frank came from the Concerned Citizens Committee, (CCC), over the sewer and water bylaw. Hubert James "Pat" Barron, a pre-fabricated home salesman, felt that developers would benefit greatly over the bylaw and should therefore pay a greater share of the cost. His committee painstakingly mapped out all of Frank's holdings that would directly benefit. Barron said, "It's beginning to look like those pre-World War One maps of the British Empire in which the sun never sets."

Frank was not the only one under the spy glass. A number of mayors from various towns were being watched quite closely. Frank had not made maps of his properties but noticed that the bylaw "covers a circumference of about ten square miles. It means the whole city, more or less, will get sewer. If there are parcels our company is benefitting from, and I'm sure there must be, there are thousands of other parcels too." He said that that was too broad an area to warrant him vacating his chair. He remained seated for the third reading of the bylaw and was registered as having an affirmative vote.

When the water bylaw came up Frank decided not to vote on it because he had a summer home on Protection Island where the one of the water mains would go. His decision not to vote was not based on the fact that he had interests in two companies that together owned 21 more lots on the Island. The bylaw didn't need his vote anyway. The Island needed a water line and got it.

Lots of money was spent. There was no other municipality in B.C. that took advantage of provincial funding to the degree that Ney's Nanaimo did. When a town grows from 3 ½ to 52 square miles in size, a whole lot of upgrading is needed. Once Frank had done all his homework, government grants had paid for 80 per cent of the installation of water and sewer facilities.

In all cases of conflict of interest Frank was exonerated. Reporters asked how he felt about his critics and he happily stated that he loved them. He looked at his critics as his best friends because they tell him what he's doing wrong and he appreciated the help they gave him.

"In my ten years in public office I've never had an alderman accuse me of using my office for personal benefit, and not all aldermen have been my friends. My conscience is clear. I don't have to do that sort of thing."

Bill Ney was the general manager and the second largest shareholder in Frank's largest interest, Great National Land. Bill was telling his big brother that he felt it was time for him to quit politics because he was away from the company too much. Bill was also getting tired of the company having to tread so carefully in any dealings with the city. He wasn't finding Frank's position as mayor to be much of a benefit at all. Frank believed that the company neither lost nor gained by his dual role. He also felt that any way of bettering the city betters everyone, including his companies.

It was up to the people to decide whether Frank was a crook or not when they hit the polling booths. Frank had decided to run again and in 1978 he won the election once again and rode on the shoulders of his supporters while the cameras clicked away.

Every election saw the conflict of interest topic come up. As always Frank would restate, "Certainly I have a conflict of interest; I'm in the real estate business and I'm very worried about the taxes. But everybody has a conflict of interest and that's how a democracy works in our Government."

Frank Ney A Canadian Legend

"In all my life I've never had anyone come to me and say, 'Frank, you've been dishonest.' Not once in my life has anyone ever said that to me."

Frank's home movies centered around boating, skiing and swimming. The birthday parties were sheer madness.

I think that everybody who knew Frank Ney would acknowledge he was a pretty capable politician. After all, you don't get re-elected as often as Frank did unless you've got some political skills.

I've got some vivid and warm memories of watching Frank operate in a crowd. He'd be talking with me or others standing near me—listening and looking but also keeping an eye and ear out for others in the room. If he saw somebody he didn't know, he'd instantly interrupt whatever somebody might be saying and ask, "Who is that fellow or woman over there?" Then he'd ask what the person did for a living or for some other bits of helpful information. And then, surprise, surprise, Frank would excuse himself, walk over to the person you'd just named and greet the person by name and offer some observation on what she or he did for a living or whatever.

You can guess what kind of an impression Frank made by doing this—and I would have to write a very long list of people to name everybody who has said to me that Frank Ney never forgot a name and always remembered who you were.

A pretty capable politician, don't you think?

Dale Lovick, M.L.A. Nanaimo

Frank displayed another name memorization technique to a doctor friend of his at the Green Mountain ski hill. They were joined by another gentleman, this one a dentist. Frank asked him how his last name was spelled. The dentist told him that it is with TWO L's. This was not exactly the clue that Frank was after. The doctor later took Frank aside and told him, "It's Scott!"

His mind was always racing, like tapes going around. He always had a lot on his mind.

He always called me Dorothy. At first we corrected him. At one point I asked him why he always called me Dorothy. His answer was, "Well, you look like a Dorothy." After a while we just let it go and went with the names he gave us.

Audrey Thomas, Organist/Pianist

Frank told a good story, "I'll never forget when the queen came, I'd thought I'd put a bathtub race on so I put on my robes with my big chain and the General said, 'Ney you walk in front of the Queen'. 'Oh,' I said 'I can't walk in front of the Queen'. He said 'it's perfectly alright'. So I walked down the pier, the Queen was behind me, then two people behind her and all around her. As I walked out on the pier I looked around; every hotel, every pier had people with guns on with telescopic rifles! And I said, 'What's going on?' He said, 'We have to do that in case there's anyone trying to assassinate the Queen'. 'Well' I said, 'they're not going to be able to see the Queen. They're going to think I'm the Queen with these bright robes on'. He said 'That's the idea Ney'. And I learned that day that being a Queen isn't all fun. She's a very brave and wonderful lady."

Queen Elizabeth had paid two visits to Nanaimo in the 1950's. There was not a lot of hoopla then. The thousands who lined the streets stood in silent dignity. It wasn't until the spring of 1971 that she made her return. Frank had arranged a variety of tastefully entertaining events for her. This time an estimated 50,000 island residents were out in force to greet her with cheers and waves. The Mount Benson Legion Pipe Band played their tunes and children performed in special Indian clothing. This was all a warm up for the "Queen's Plate Bathtub Race." She had heard of the event but was was never able to attend one. Frank had decided to bring the race to her.

Other races start in Nanaimo and end in Vancouver. Only the tubbers themselves get to view the entire course of the race. The Queen's race was unique in that it had an oval-shaped course. She got to see the start, middle and end of this one. 17-year-old Duncan Tait had lapped most of the 22 tubs by the time he won the race. He was thrilled to have the Queen present him with an engraved silver plate. Mayor Frank Ney then presented the queen with a totem carved by the 94 year-old Jimmy John, whose art showed a timeless quality which so fittingly represented life on the west coast of Canada.

Frank was in his office with Queen Elizabeth and Prince Philip. Frank offered drinks to a polite refusal.

The Queen and the lady-in-waiting slipped off to the washroom and Frank says to Prince Philip, "Now she's gone out, would you and I like a drink?"

Anonymous

Re-elect Frank Ney, Again

Frank's attitude was just as though it was anybody off off the street. He was so natural. He just plunked his bathtub hat on Philip's head. A lot of people wouldn't do that. But that's Frank.

Helen Sponaugle,
17 Years as Secretary for Mayor Ney

The queen made yet another appearance in the spring of 1983. Frank dressed in his mayor's robes, complete with bow tie and military medals. He escorted her from the waterfront up to a podium that was set up with a microphone. The concert band was assembled and awaiting their cue to start "God Save the Queen." Frank announced, "Ladies and Gentlemen, O Canada", and confused everyone. He changed his mind and said, "It's supposed to be "God Save the Queen." Who put this thing together? City Hall?"
The crowd had a good laugh.

Queen Elizabeth in 1971. She returned a decade later and the sun broke through the clouds for her appearance. Frank said that he was delighted by her "devine talent of blowing out the weather at the appropriate moment." Some onlookers were not amused.

Frank's attitude to his position as Mayor seemed to alter, that he was a representative of the city, a figure head, a P.R. person, even the father of the city rather than a strictly political figure.

After I appeared as "Shylock" in Shakespere's "Merchant of Venice" he came up to me and asked if it wasn't a rather controversial play to put on in this day and age, as being possibly offensive to Jewish people - but he gave this criticism in a very tactful and indeed gentle manner.

Tim Lander, Poet

Geoff Mathews recalls a phone call he received that same year. Frank had decided that it was time to put into effect his dream of having a natural gas pipeline to Vancouver Island. There was no way that he could accomplish a task of this magnitude by himself so he decided to form a Nanaimo gas pipeline committee. He asked Mr. Mathews for about 20 minutes of his time each week. This idea was an agreeable one and turned into an epic of thousands of hours over almost nine years. The committee was formed and they pushed the project through a succession of three prime ministers, two provincial premiers, and four or five energy ministers.

It was hard to say "No" to Frank's enthusiasm. He had quite a vision about natural gas and its benefits. He phoned approximately a dozen people to be on the committee. He didn't ask, he just said, "You're going to be chairman."

We always had 100 per cent support of Frank Ney. He really helped us go the whole nine yards.

Geoff Mathews, Pipeline Committee Chairman

Members of the Pipeline Committee insist that the Island never would have seen natural gas flowing without Frank's leadership. Frank maintained an ideal relationship with his committee by keeping his nose out of their affairs and only stepping in to use his vast political influence when it was needed.

When Frank first spoke of a pipeline, everyone looked at him and said, "You're crazy." But he had vision. There was no personal gain for the mayor. He just saw that he could make people's lifestyles and the environment that much better for the project.

He had a huge network of politicians across the country. He could just get on the phone and call a lot of powerful people. They always knew him, or of him, and he knew how to get his message across. He also championed the cause every chance he had. But he generally left us to sort out the tactics and the war ourselves."

Larry Hume, Pipeline Committee member

When it came time for an election, the other candidates all knew that they couldn't outdo the popular pirate in sheer exposure. They had to try different approaches. Mr. Graeme Roberts felt that he could beat the incumbent on one of his weaker voting tactics.

He hated door knocking. He wouldn't do it. I told him that I do it. I get to meet people, although I don't always know how useful it is. Frank told me, "I tried it once. I knocked on the door and I got this woman out of her bed in curlers and dressing gown. She was very upset. The second one had been baking bread and she came to the door with her hands covered in flour and I said that was it. I have never knocked on the door again."

Frank never seemed to take the campaign seriously. He enjoyed it, he loved the signs all over the city. He loved going to all-candidates meetings. Because he was everywhere, campaigning every hour of the day, he was a natural campaigner in his own way, not an organized one.

Graeme Roberts

The most famous of his 4 pirate suits. This postcard sold thousands of copies. Thousands more were brought to the dump when he lost an election. The distributer thought that nobody would want them.

For the first time in seventeen years, Frank sat in the council gallery watching another person being sworn in as the new Mayor. The television cameras were there that evening in 1984 when Frank was given a standing ovation upon receiving the highest honour the city could bestow upon a citizen. Graeme Roberts had won the election that year and was proclaiming Frank a "Freeman of The City of Nanaimo." In presenting him with a scroll and medallion he said, "Everyone that is watching tonight and all who have lived here for the last seventeen years who saw you serve so well, so dedicated and so sincerely as Mayor of Nanaimo...are with me tonight in paying respects to you as a person, a servant and a very dedicated Mayor."

Frank responded, "This is an honour I deeply appreciate. I will carry it off with dignity and honour. I will always have a love affair with the city of Nanaimo...." He was then presented with a brightly wrapped gift "from the citizens of Nanaimo to Black Frank." He ripped off the paper to reveal a beautiful large brass telescope with an engraving that expressed appreciation from the people. He assured the crowd that he would use it to watch for "villainous pirates from the east."

Mayor Roberts is a fine man with a good ideas and a smile for the cameras. With all due respect to him, the word around town at the time was "the reason he got elected was that Frank had been mayor for so long that many people didn't bother to make it out to the polls that year. They figured that Frank would win anyway, so why bother making the trip to the ballot box?"

My mother was quite ill at the Nanaimo Regional Hospital. Around that time there was a local election with Mr. Ney running again for mayor. Well, my stepfather and I had been so stressed out with my mother's illness that we didn't vote. Well, we never heard the end of it. My mother informed us that if she could literally leave her sick bed to go to the main floor of the hospital to vote we could surely vote as well.

Diane E. Ursel

By the time election time rolled around again, things had changed around again and Frank was once again to wear the blue mink-trimmed mayoralty robe and chain to City Hall. This was to be his last term as Mayor of Nanaimo. He had said, "I love the excitement of politics. I like people and I like to know what's happening. I've seen Nanaimo come a long way in my time, and I want to keep on doing what I'm doing because we've got a long way to go yet."

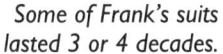

Some of Frank's suits lasted 3 or 4 decades.

Military medals are proudly displayed on his robe. He loved having people sign the guest book at City Hall.

When Frank was re-elected as Mayor in 1986 at 67 years of age he claimed, "Older men are wiser men. I've got the body of a man of 40. I'm ready to go. There is no fox like an old fox." He said that his experience as a former hockey player has taught him a lesson; "Anytime you've lost, you look forward to a rematch. Because you are beaten doesn't mean you're out forever."

In 1980 he had made the same claim, "Winston Churchill was in for a long time and there are many politicians that have been in for a long time. I think that if you tire out, if you lose your enthusiasm, then you have made your contribution obviously. As long as you're enthusiastic and you have a love and loyalty in what you're doing, I think there's nothing wrong with carrying on."

We'd do financial reports and his memory was tremendous. He could remember the report up to a year previous including the figures.

Bob Rowledge, Former City Finance Director

1988 saw the Hell's Angels motorcycle club hold their fourth annual festival on the fourteen-acre site dubbed "Angels

Acres." About five thousand Hell's Angels and friends attended, including people from England, Ireland, Holland, Germany and Brazil. Locals were also invited to participate in the party that included a half dozen local rock bands. Frank really wanted to go to the bash and came as close as driving by the site. He was living an awkward life by being so popular. Everywhere he went he was news. He felt that if he let loose at the biker's party a lot of people would have the wrong things to say about it. He didn't need the hassle of a new set of rumours and declined on joining the party.

Instead of attending, he viewed the weekend event from a distance. After summing up his feelings about having his town full of Hells Angels, he told the press what he thought about the whole thing. "The bikers came up here last year and there wasn't any disorderly conduct. We only had two complaints - phone calls about the noise from the bikes. Last year the bikers spent over $500,000 during the long weekend and merchants appreciate the extra business. One lady from a service station told me she sold more gunk in one day than she had all year. It's all nice clean money for us. They come to town, they pay cash and they're gone in twenty-four hours. What more can you ask from any other tourist?"

Bill Reid, Tourism Minister for B.C., bestowed on Frank the honor of Ambassador of Tourism for 1988. Said Reid, "Frank Ney is an individual who has considered tourism our number one industry for years. In every sense he has defied the skeptics. Designation as an Ambassador of Tourism is our symbol of great respect." While that award was being presented, Frank was in Bremerton, Washington, with the world's largest bathtub, to promote the bathtub race. He was back in time for the Empire Day parade and then out again for a parade in Victoria.

I grew up in Toronto and remember seeing two Mayors on the national news. One was from Australia and the other was Frank. They were drunk on a lawn with bottles in their hands, swaying. I thought that was pretty wild. Later in Nanaimo I was playing in a band at the Columbus. It was one of the smokier bars. I was surprised to see Frank there slum-

ming it. It shows that he wasn't uppity or pretentious, I mean he was a millionaire and could hang out with regular characters. Anyway, I tried to sell him a shirt but he would not buy one. I thought "You cheap-o ." He obviously didn't throw his money away.

Steve Palin, Musician

The orange and blue pirate suit had come to represent many memorable events, and after twenty years of service, it became a victim of the auctioneer's gavel. At a fundraising auction in the 1980's for the United Way, Frank's tasseled piece of history, complete with boots, sword and breeches started with a bid of $5. Of the $10,000 raised that evening, $600 of it came from the famed suit. Said Black Frank at the time, "After 22 years, it's been viewed by 550 million people in 58 countries, and it's helped to bring much publicity to Nanaimo. It's been through a lot of wars in salt water. As soon as I wore it, I noticed the television cameras. It's served me well."

Frank had no idea that his suit was being auctioned, since his son Russell snuck it out of the Ney house. To add to his surprise, a sharp new crimson, black and gold pirate's jacket with a gold vest was presented to him by a very similarly attired Jerry Berry. Garry Ford, representing Nanaimo Realty in a spirited bidding war with Tom Harris made the final bid. The company wanted to buy it back with a thought of putting it in a glass case. Frank loved his new suit and slated the Grey Cup parade in Vancouver for its debut. The glass case was a passing fancy, and the old suit was still to be spotted on Mr. Ney's back from time to time.

You know that huge dinner that was held for Frank, well they presented him with a brand new pirate suit. He tried it on and he hated it. He put it in his closet and used his old one.

Anonymous

Re-elect Frank Ney, Again

He was definitely the one boss in my life. I gained more respect for him as I went along. He encouraged me to continue my education through night school. I was impressed with his patience for things both big and small. I prepared lengthy schedules for him each day, and he would insist on keeping to them out of a sense of profound duty.

A lot of people used to laugh about Frank attending every funeral, every 50th anniversary, every wedding. But he did it because people really wanted him to be there.

Roxy Jones, Frank's last secretary at City Hall

Not many people got a chance to experience what it was like to be Nanaimo's mayor since Frank dominated the position. The United Way played their part in alleviating this concern by hosting another auction. The grand prize, for anyone who was willing, was a shot at being mayor for one day. Fred Bates laughed when he won. He had always joked about Frank's tardiness and said, "I'll show Frank how to get to functions on time." He was then handed five pages of typical Saturday duties.

Saturday at 7 a.m. saw Mr. Bates at breakfast meetings. Five costume changes later, he was free to go home at 2 a.m the following morning. He had lost his overcoat, amongst other things, and had appeared late at several events. He showed up looking fairly exhausted at City Hall on Monday and apologized for laughing earlier. He mentioned to the secretary, "I don't know how he does it."

Frank and I flew to Vancouver one day to deal with an important policy issue regarding B.C. Ferries. Frank was notorious for not dealing with 'business issues' at City Hall so it was a bit of a coup to get him to actually attend a meeting of Mayors to deal with a mutual problem.

Unfortunately, when we stepped off the float plane in Coal Harbor, there was a television crew there taping (some other newsworthy person), who was getting on the plane. The television crew recognized Frank and he immediately launched into his, "jewel of the west, sunporch of Canada, Bathtub Capital of the World, low taxes, sound administration, eight bells and all's well in Davey Jones' locker" routine. After that the work day was over for Frank. Provincial or even national coverage for Nanaimo at 8:30 in the morning and any civic government problems were immediately inconsequential and completely unimportant. All our work to get Frank on focus was destroyed in a moment before the camera.

Gerald Berry, City Administrator

The city staff took a one-day ski trip during 1990. Frank was enjoying his regular routine of walking, talking and shaking hands with all those around. By the end of this active day he was sitting on the tailgate with another fellow drinking what appeared to be port wine. Jerry Berry walked by and Frank enthused, "Jerry boy, did you see that fellow up their skiing, he's 72 years old." Jerry just had to remark, "Your Worship, so are you."

Two feet of snow, and all's well!

Re-elect Frank Ney, Again

Frank Ney was defeated as Mayor for the last time in 1990. Immediately after the election he was appointed Nanaimo's official Goodwill Ambassador. It was a post Ney had filled for years, and it was in every one's best interest that he continue.

It was a dark and rainy Sunday afternoon about 5:30 or 6:00 in the evening. I was on duty as a commissionaire at the main gate of the Nanaimo military camp, watching the rain spatter against the guard house window and the light fade over the Gulf of Georgia, I recall wishing I was at home with my wife. When out of the rain I noticed Frank's little yellow car come scooting out of 808 sqdn, located at the base of the guard house. I waved, expecting him to pass by, but he stopped at the gate, hopped out of his car and came inside.I thought, "Oh my, - what's wrong," but as he came through the door I could see the twinkle in his eye and I relaxed. Frank looked at me and held out his hand and in it was a tiny miniature bathtub, a souvenir of the bathtub races and a card with a "City of Nanaimo" pin attached.

Laughing, he shook my hand and said, "This is my last official act as Mayor." And I really believe it was, because as of midnight a new mayor moved into his office. I shall never forget that.

John AJ Harte, Commissionaire Military Camp,
Nanaimo B.C.

The island highway, with all of its huge trucks, runs right through the town center of Nanaimo. A proposed trucking route had been designed for the outskirts of the city in an attempt to alleviate this traffic problem and give the town room for the traffic of the future. Frank liked the idea, and he felt that it was his stand on this issue that lost him the election. A lot of people were strongly against the new bypass route, and rumours abounded that Frank was once again pushing in favour of having all his real estate holdings benefit. Frank's shareholders knew otherwise.

During his tenure, he received more than twenty five awards and citations for his service to the city, business and community groups. His twenty years as Mayor is a local record, well ahead of Nanaimo's first Mayor, Mark Bate who served for twelve years off and on between 1875 and 1900.

His final Mayoral defeat didn't dampen Frank's enthusiasm or halt his schedule. As he looked through his bulky daily planner in the Modern Cafe during the spring of 1991, he related, "I've got so many darn things to do. That's the story of my life. My calendar is just as busy as it ever was. The only thing is, I'm not having to go to long meetings anymore."

I have known Frank since the '50's. The one time that I saw him actually look sad was right after he lost his last election. He was at the Nanaimo Realty office. I imagine he felt that it was the end of an era for him, a part of his life was over.

Anonymous

On the subject of his appointment of Goodwill Ambassador, "This was an idea that was actually supported by a lot of my political opponents, which made me scratch my head a little. What they're saying is, 'If you keep going to the parades, we'll pay you out-of-pocket expenses'. I'm very happy to do it because I think it's good to spread Nanaimo's name around. I'm getting invited to a lot of things."

"Now I'm going to more movies and hockey games and skiing and skating. I'm eating more popcorn and hotdogs and leading an unsophisticated life. I have more time for my work as a notary public and in real estate, but I'm still involved in a lot of committees."

A Good Time Was Had by All

OF ALL THE LABELS ONE MIGHT PIN ON FRANK, perhaps "promoter" is the all around most suitable one. He loved to take a good idea and run with it. Every person living in Nanaimo at the time could look forward to seeing him at every event. You could always share a laugh or an enthusiastic remark. It was not difficult to spot him in a crowd. There he was, shaking hands, with a big smile. Some say that his presence made the event. It was not unusual to be asked, "Did you see Frank Ney there?"

As for his clothes, he liked happy, bright colours, which he said gave him a lift. He didn't like to dress in a "sloppy coarse way" and although he larked around, he always did it with class.

Other than those who despaired the "lack of dignity" a Mayor projects in a pirate suit, everybody loved the way he dressed. His range of outfits quite suited the occasions for which they were donned. You may have seen him as a Mississippi gambler with black pants, topper, tails, giant vest and gold-topped cane. This was the main media image of the man until 1968. He was the "gambler" at the first bathtub race, but when the event paid off he celebrated by reviving the Pirate Look for the next quarter century of bathtubbing. The Mississippi Gambler outfit was never moth-balled into obscurity. It became well-known to children growing up in the 1970's as Frank's "Easter Suit."

The highly recognizable mayor was also seen at various functions respectfully clad as a local Indian, World War 2 veteran, authentic Scotsman, sea captain or sharp businessman. Whatever the costume, it would always fit the seriousness or comedy of the situation. Perhaps because he was a busy man with a lot on his mind, his attire at times contributed to the hilarity of the event. Hundreds of people once saw him make an impressive speech in a full white outfit, with bright red underpants showing through. It has been said that he would show up at a friend's wedding impeccably dressed, but missing a shirt. He was also spotted in safari gear riding an elephant in a circus parade. At a VIP dinner, you could spot Frank looking immaculate in kilt, mess jacket and campaign medals. The next morning you may have noticed him in a clown suit, skating at a children's skating party.

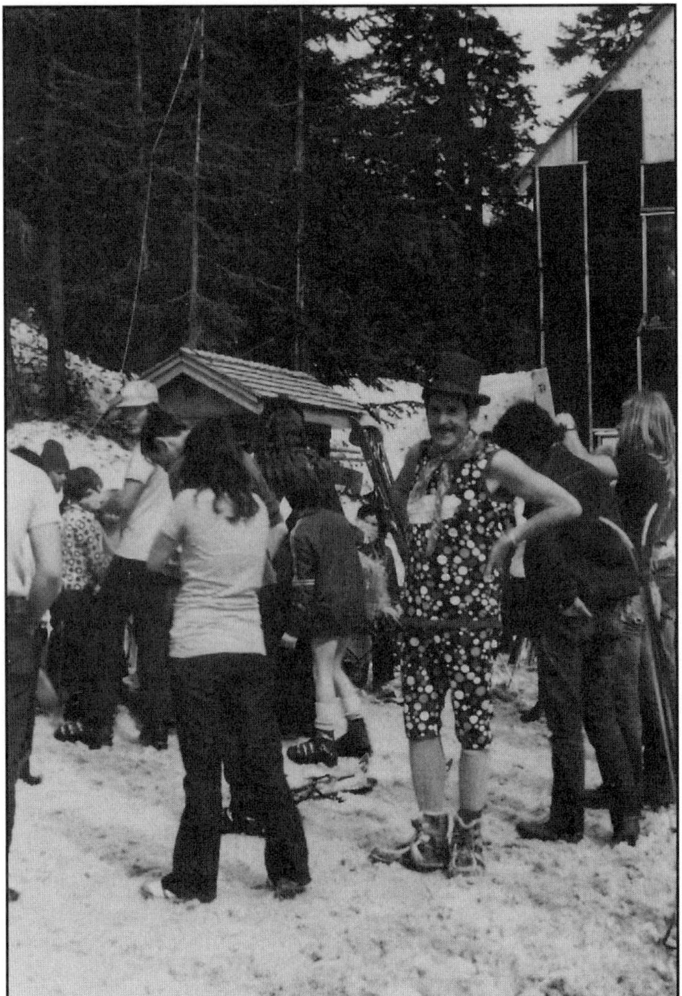

"Yellow socks and green hat"

A Good Time Was Had by All

When asked about being embarrassed about being seen in crazy costumes and circumstances, Frank replied, "I wave my orange plastic sword, and I say 'eight bells and all's well in Davy Jones' locker,' and they all laugh at me and I turn around to them and say 'wait 'till you get your tax notices! That will take the smiles off your faces.' They shake their fists but they're laughing while they shake their fists, so we have fun." It didn't matter much whether he wore a business suit or a 1920's bathing suit. The charm of the man always radiated and attracted people. They recognized him as a man who was going places.

You never knew what costume Frank was going to turn up in. You really had to keep an open mind.

Frank Graves

....His antics undoubtedly made him amongst the best known of municipal mayors on earth. Along with his personal fame, his beloved town of Nanaimo gained a reputation as a place of many ceremonies. He was not at all shy about his PR activities.

Olivia Chambers

I was in an old-fashioned bathing suit contest that Frank was with. I got second prize, and I am not young.

Kathleen Goodacre

There were some things he wouldn't do. When the Queen came to town, a lot of people phoned him, requesting that he wear his pirate costume. Frank said, "I wouldn't do that. That's cheapening the whole thing. But on a holiday occasion it can be done and if the kids at the school want me to wear my pirate costume I'll do it, you know. It's a very fine line but if you go over it you just look like a sloppy, silly foolish person. You've just got to stay on that razor's edge all the time."

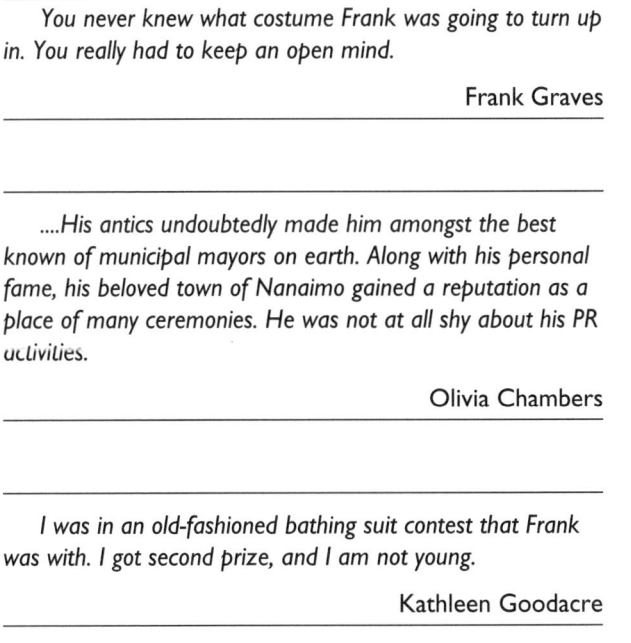

The passion for sports was never lost with Frank. The local celebrity status that he held could get him into any event for free. However, Frank would have none of that. He paid his own way to every sporting event he attended.

Nanaimo is represented by the Nanaimo Clippers in the Junior B hockey league that covers Vancouver Island and some of Mainland B.C.. For many years there was a special event that took place between periods of their games. The winner of a draw would be escorted out to stand on a piece of carpet by the center line. In front of the entire crowd, the winner would be handed a hockey stick and puck. If the participant could score a goal, a cash prize would then be won.

It would have been easy to score if it were not for the piece of plywood in front of the net. There was a small square cut into the wood and nobody could seem to get the puck through from that great a distance. After each weekly attempt more money was added to the pot and by the time Frank's name was drawn, there was over $100 to be won.

Many people insist that he went to every hockey game that was held in Nanaimo.

Just like many before him, Frank was walked out to the center line and handed a hockey stick. He blasted off his first shot at the net and it banged off the plywood. He had just barely missed the hole. Gallantly he then removed his jacket and placed it on the carpet. His second shot was another near miss. This time he took off his tie. One last time he slammed the puck at the net and eleven hundred spectators cheered as it breezed into the slot. Some said it was a total fluke, others recognized skill, while Frank simply stated, "It's a good thing I got it, otherwise I would have been naked out there!"

Hockey was just for fun after Frank had finished his stint as one of the great players in pre-war Europe. He got downright silly with his approach to the game during the '60's. The Jaycees and the Lions service clubs had it out on the ice in front of a large crowd who were awaiting a scheduled Pacific Coast League exhibition with the Nanaimo Clippers up against the Whalley Flamingos. Frank had planned a few laughs when he announced his intentions for the event. As the Jaycees' chairman he was qualified to state, "Dress, is optional. It's not important whether members can skate or not. We want a clean fight though." Two-fifteen minute periods were planned with stretcher-bearers available for the "fallen." Frank had sent a "rather informal" letter to the Lions Club, challenging them to the game. He gathered up fifteen players and many began to borrow skates for the big night.

The Jaycees were doing some good work for the community. They had collected over 800 pints of blood and $400 in dimes. The hockey game was set to add some fun and contrast to the workload.

Both teams claimed victory after the wild and weird game. A skirmish early in the game resulted in two players playing the duration of the game handcuffed together. The Jaycees, enlisting the services of a live cougar as a goaltender, kept the Lions away from the net. Frank was star of the show dressed as a ballerina with a lacrosse stick. He ended up in the penalty box for smoking.

It got sillier yet, as the RCMP went up against the lawyers and teachers in an evening of ice "shmockey." There were three teams, three nets and three reasons for spectators to laugh. Frank fit on neither team and had to be happy blasting around the ice on a pair of speed skates complete with extended blades.

Fun for Kids

> *The family always remembers hearing "Ho ho ho! It's Christmas eve!" as he strolled down the street in his Santa Claus outfit with his children's toys in a bag over his shoulder. The younger kids on the street thought he really was Santa Claus."*
>
> Stan and Molly Dakin, Frank's long-time neighbours

FRANK SAID THAT HIS FAMILY is what he cherished the most,valuing every minute of the time that he could spend with them. He never spanked his kids. Instead, his idea of disciplining a child was to follow the kid around and harangue him or her until he was satisfied that he had got his point across. He would even follow his child into the bathroom and continue, ."..now why would you go and do a thing like that?..."

He always welcomed his kid's friends and everyone else's kid's friends as well. "I take them skiing. I take them on holidays on my boat in the summer. One summer I went out on the boat and I took 25 kids with me." Children from less affluent families could participate in sporting events and Christmas dinners made possible with Frank's help. He loved to help people when he could and completely respected their need for privacy. Most of all, he wanted people to feel good about themselves so they would have the confidence to live out their dreams. His charity was performed in the spirit of encouragement.

"My greatest moment is when small kids call me Frank."

Frank was very much in favour of young people socializing with each other, regardless of their family background. He did not like to see anyone isolated. During a 1950's interview with Woodland Junior High School student Marion Green, he related that the "give and take" of life are learned at school. While discussing the role that education plays in character building, he said, "The school environment tends to eliminate social and religious barriers and teaches humility as well as moral integrity. Other qualities learned are honesty, sympathy, courage and fairness, all of which lead to an enriched personality. Educational benefits cannot be overstated."

When Frank became the mayor, his personal philosophies began to carry much weight in public. He felt that a day-care center for children would be an economic asset for the community. More importantly, he insisted that it would be a vehicle which would help mend broken lives and create a better society. "The children the center will care for will have the opportunity for a better start in life and they are the leaders of tomorrow." He believed that the need for the facility was so great, and that it would be so successful that expansion plans would soon be necessary. As he made a personal donation to the Children's Non-Profit Day Care Centre, he publicly urged others to do likewise.

There were plenty of good quotes to be heard when Frank became a mayor. "We are born free but not wise. It takes a liberal education to make free men wise. The greatest legacy any family can leave a community is a well-educated child." Occassionally Frank had to justify the high cost of public education. People who didn't have kids were not thrilled about paying school taxes. Frank would explain the benefits of education for the whole of society as well as for the individual. "The roots of education are bitter, but the fruit is sweet. The only thing more expensive than education is ignorance."

Mr. Ney has been involved in the organization of young people since his own youth. He took thousands children on outings over the years. Sometimes it would just be for a walk. Often it would be a sporting event and the walk would be an afterthought which took place between the car and the Dairy Queen.

It is true that he often attended children's skating sessions where he would join them on the ice and skate at their level. The man who was a professional athlete would fall down with the kids and have a grand old time. It is sometimes hard to find a 50 or 60-year old man who is willing to volunteer to fall down on a sheet of ice.

Fun for Kids

Years ago he picked the kids up and took them to the parade in Victoria. They rode down in the convertible and I think they were in the big bathtub in the parade. He bought them all lunch and gave them lots of treats.

Laura Large

He truly could have been a professional entertainer. He wooed a crowd of young people with his shenanigans at a charitable event in Vancouver. He relates so well to the children. He kept hundreds and hundreds of children enchanted while they were waiting in the cold.

Joy Leach

I brought my son to meet Frank when the boy was four years old. Frank took him out on his boat, let him steer, dressed him in a sailor hat in his office, and guess what? - that little boy, now nine, still remembers his dad's friend, Frank Ney.

Malcolm Barr, Washington D.C.

I was general manager of Paradise Mobile Homes, a subsidiary of Great National, in the early seventies, and lived on the sales lot. My wife was on the sales staff. Although we had very little personal contact with Frank Ney, he made a point of visiting the sales lot a couple of times a year. He would drive in and stop his black Lincoln Continental abruptly, whereupon the doors would fly open and a mob of kids would jump out and scatter all over the property. I once asked him if all these kids were his. He replied, "Probably most of them." Frank would chat with us for a few minutes and then blow a whistle that summoned his pint-sized passengers. They would load up and take off as abruptly as they had arrived.

In the ensuing years, when I met Frank on the street, he would always stop for a brief chat. He never forgot my name but my wife's name, Donnely, was beyond him, so she got "Mrs. Bill", an appellation she found less than amusing.

F.H.D. Bill Fitzpatrick, aboard "Irish Coffee"

I used to chair the community picnics at Bowen Park on B.C. Day and he'd always be there. He came with a ball and candy for the kids. It wasn't just a run through the park. He'd take the time to talk to the kids, and he always had time for the parents too. It always made people so happy, being around Frank.

Muriel MacKay-Ross

One fine day Frank found the time to relax in his garden. Two small kids were walking by when Frank called out, "Do you guys want some bottles?" The youngsters eagerly accepted. Frank told them that they were inside the house and lead them in.

Frank and his new friends gathered up pop bottles and found a few boxes to put them in. Frank looked at the boxes and at the kids and said, "Well, we may as well put them in the trunk." Once the bottles were in the car, he said, "We may as well drive." The gang cruised off to the grocery store where they cashed in the bottles. After Frank had the clerk give the bottle return money to the kids, he drove them home and let them know, "If you ever need anything, or if you're ever in any trouble, let me know and I will always do what I can to help."

Frank extended his offer of support to all the kids of his era. Eleven-year-old Todd White was a big admirer of Mr. Ney in the early 1970's. He had found that the Mayor's office door was always open to him and he gradually became a familiar young face at City Hall. Todd approached Frank at his desk one day with an idea: "Do you think I could be "Mayor" for a day?"

Frank took this request as seriously as those he received from any citizen. He asked Todd, "Why do you want to be 'Mayor' for a day?" The young man simply told him, "I think it would be fun!"

Since he had no problem in finding the logic in this exchange, the Mayor brought out his calendar. A suitable date was agreed upon and on that day the City Council had a surprise. In the Mayor's chair sat a much smaller person. Todd sat through the entire meeting and got a taste of what the routine is all about.

Frank attended a bicycle drill team event for kids. There was one little boy, who didn't win, that was quite upset. He was having self esteem problems and all that. Frank walked over to him and talked about all that stuff with him. He then invited the little guy for a cruise on the Blue Girl.

About a week later he made good with his promise and invited the boy and his mom aboard his boat. I was one of the other people who came along and we all had fun. He was always doing nice things for people.

Anonymous

When they raised the flag for some kind of games Frank got our son to go to City Hall and assist him. We still have the picture that was published in the paper.

Hewitt Reavley

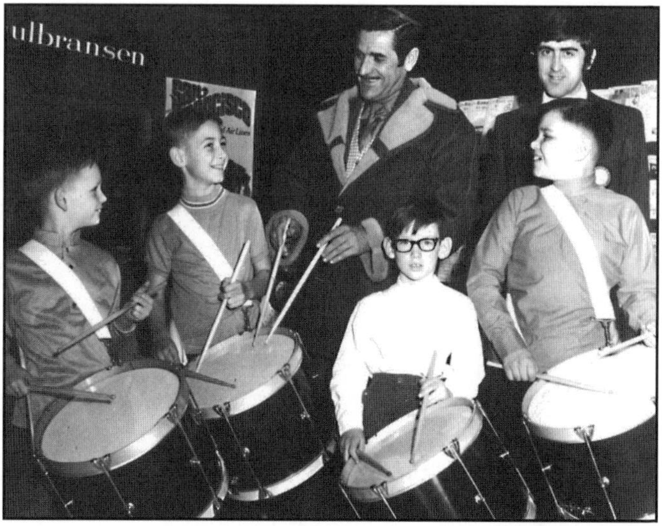

Some people chose to believe that all his good deeds were just attempts at drumming up more votes.

Alan Wright was 12, when he and Dan Watson found $1700 cash. When Frank heard that the two youths were returning such an incredible find to the rightful owner, he was very proud. Inviting the boys, the RCMP Superintendent and the press to his office for a celebration, he presented the two with a $100 bill and commended them as a fine example for the youth of the nation to follow. More than anything Frank wanted kids to be honest. He felt that everyone could succeed if given the chance and encouragement.

As the wife of an alderman who attended many of the bath tub days as a representative of the district of Coquitlam, I got to know Frank quite well. The center of all activity - no matter how long the day or what the event was - Frank was right there in the middle of everything. The perfect host, with all the V.I.P.'s around. He treated everyone with a flair that only Frank could do. He was promoting and selling his town, and doing it well.

On one such trip we had taken one of our young teenage boys with us. The lad felt very out of place, and somewhat dejected at having to be with these people. I happened to mention it to Frank, and without a word, he walked over to the kid, sat down and talked a full half-hour with him - ignoring everyone else.

This was the side of Frank Ney I admired - thoughtful, considerate, compassionate, understanding - who would take the time to reach out to a young kid. That kid now lives in Nanaimo - the city that he felt was friendly due to a truly great man - putting a kid first.

Dolores Boileau

Old Folks Had Fun, Too

HE WAS MUCH THE SAME WITH THE OLD FOLKS. The elderly got rides into town with Frank whenever he spotted one on the go. Every month without fail he awarded seniors with birthday gifts from the city. He would fill them in on all the news of who's having an anniversary and where the relevant parties were at.

The day on which he finally became a senior citizen was a happy one for him. He was proud to receive a card that allowed him to be an official member of seniors' clubs. He walked right into the newspaper office and raved about coming of age.

Frank made sure that his Jolly Roger hats were well distributed. He always brought a gift.

Old Folks had Fun, Too

During Frank's political career he admired Sweden's method of increasing accommodation for senior citizens, and sought to follow this country's example. "We could look to Sweden, even if it is a socialist state. Free enterprise with a touch of socialism has made Canada one of the most prosperous countries in the world today."

I had a house quite close to the Nanaimo Realty building. I decided to sell it. When the sale was discussed, Frank Ney heard about my concern. I fed the birds every day and I also had a rabbit. Who was going to continue this when I'm gone? Frank told me not to worry and that he would take care of it.

After the house had sold I would walk by every so often. Much to my delight the girls who worked for Frank were out feeding the birds. Frank took the rabbit to a farm in Cedar and dropped by to visit the little bunny when he could.

Mrs. Cuthbert, Retired

My mother lived alone in an apartment. One evening in summer, Mr. Ney called to take her for a ride with several children also in the car. They visited a lady in Lantzville who had received a present of two rabbits from Mr. Ney. She asked him to come to her place as she now had 24 rabbits, just too many. It was a hilarious time as the children tried to catch and box the rabbits. I don't know where they were

taken, probably to Bowen Park as there are many there now. It was a memorable outing for my mother who was 92 years old.

Vera Cowan

Mr. Ney was a good friend of mine and I had the honor of his friendship for 45 years. He was the first one to arrive at my house on my 80th birthday and retirement on July 9, 1989. He brought a book (the story of Nanaimo) and a jolly giant bathtub hat. Frank was always ready and willing to listen to anyone and help in any way he could.

Mr. K. W. Blaser, Retired driving instructor

He helped my mother get a house on the reserve.

Willy Good, Artist

We are seniors and as such we were always visited at Bowen Park Center by Frank on any special occasion, sometimes late but always with that special greeting of his.

He always made it a point to appear whenever the seniors were going on a tour and to wish us Godspeed and present us with a lapel pin from the city of Nanaimo.

Mary Warner Huddlestone, 86 years old

He rarely missed coming up after a birthday party. One time he read out to the group his large schedule of upcoming appointments, much to the amusement of the crowd. Regardless of his business, he would still be there, even making a point of sending each senior a signed Christmas card.

Old Folks had Fun, Too

When the seniors went on a bus trip, he was there to greet them. One of them lived alone. So when he took her home and helped her into her suite, he checked to make sure that everything was OK. No one asked him to do that, and he had a meeting that night.

Anne Graves, Seniors Co-ordinator

.....Frank was notorious for arriving in the wrong place. On one occasion he was to attend a seniors' picnic on Newcastle Island. Frank arrived on Gabriola Island and said, "Where's the picnic?"

Anonymous

My husband and I were seated at long tables set up in East Wellington Hall for the occasion of the Golden anniversary of long time friends of ours whom we had known in Vancouver. They had moved to Nanaimo some years before and when we decided to retire to Nanaimo, they promptly took us under their wing until we were oriented with this beautiful area.

As the meal was served we had a chance to talk with the friendly people near us. I was absorbed in stories of early Nanaimo when someone came along the narrow aisle behind the diners. A hand came over my shoulder, and a gentleman shook hands with me and my husband and moved along behind the seated guests, shaking hands as he went along to the end of the table. He stayed a while, chatting and laughing with everyone until he went out the door.

"Who was that?" I enquired as our host came along.

"Oh. I'm sorry, I should have introduced you - that was our Mayor Frank Ney. He never misses turning up at local celebrations."

"Then he'll be this city's Mayor for some time!" my husband ventured, and found joyful agreement on all sides.

Mary E. Urquhart, Retired

He was famous for dropping in on all sorts of events in Nanaimo, especially birthdays, anniversaries and so on, bringing his good wishes and a little gift. I just wanted to mention that on my 95th birthday, my son arranged a surprise luncheon for me at the Northbrook restaurant on July 17, 1990. Eight of us were having our meal when Frank Ney dropped by, totally unexpected, to wish me a Happy Day and present me with a miniature bathtub and Nanaimo pin. it was typical of his concern for all the people of his city and I just wanted to express my admiration for him and all he did for our city and its people.

I am now in my hundredth year, having come to Nanaimo at age 13 and having seen many changes, and the tenure of many mayors, but certainly Frank Ney was the most memorable among many fine men who gave their time and efforts to make Nanaimo a better place to live in.

Best wishes for the success of your book which I shall look forward to. Although I am now blind, my son will read it to me. He is John B. Shepherd, now retired from his Optometry practice in Duncan.

Sarah J. Shepherd

On the Slopes

As a young man, Frank had spent a great deal of his recreational time skiing in Europe. A large number of the black and white photographs he kept with him were from his early skiing trips. When he settled in Canada, he never left this passion behind him.

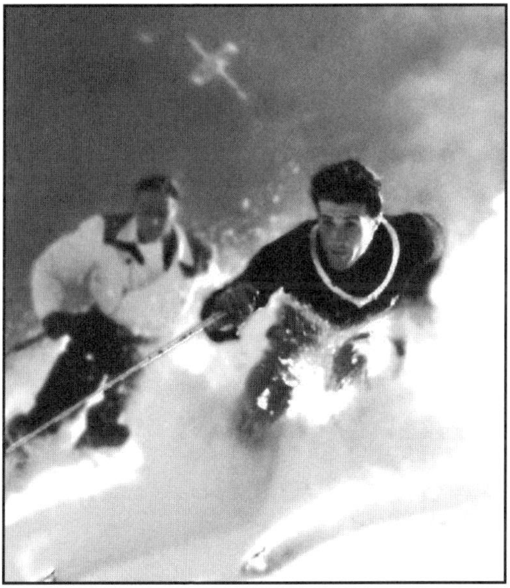

A young Frank flying down the slopes at Banff. His early photos show his gang of close friends, numerous girlfriends and plenty of skiing.

As a child, Dell Plensky lived on the opposite side of town as Frank. An active skier, like Frank, she had seen him on the slopes and certainly knew who he was. Being too young to drive, she found her way up the mountain by hitch-hiking. When Frank became aware of this, he simply wouldn't have it. At first he pulled over and had her pile into the car with the rest of the kids. Soon, like the others, she was being picked up at home.

With all the many stops to pick people up, stops to pick things up, and stops for kids to go to the washroom, the entourage would often not arrive on the slopes until early afternoon. On one such occasion, Frank had all the kids phone home to inform their folks that they were staying over. He rented hotel rooms for everyone and the next day they all got an earlier on their day of skiing.

Dell continued to join in the fun with Mr. Ney's entourage until she was into her mid-teens. She still loves to speak of the fun times everyone had together.

In January of '90, Fred Maguire was sitting in the lounge at Mount Washington. Frank walked in, sat down to join him for a drink. Frank mentioned that he had been out cross-country skiing with a friend, had worn the fellow out and was now stopping for a few minutes before going downhill skiing. Frank was in full form, he was the Mayor of Nanaimo, in good humour, talking to everyone in the place and all set to go out and do some more skiing. Frank was in his early seventies and had for the last number of years been somewhat forgetful. After drinking his glass of red wine he got up from the table and went out to do some more skiing. Fred stayed in the lounge.

About twenty minutes later Frank came back into the lounge with a bemused look on his face. He said, "You know, Fred, I've never had anything like this happen to me in my life." "What was that?" Fred asked. "Well, here I was in the line-up to the yellow chair. I went to get into the lift and the young man, I can't remember his name, said—'Mr. Ney you can't get on there.' 'Why not?' I asked. 'You haven't got any skis on!'"

Most people wouldn't admit to such foolishness. However, Frank saw the humour, as did Fred, and they both roared with laughter.

Fred Maguire, Nanaimo Realty

Frank was more of a recreational skier than a competitive one. He participated in the Famous Mayors' Ski Race at Forbidden Plateau as part of the Comox Valley Winter Carnival. The mayor who won the race removed an "Entering Nanaimo" sign from the bottom of the hill and gave it back to the loser, Frank Ney.

Lisa Gould, Montreal Quebec

I had a company in Duncan and was living there. One day I went skiing on Green Mountain. I came part way down the mountain and saw that a man had stopped over by the trees. I thought that maybe he was in trouble so I skied over to him. When I got over to the man, I realized that it was The Frank Ney whom I had seen pictures of and heard about. I asked him if there was a problem. He replied, "Oh no problem, it's just these damn mosquitos biting me," as he smacked the shoulders of his big ski jacket.

I had never seen any mosquitos on the mountain in the dead of winter, and if I did they would have a tough time stinging through the heavy clothing. It was certainly good for a laugh!

Anonymous

Frank Ney A Canadian Legend

As a girl growing up in the area, my family and I spent many weekends skiing and eventually working on Green Mountain. Frank Ney and his family were very much a fixture of the mountain.

Mr. Ney made this time especially fun during the evenings by taking the young skiers (and most of the time the older ones followed) for an adventure out-of-doors on the elusive "white cougar hunt." We'd follow him up and down the hills listening to him tell about the times gone by and the favorite spots of the "cougar." By the time we returned he'd always give us a treat for participating in the hunt (usually a wagon wheel). I always remembered him for this as the big person who paid attention to us young ones. Thank you, Frank Ney.

Donna McNab

.....In the early 70's Frank Ney was a familiar sight on the ski slopes of Green Mountain. Even there he made a fashion statement dressed in woolen knickers and knee high tartan socks. At the top of the mountain there was an overnight lodge run by the Snowbirds' ski club. Every Saturday night you'd find about 45 overnight guests enjoying the beautiful mountain life. Frank was usually there along with five or six of

his kids. After dinner he'd round up all the youngsters and off they'd go .... "COUGAR HUNTING!" He'd take them all for a good hike which put them to sleep nicely, and gave their parents a bit of free time. He even had ribbons printed up for all of the kids, labelling them as "COUGAR HUNTERS." Our time spent on Green Mountain was made all the more memorable by Mr. Ney's presence.

Sidney Zubach Easterbrook

Frank became a regular at Green Mountain. It was only an hour and a half drive from town and Frank, being a skier from an early age, somehow made the time to have some fun on the slopes.

The drive to the 4800' mountain was capped off with a steep four and a half mile logging road to the Day Lodge. This twisty road was closed to the public on weekdays because it was owned and used for logging purposes by a giant corporation. Among 200 coastal moutains surveyed, Green Mountain ranked tenth in the amount of snow-fall. Three feet of snow fell in two days in 1971. Frank and his convoy made the trip up on December 29 of that year to ski the 11 or 12' of snow that had piled up.

Frank was absolutely delighted to be trapped with 60 others and nothing to do but ski. The road conditions made it dangerous if not impossible to leave. After the first night some of the young people had run out of money and had taken temporary jobs at the cafeteria to buy food. Frank suggested, "They are getting their first lesson in business."

When the road was cleared enough for Frank to finally make it back to his office he let it be known that he was in "fighting shape" and that it was an exciting adventure. He had always said that Green Mountain has tremendous potential because it is so high and the snow stays much longer than at many other ski resorts. This was why it could remain open longer in the season. The area had been approved by the Associated Chambers of Commerce for Vancouver Island as a recreational spot to explore for further development. Frank had some ideas in that regard!

Green Mountain had quickly grown from being a facility with regular familiar patrons to one of the major recreation ski areas in the province. Over 1000 skiers per day had been using the slopes during the weekends of 1970. Frank used his position as MLA to make strong pitches for the mountain to be included in the paper on park development on Vancouver Island which was being prepared by the Department of Recreation. He insisted that "skiing is one of the world's fastest growing sports and this mountain sits at our doorsteps waiting to be developed." He said that it should be given full provincial support from a park and road improvement point of view. Frank believed that there was a world class tourist facility there ready to be realized. Having skied the great hills of Europe, he had a strong basis of comparison.

Unfortunately the facilities at Green Mountain were hit by vandals in the early 1980's. The towlift engine room was burnt and everything was damaged. The association that existed at the time disbanded and people just gave up. The recession had hit everyone. No one had the funds required to fix the ruined tow motor. To put the whole thing back in shape was beyond most people's priorities. Frank was very much saddened that Green Mountain was no longer there for the people to enjoy.

For the remainder of Frank's life, one of his greatest hopes was that people could revive Green Mountain. Whenever he ran into people who had been involved years ago, he would try to raise interest by asking, "How can we get it going again? What can we do?" He would have liked nothing better than for a group of people to get together and make it all happen again.

The mountain is now happily retired as a wildlife refuge, and the kids who had participated in its early "cougar hunts" are now all adults. Frank never did stop skiing, and he never stopped taking kids on outings.

All Aboard

....In 1957 I was Managing Director of VIGAS, and we bought a house at 850 Beach Drive just three houses from Frank. We got to know them quite well.

In 1958, a year after we arrived in Nanaimo, Frank invited John Dunham, then manager of the Blackball Ferry operation, Dr. Herb Welch, and me for an evening cruise and fishing on his boat. I don't remember the name of the boat but it was a cabin type about 20' long with an outboard. We did a lot of cruising but I don't remember any fishing. I do remember there was a bottle of rum on board.

About midnight someone suggested we go ashore on Jesse to explore a bit. John was at the helm and we were slowly approaching that sloping rock and sand area on the SW part of the island. I got up on the bow with the painter in my hand to jump off when we noticed the ferry was going by. Someone shouted, "Watch out for the wake of the Blackball." Just then the wake hit us, the boat tipped about 45 degrees and I was tossed into the salt chuck. I swam ashore and got out on the beach and there was the boat half full of water pitched up on the shore about 4' above the water level. The outboard had been knocked off and the other 3 guys were standing looking at it. Now, we had a problem.

We walked up to the high part of Jesse and looked at the houses opposite us on Stephenson Point Road. We decided we would try shouting for help. Pretty soon we spotted a porch light blinking. It was Madge Taylor who had been a Wren during the war. She was blinking Morse Code at us but it was lost on us. The only one who might have figured it out was John who had been in the Royal Navy during the war.

Through the shouting method, we learned that help was on the way. In about 30 minutes an outboard from the Anchorage showed up and took us back to our starting point. I never learned how much the repairs cost, but it must have been kind of expensive. I have always been very happy that the boat didn't land on me while I was in the water.

Dick Bond

THERE ARE HUNDREDS OF PEOPLE who often recall outings with Frank on his private boat. Early into his life in western Canada he discovered recreational boating. Local folks recall how he hosted innumerable trips and events on his wooden cabin cruiser *Jolly Tar* during the 1960's and early 1970's.

Frank's early wooden boats were not fancy, but the improtant thing was that they held a lot of people!

All Aboard

Some boats sit at their mooring all year waiting for a cruise or two in the summer. Frank's boats were not like that. They always got a lot of use. An old friend named Ken laughs about a trip to Gabriola where Frank had only two drinks with friends and then claimed he was in no condition to skipper back to town. Frank went down below, while Ken served his apprenticeship in driving a boat at night.

On another trip Frank put the engine into a wrong gear and Ken heard a scrape on the hull. When he checked the bilge, Ken found about a four-foot gash. When Frank was informed of it he asked, "Is it above or below the water line?" Ken told him that it was above. "Well," Frank continued, "Let's go!"

Because I played guitar and could get a good campfire sing along going, Frank often asked me to go along on his endless overnight campouts on the Gulf islands. I was always happy to go as I was assured a good time, but I always made an weak excuse not to go, as it cut into my sales and I would come home more tired than when I left. Frank would invite me to bring my ukulele, my mandolin or banjo. He always meant "guitar", although he never said so. I always went along and was never sorry.

After a night around the fire and a couple hours of sleep on the ground or on the deck of Frank's boat, I would awake to the smoke of the engine and Frank yelling something to the likes of, "Wake up you swabs!" We were riding on Frank's enthusiasm and unlimited energy, and constantly meeting interesting people.

On one occasion the guest of honor was a famous surgeon who had written some heavy duty medical books. Frank's answer to the good doctor when asked where he got his endless supply of energy, was, "Oh, it's easy, doc, all I have to do is eat a couple of oysters, raw and on the half shell." Well, Frank blew it that time because the doctor absolutely insisted on watching this with his own eyes. Since there was no way Frank could or would do this little trick, he would always make some excuse like, "Oh I just had a couple." Thus Frank was able to evade the performance, until one morning when the doctor was up and about early. He told Frank that he was going to stick to him all day until he saw someone eat an oyster right out of the sea. Frank was by this time beginning to sweat bullets. He came over to me and asked me to accompany him to the boat on the pretext of pumping out the bilge. Once out of earshot, Frank asked me if I would get him off the hook by eating the raw oyster for him. I said that there was no way. "But Kenny," he said, "I know how many hot dogs you can eat around the campfire and I see you eat all the leftover toast and jam at the breakfast meetings." So even though I had never eaten or had any intention of eating a raw oyster, I agreed to do it. Frank said, "I'll be your friend for life." A promise he kept.

Ken Gogo

In the fifties when we cruised the Georgia Strait at three knots per hour we'd often not see a boat all day. Once we were down to half a loaf of bread. Captain Ney laid down the rule, one slice twice a day and one cup of water. We spotted a small island with a store. We purchased groceries with cheques written on Kleenex after explaining we were lost. It was years before Frank bought charts and quit using the free gas station road maps.

Arriving in Cowichan Bay in a putt putt captained by Frank Ney, the crew of Joe Isherwood and myself went into the sea side cafe. Frank had his captains hat on so some of the ladies asked if they could see his yacht. Frank pointed to a freighter anchored in the bay and said, "Fine, it will have to be tomorrow, I have 30 of the crew holy stoning the decks. It's too slippery for visitors tonight."

Ron MacIsaac, Lawyer

All Aboard

There were a few rules aboard Frank's boat. First off, have fun, and secondly, don't kill any bugs. He really didn't like to see anyone hurt, and that included our friends in the insect world. This became fun in itself when flies became a bother down below. There was to be no swatting flies or stepping on spiders. However, it was easy enough to put them in a cup and give them their freedom elsewhere.

Guests aboard Frank's boat always had a story to tell. There were trips when rabbits and dear were amongst the crew. Frank had decided to set animals free to breed on numerous islands. Any visitors these islands today will see that they were quite successful in this venture!

The folklore associating Frank with boating mainly centers around his 34' Canoe Cove *Blue Girl*. This is the craft that became synonymous with Black Frank. She was loaded up for every maritime event with groups as diverse as major sports clubs to cub scout troops. Can you picture Frank at the helm with thirty cubs on board? The *Blue Girl* has probably played host to more functions both formal and informal than any other cruiser on the coast. She was indeed a common sight in and around Nanaimo's beautiful harbour.

Black Frank was completely unflappable. One day, the pirate was on the bridge delivering inspiring bathtub mottos through his megaphone to other boaters. Suddenly the flare gun in his other hand went off. The burning ball of phosphorescence ricocheted of the aft deck and again off the bridge before it blew the megaphone right out of Frank's hand. A couple inches closer and he would have had to add an eye patch to his attire. In his usual graceful manner he picked up his megaphone and continued; "Sunporch of Canada..."

Frank didn't grow up around the water, and the popular opinion is that he really knew precious little about boating. He made countless requests for tow-ins and other forms of assistance over the years. On one such occasion Frank was returning his guests from the finish line of the bathtub race. He spotted another craft across the way, pointed his sword and said, "Avast! Ship out yonder! Let's go welcome them!"

One of his sons was aboard and warned him, "Whatever you do, don't shut the engine off or it won't start again." They cruised up to

the mystery craft and Frank reached for the ignition. Everyone aboard yelled, "Don't shut it off!," and he did. As predicted, the next time the engine was to start was after it had been towed to shore and attended to. Frank's reaction was the same as all other simular incidents.
He laughed and said, "Don't worry. It's not a problem." If anyone disagreed, he would add "Don't take life so seriously!"

These were not fast boats. Frank always travelled at a slow clip. He would doddle around and look at things. Guests could be shocked into having fun as he acted out imaginary disasters such as, "Oh no! We're up on the rocks!" for the benefit of a guest from the prairies who was unaccustomed to the ocean.

The local police remember other incidents that were not quite so imaginary. The head of the RCMP once had to leap into waist high water to push the *Blue Girl* off a sandbar, only moments after Frank had said, "Not to worry, there's a lot of water here." The police were not about to get upset with Frank. They recognized him as the man single-handedly responsible for the continuation of marine rescue service in Nanaimo.

Guests on the Blue Girl often got wet. The reporters on board to cover the bathtub race, got used to Frank stopping the boat in the middle of the Strait each year to invite everyone for a swim. This became a tradition in itself and soon everyone brought their bathing suits along.

Bill and Frank Ney once pooled their money to buy new robes for a church choir. Frank would occasionally stroll in to their rehearsals on warm summer evenings and invite them all aboard the Blue girl for an hour or two. Most would accept the offer and have a very good time with their fellow parishoners at sea. There was never just one social circle that got all the invitations. All Frank expected of people was their willingness to have a good time.

Blowing a high pitched whistle on the bow of the Blue Girl. He took his brand of pirating very seriously and became agitated whenever the flag waver slacked off.

What a tightwad! I saw Ney paddling from his anchored boat at Silva Bay. He had only one oar and it was broken in half so it was actually only half a paddle. I yelled out to him and he said he was going ashore to buy a new one.

A while later I saw him rowing out to his boat again with the same broken oar. I told him that he could buy a new one at the store close by. He shot back, "Not at those prices!"

George McDougal, *Sandworks*

A couple college girls asked us for the time on the street. We were talking when Frank walked up and said, "So would you all like to go for a cruise in the chuck with the Mayor?" We joined some other people and had a great time on his yacht.

Anonymous

On the morning of August 8, 1980, Frank's Blue Girl *dropped anchor in Kanaka Bay off* Newcastle *Island. She had been magically transformed that day into a wedding chapel at sea as Kathleen Schmidek and Douglas Cooper exchanged marriage vows.*

When Les Varro first heard that Kathleen was hoping to be married on a boat he immediately began "making waves" of his own. Les and Al Lupton came up with an exciting idea. When they approached Frank regarding the services of the renowned Blue Girl, *his immediate response was, "Yes, why not?" A clear and endless sky, calm blue sea and an accompanying choir of seagulls set the enchanting scene which Kathleen and Douglas will always treasure.*

At the end of a most touching ceremony and the signing of the register, Frank, with his warm broad smile and a twinkle in his eye, hoisted the pennants and passed around the bubbly. With her whistle resounding in celebration across the bay, the Blue Girl *slipped proudly into the harbour.*

Frank obligingly took the time out from a usual busy day's schedule to mingle for a while and grace us with his presence at the backyard wedding reception which followed that afternoon.

This very special event will most certainly always bring back happy memories for all those concerned, and fondly and forever remembered will be the generous and kindhearted gentleman, Frank Ney, who without the least hesitation made a certain young lady's wish come true.

Flo Preston, Sorrento B.C.

My brother got married on Frank's boat - during the beer strike. You couldn't use the head because it was full of beer. There was whiskey in the magazine racks. Frank and I jumped off the fore deck. We were all swimming in our underwear.

Al Heise, Mechanic

On a visit to Nanaimo in August 1990 to have a reunion with my brother, we happened to bump into Frank Ney while on a walkabout downtown. After exchanging formalities, he invited us for a trip aboard his boat. We arranged to meet one afternoon on the dock. And much to our surprise there he was waiting to take us out as promised. We really did not think he would keep his word when we left him that sunny morning but he was good as gold.

After offering drinks all around, he duly took us for a delightful trip around the bay and explained the history of Nanaimo to us. He was truly a very colourful character who delighted us with his tales from around the world. One of the highlights of our visit to Nanaimo that year had to be the trip around the bay with Frank Ney. Where else in the world would you get the Mayor of any city to take you out for a sail aboard his yacht.

Deborah Nicholls, Dublin, Ireland

Once he invited me out on his boat and I told him I couldn't make it because I had to meet some people. He said, "Well, bring 'em along!"

David J. Strang, RBC Dominion Securities

Several years ago my wife, Cora, and I spent a very enjoyable three hours with Frank Ney. It was a warm, sunny summer afternoon. We had been out for the weekend on our boat La Bonne Vie *and had anchored in Pirates' Cove. About 4:30, in came the Blue Girl, his boat, with first rate cook Bob Inez, and about a dozen holidaying kids aged about twelve. They had been away for a few days and were returning home. A requirement for passage was the ability to swim.*

Frank hoisted the black skull and crossbones, and "avasted" us, and circled our boat. We put the fenders out and they tied up to us. It was a hot afternoon, they had the "coolants" and vegetables. We had a mess of fresh filleted ling cod and fock fish, so we boarded the Blue Girl. *Bob Inez did the cooking and the other three adults moved to the top deck.*

A great time was had and we enjoyed the excellent dinner prepared by Chef Bob.

All good things come to an end eventually, so the Blue Girl *cast off and started to head for home. Unfortunately, a head count was not conducted, and Frank had to return to our boat for the missing passenger. A very enjoyable experience!*

Bob Barclay

Bathtubmania!

Guests got mobbed by tubbers at City Hall!

NOBODY EVER IMAGINED THAT the first bathtub race, lark that is was, would ever snowball into the international spotlight in such a grand fashion. The success of this race really did catch everyone by surprise, and no one wanted to see such a good thing come to an end. Forty people jammed the hallway and stairwells at city hall in a bid to carry the race to perpetuity. Almost all of these bathtub fans were from local service clubs, who were offering to support the race in any way they could. The city council, led by Frank, had no problem deciding to sponsor the race. Glen Galloway was certainly excited with the thought that his idea of racing bathtubs was not going to fade into oblivion. He boasted; "We don't need the (Vancouver) Sea Festival or Empire Day - we can stand alone in this venture!" Frank was there to remind everyone: "Someone has to set things up on the other side. We haven't taken over Vancouver - yet."

The great race lives on. Nanaimo is a funny town. Amongst the old windows and other discarded household items found in the back alleys, one can spot the odd hull of a racing bathtub. As old tubs are discarded, new ones are being built, and people are building faster, better tubs every year. Frank had once said, "I find that corn is better than culture for getting people interested in doing something." People now say that Frank planted the corn which became our culture.

In 1968, when the Loyal Nanaimo Bathtub Society was formed, Frank was given the honorary title of Admiral of the Bathtub Fleet, which he held for life. He handed over the job of organizing the fine details of the race but still worked to showcase the Nanaimo Marine Festival and the bathtub races to the world with great success. The bathtub race was born into this world wearing a crazy reputation. If Frank was going to continue the project, he needed to look the part. He did more than just that; in fact he looked noble as he seized the opportunity to wear his colourful pirate suit.

Since Bill McGuire and Don Rose were extremely heavily involved in bathtubbing, they accompanied Frank to the Grey Cup parade in Toronto one year to promote the race. One day the gang was waiting in the lobby of the Sheraton Hotel for another person to arrive, so that they could go to a reception. They got tired of waiting and decided to call a cab.

Frank went out to hail a cab in his pirate suit. Instead of getting a cab, he was handed the keys to someone's car. The Admiral Of the Fleet had been mistaken for a parking attendant. His smile and courteous manner earned him a good tip.

Anonymous

I was cruising down the road one night and noticed that Frank was driving the car in the next lane. I yelled out, "Hey, old Franky-Boy," and he gave a whooping, "Hey boys!." I yelled to him that his headlights were not on. His reply was, "I was wondering why they pulled me over back there." He continued down the road. Never did turn them on.

John Davidson, Plumber

Bathtubmania!

The 1969 bathtub season saw the introduction of the bathtub trade dollar. Dollar coins are issued every year and are legal tender in Nanaimo until the date marked on the coin. They are more commonly kept as prized keepsakes by coin collectors and bathtub enthusiasts. Bathtub coins depicting the famous Bastion on one side and the official crest of the World Championship Bathtub Race on the reverse have gained international attention. A feature article in the World Coin News was followed by articles in other major publications. As a result of this extra publicity mail orders came in from many points in the U.S. and Europe. What's an event without merchandise?

I came to Nanaimo in 1969. Our business at the time was Catto and Peirson Photography. I had heard of Frank Ney and his pirate suit and the Bathtub Race. On Bathtub Day, I went down to his boat Blue Girl *to meet Frank and ask him to pose for a photograph before the race. I had a lot of equipment with me and was standing there with one foot on his boat and the other on the dock. The boat started to move and Frank and another person pulled me on the boat,and Frank said he would pose after the race got underway. I took all sorts of pictures on that trip, so I was with him all day and never got back to Nanaimo until one a.m. So I saw the start of the race and the finish. Frank was very excited and full of enthusiasm during the whole trip. A really enjoyable day.*

Like so many other people in Nanaimo, I considered Mayor Ney a good friend and a man who really loved Nanaimo.

Jim Peirson, Photographer

Nanaimo became bathtub crazy as huge crowds swarmed the town every year to help celebrate the weekend. Fred Maguire took the initiative in the summer of 1974 to cruise all around Vancouver Island in his bathtub. That is no small feat, and he is no small man. The Island has a circumference of 1610 km and Fred stands about 2 metres tall. That is 1000 miles and 6' 4½" for those from the old school of bathtubbing. Many fine folks wouldn't dare to test the nearly open ocean of the west coast to any small vessel, let alone a tub! Despite suggestions of lunacy, he completed the circumnavigation in 10 days.

Party crowds will party loud. There was a time when B.C. festivals had definite crowd control problems and Nanaimo was no exception to this unfortunate trend. At its worst Frank found himself downtown hollering for peace through his megaphone to 600 intoxicated folks as they slashed tires, trashed police cars and broke windows. This continued until 4:15 a.m. It was a black day for Nanaimo. At its worst, a speeding car broke through the police lines and headed right towards Mayor Ney. Frank spoke of his 1975 experience, "I ran for my life! I jumped behind a telephone pole, and they hit the pole." The twenty-two year old driver was charged with attempted murder, and later pleaded guilty to a reduced charge of dangerous driving. The case resulted in two years probation.

Mr. Ney looked over the city's damages and was left with two choices: cancel the bathtub festival or try one more time. He loved the whole idea of the race and didn't want it to end this way. He felt that the kids would stay out of trouble if they were entertained. And so he decided to keep the entertainment constant, beef up the security and give the festival another go. The perserverance paid off and the race grew to be telecast in sixty-five countries. Problems with crowds never did pop up again and the entire weekend grew to be consistently safe for kids of all ages.

Many reporters enjoyed trips on Frank's boat. It was the only way to get him in one place for an interview!

When the "National Enquirer" entered a tub and subsequently reported on the race, they had nothing but good things to say about it. They were thrilled to have set a new world's record in the heavyweight class. The 90.9 kg, (202 pound), 38-year-old skipper Art LaLone flipped right over the bow at the finish line. He rolled onto his feet and staggered his aching legs up to ring the official finish-line bell. He had piloted the plywood-hulled tub across the Strait at a constant 25.76 kph, (16 mph). That's pretty fast for a tub carrying such a large man. LaLone was presented with the Tubby trophy, an elegant, two-foot tall model of a pig on a pedestal flanked by two bathtubs.

My husband and I and my mother went to Vancouver to see the finish of the Bathtub Race several years ago.

After the race we were at the outdoor theatre, Kitsilano, waiting for the awards. My mother talked to the lady sitting next to her, and remarked that she knew Mayor Ney very well. The lady did not believe her. Just then Mayor Ney, splendid in his pirate costume passed by us. He stopped, came back, gave my mother a hug and a big kiss. The lady looked on in amazement and said, "I guess you do know him."

Vera and John Cowan

It has been reported in the media that Frank was a member, or a director, a patron or honorary member of at least seventeen local and provincial organizations. Being the admiral of the Loyal Bathtub Society was his favourite...

As a longtime member of the society I've been fortunate to have had the opportunity of travelling with Frank to many bathtub related events in the USA and across Canada. One memorable trip was to Toronto in November of 1982 for the Grey Cup parade. The world's largest bathtub was chosen as a float to represent British Columbia....The tub and Frank were a big hit, with Frank bellowing his famous lines...."Alright, you little kiddies, throw your bubble gum and candies into the big bathtub or I'll cut your little scurvey heads off!" " I'm a young bachelor from Nanaimo and I'd like to sing you young ladies a love song." Then he'd sing his rendition of 'Waltzing Matilda' very poorly I might add. And "Shiver me timbers! Shiver me timbers!"...

Upon arriving in Toronto, Frank asked me what two teams were playing in the Grey Cup. I told him, "The Edmonton Eskimos and the Toronto Argonauts." He said that made it easy; he would root for Edmonton, the team from the west. Then I mentioned that Carling O'Keefe, our sponsor for the trip, owned the Argonauts. Upon hearing this, and being the politician he always was, he went out and bought a Toronto team button and an Edmonton team button, putting one on either side of his pirate costume that he wore everywhere he went in Toronto along with that pirate flag that knocked over more things than I'd like to mention.

Before going into the many receptions and functions we attended, Frank would always ask who would be the host and who would they be rooting for. He would them tuck his plastic sword in the appropriate side, covering the other team's button and proudly displaying the right one. These two buttons still adorned his pirate costume in this year's Nanaimo Marine Festival parade....

Bill McGuire, Realtor

The world's largest bathtub has hit parades in many cities. She is seen here with the Royal Yacht Britannia.

Nobody could ever count the number of parades Black Frank was in. Over the years he rode in the World's Largest Bathtub with lots of kids. The 11-year-old David Pederson recalls meeting Frank in a parade and this time it was Frank who hitched a ride home. Aunty Pia loaded her nephew and her mayor into her beat-up 1982 Honda Civic and cruised off. They thought that it was funny having the mayor in the car and were glad that he didn't have any pretensions. A Honda Civic was rather a tight squeeze after seeing the sights from the vantage point of a giant bathtub on wheels.

The Admiral Of The Fleet made use of bathtubs of all sizes. He gave away hundreds of small ceramic tubs as gifts and prizes. A grand old classic tub graced the front door of his new office building. He even had a striking yellow one placed in front of his house as a gift from his family.

Every year Frank looked for new ways to make Bathtub Weekend fun. He wasn't the only one. In the 1968 race, Barry Clark had made a 32-hour voyage across Georgia Strait equipped with paddles and a true spirit of adventure. In the mid 1970's, he rescued Frank from a kidnapping attempt. Frank had taken the 3-hour tour on the old CPR ferry from Vancouver. He was certainly not alone on that ship. The Vancouver Sea Festival people had met with the Bathtub Society during the crossing.

Skiing down the hill at Bowen Park.
"It just proves that bathtubbing is a year-round sport here."

As Frank was about to disembark, he was grabbed by about a dozen men. "They had a villainous look and I knew immediately they were from Vancouver." He managed to break free and left the ferry by way of the freight deck, "tricking those dastardly Sea Festival rascals." Barry Clark didn't fare as well. He had made a valiant attempt to rescue the famed mayor and MLA, but ended up in Vancouver with no money to pay for a return ticket. The road to heroism is occasionally paved in misfortune.

There was never a shortage of ideas for projects in Frank's life. He loved to encourage other people's ideas while at the same time offering many ideas for others to work with. He once wrote a letter to the Canadian National Railways asking them to consider broadening their operations on Vancouver Island. The company could reclassify Nanaimo as a distributing point and create competition for the Canadian Pacific Railway. This would result in an improved freight rate for the city. Frank's letter contained enough detailed information to warrant a meeting with one of the big company men.

When Frank sat down with the representative from the company that employed more than 96,000 people, he had more than railways on his mind. Frank spoke of tourism, and of bathtubs. The two men discussed the possibility that the CNR run a "Bathtub Special" passenger train from Halifax to the west coast. "It would be a natural. They do it for the Calgary Stampede and the Grey Cup and things like that. Why don't they run a train right across the country and pick up the mayor of every city en route?"

The idea itself made good press, but was never put into practice. With the constant mental juggling of ideas, some have to be put back on the shelf in order to keep the others in the air.

A swamped tubber is not an uncommon sight.

Black Frank never missed a race. Every year he would assail the crowd with one of his famous speeches. His *Blue Girl* graced the scene of many maritime activities. With megaphone in hand, he would stand on the bow as the boat crashed through the big waves. He was never alone on these trips. There was always a fine regiment of family and friends and most often a fine piper. He would often have Norm Porter's Dixieland band follow him aboard a navy ship on trips where music was needed to calm the savage sea.

Days before the race, the *Blue Girl* could be seen cruising or anchored with a flotilla of smaller craft tied to her side. The crazy fellow swimming around in the busy waters could be identified as

Frank Ney, and it took very little coaxing for him to find the right moment to yell a respectable greeting your way, or at least wave a bottle of rum at you.

Local folks developed a sea-tale about Frank getting drunk on bathtub weekend and steering the *Blue Girl* into a police boat. This myth has its roots in a true bathtub story that took place during the start of the 1986 Expo summer race. Frank was down below gathering his plastic sword and other accoutrements required for his appearance at the finish line. His regular skipper was at the helm bringing the pirate back to shore so he could catch a quick flight to Vancouver for the ceremonies. The harbour was filled with boats. It is typical on such occasions for at least one idiot to be speeding through the maze of yachts. One such fool cut in front of the *Blue Girl* and the captain cut to the starboard to avoid disaster. In doing so, the *Blue Girl* sideswiped a RCMP water-cruiser.

One of the cops aboard, shaken up and bruised, was not thrilled and laid formal charges on the captain. Frank was unaware of all of this as he sorted out his pirate luggage in the cabin. The story got twisted out of proportion around town and finally the captain was acquitted of all charges. No serious harm was done, and Frank did make his flight on time.

The Expo summer had long been anticipated by the Admiral of the Fleet. Special guests from out of town received hearty welcomes to the Bathtub Capital. Frank arranged a financial package that facilitated a pioneering Australian tubber to once again stir our waters. Gary Deathridge had won two earlier races and was active in introducing the sport down-under. This honoured and appreciated guest was lucky not to have met the fate of the two-masted schooner *Bluenose II* as it sailed into the harbour.

As most Canadians are aware, the *Bluenose II* is an exact replica of the 1921 *Bluenose* which adorns the Canadian dime. After being launched in Lunenburg, Nova Scotia in 1963, she immediately sailed into the Canadian history books. Captain Don Barr had been a resident of Nanaimo before he made a return visit to the bathtub capital behind the helm of the *Bluenose II*.

The Bluenose II *was scheduled to pay a four-day visit to Nanaimo on her way to Expo 86 in Vancouver B.C. This was a reasonably publicized event and hundreds of people stood on the shore awaiting her arrival. Frank Ney found this to be a magical opportunity to organize a welcoming committee.*

As the famed schooner approached the harbour, Frank and his gang of pirates, including drama students from the Malaspina College, started firing cannon shots from their ship. They waited until the Bluenose II *reached the pier before they forced their way aboard. Frank and his pals, all dressed as pirates, initiated a bloodless 10-minute battle. When the battle subsided, the* Bluenose *captain had been evicted and forced to walk the plank. As he reached the end of the plank, he received a full pardon and was presented with a box of Nanaimo bars. Musician Mike Thomas provided attack music while the crowd of spectators gaped in hilarious amazement.*

The captain was not too shy to admit that he had never had so much fun.

Annonymous Old Man of the Sea

The pedal-powered tub had three different paint jobs and a tiller on the bow. One hand steered while the other held the flag.

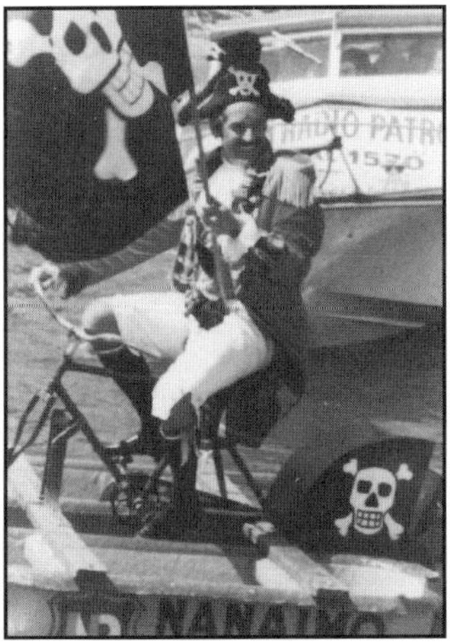

Frank Ney A Canadian Legend

One of the few times the Mayor of Nanaimo went down in defeat was during the Campbell River Water Festival. Five Vancouver Island mayors competed in a bathtub race and Black Frank came in plum last. He boarded his one-man-power sternwheeler bathtub and lined up with the five other tubs. All the others had 6 hp motors. Frank pedalled furiously down the course while waving at the crowd of 5000. You can bet this made good press.

"It was a good race, and I must say that I was overwhelmed with the beauty and delights of the lake and the warm hospitality of the seaside cottages." Frank had nothing but good things to say about the town and its surrounding real estate. He had seen quite a lot of it lately as he had just opened an office there.

In 1978 I had a Japanese student who was attending Malaspina College for 5 weeks staying in my home. She got very excited when she heard that there was to be a bathtub race as she had heard about it at home in Japan on T.V.

A friend at work suggested that I ask Frank Ney if we could ride in his boat, The Blue Girl *during the race. He said, "Frank will invite you for sure!" When I called to ask, he said that he was all full up for the actual race with lots of dignitaries but he could take us on the Junior Bathtub Race. This turned out to be just perfect because she had the company of the young Queen candidates and this event became one of the highlights of her trip to Canada.*

To thank Frank for this boat trip, I invited him to a special garden party I held. I never received a reply and assumed he was far too busy to attend. The day of the party turned out to be lovely and sunny. The gathering was a huge success and in full swing when a loud whistle was blown. Everyone looked up and there was Frank all dressed in his pirate costume for his Newcastle Island Swim. He came down the stairs into my garden and graciously accepted refreshments and then went to greet each and everyone of my guests. I was so happy and proud. It had been like a very special entertainment had come to my party.

However, I soon found out who were my friends! Some said, "How come he came to YOUR party?" Others said, "Why was he here? I never have liked him," etc. And one fellow very mean-spiritedly said, "Oh, I can see how you got your job at City Hall."

Again I say, "Thank you Frank. You always gave to us your very best

Clare Mosher

Black Frank has been the only Mayor in the known world to have made the orange distress flare his personal signature. Everyone noticed the sharp-looking pirate as he bellowed wisdom though a megaphone while holding a tube with red-orange smoke billowing out. He also made a tradition of setting a boat ablaze in the harbour as a sacrifice to the gods each summer. The red smoke from his flair was the perfect match for the flames that shot into the darkening sky above the festive sea. The atmosphere created in anticipation before the fireworks filled the sky with nothing short of magic.

Frank didn't know much about football, but he sat in special boxes reserved for him and entertained people from dawn to dusk. He was a great ambassador, always a gentleman, and he stuck out like a sore thumb. Everybody had heard of him.

Bill McGuire

Every year has seen a new original poster promoting the Bathtub Weekend or Maritime Festival as it is more officially known. The posters are consistently beautiful and always prove to be collectors' items. The 1992 version proved to be extremely popular as it was a salute to Frank Ney and the international maritime bicentennial. The artwork featured a full length shot of Black Frank with the world's largest bathtub in the foreground decked out in full sails, with rigging like the ships which plied the northwest waters two hundred years ago. A limited number of these posters were signed by the artist Mark Heine and Black Frank himself.

The bathtub race continues to be a very popular tourist attraction. It has melded into the Marine Festival which includes other local events such as the Silly Boat Race, Tunnel Boats, the Marine Art Exposition as well as numerous events in Vancouver. Frank never lost his enthusiasm and talked tubs with anyone who would listen. "When I talked to the Duke of Edinburgh, he seemed more interested in the bathtubs of Nanaimo than what was happening in industry. I was delighted to give him the information."

Talk to merchants downtown. The busiest times of the year are Christmas and Bathtub days. Frank was always aware of that.

Bob Pederson

The bathtub race is now covered by the sports network (TSN) with a camera inside the tub of veteran tubber George Johnson. George has never won the big race but he does receive the honour of being the first man with a tub wired up for television. How would you like all of North America to see you in the tub?

What the casual observer must remember is the fact that these vessels are very small and the ocean does get very rough. Anyone who has witnessed this event, or experienced it can attest to the fact that bathtubbing is a very rugged world class sporting event. There are no cash prizes to be won. Big corporations are known to donate prizes and the Bathtub Society is known to raffle them off between all the entrants. The media reports that some 600,000,000 people now watch the race every year. The race itself has become far better known than the town that hosts it.

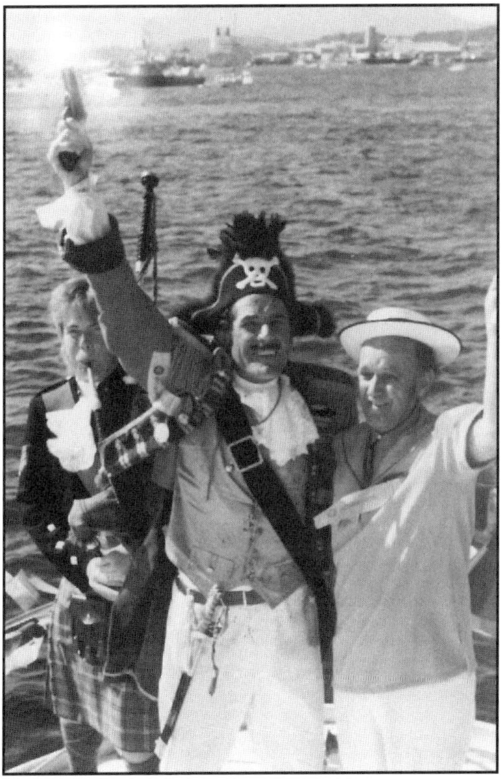

The starting gun - a shot heard around the world.

As the main pirate himself would say at the finish line of all the twenty races he attended, "In Nanaimo harbour this morning, 270 bathtubs started and 178 sank in the first minute. The crossing was an epic saga of raw courage and true bathtub seamanship. And today we have once again proven conclusively and incontrovertibly that British Columbia leads the world in bathtub technology, and out here on the west coast on a holiday occasion people prefer corn to culture, and today we gave it to them right off the stalk. ***Eight bells and all's well in Davy Jones' locker. Yo Ho Ho and a bottle of rum!***"

Frank Ney A Canadian Legend

The Admiral of the Fleet

Thousands of people have wondered over the years what this pirate is talking about with his "Eight Bells" routine. It is actually a very old slogan that began during Columbus' first trip to the Americas aboard the "Santa Maria." For a while there were almost ideal conditions aboard ship, with steady flowing trade winds making nearly all work unnecessary. A routine developed where the duties on deck were divided between two watches which alternated every four hours. Time was kept by cabin boys (grummets) who watched the sand run out of the half-hour glass, turning it when empty to an appropriate verse. This became the "Eight Bells" arrangement for changing the watch.

Frank would later state, "I take my hat off to the people getting into the race, for having so much enthusiasm and energy to get involved. When I went down there I couldn't believe it. There must have been thousands of people involved in this race today."

Frank explained his passion for promotion by saying, "People have very warm hearts and they like very down-to-earth things and what we're doing is exemplifying the salubrious climate of British Columbia not just in Canada but right around the world."

Ney suggested that bathtubbing could benefit young people seeking careers in the maritime field. He referred to it as a healthy sport and mentioned that some participants ended up joining the navy.If anyone needs further proof who leads the world in bathtub technology, please refer to the Guinness Book of Records.Here on the west coast of Canada, we take the mobility of our bathroom fixtures very seriously.

"Through Adversity to the Stars"

> *Said Frank as he organized some kind of event, "Brad, I want three bands: a country band, a Hawaiian band, and the kind with the electrical guitars."*
>
> Rob Becker, Musician

> *I had really long hair when I was a kid. I was walking down the street with another guy and said "Hi" to Frank Ney. "Hi girls!" he replied as he kept on his way.*
>
> Tom Gogo, Musician

FRANK HAD EARNED HIS REPUTATION AS A BUSY MAN. Some positions he held in the 1970's include: Director of the Salvation Army Advisory Board, Director of the Nanaimo United Appeal, Director of Fort St. John Petroleum Ltd., Director of Vancouver Island Gas Co. Ltd., Director of the B.C. Automobile Association, Director of the Canadian Council of Christians and Jews and the Director of the Vancouver Island Publicity Bureau.

Previous to this he was the president/governor/chairman/director of a host of civic and professional groups, including the Real Estate Institute of B.C. and the B.C. Society of Notary Publics. There were 23 affiliations listed on his resume by the early 1980's. With his reputation he didn't exactly need a resume, but it was fun for him to make the lists.

All of these titles were on top of his responsibilities to the Bathtub Society, his real estate business, political career and of course his large family. This was the man who attended birthdays, bar mitzvahs, weddings, funerals, dances and sodturnings. A Saturday evening could mean making appearances at as many as five social or civic functions. There was never a question of his "having to" attend every event in town. He did it because he wanted to. He kept piles of notes on the speeches he was constantly delivering. Besides being the provincial champion at the Toastmasters, he freelanced on the lecture circuit in the area. The Vancouver Lions Club heard him speak on "The Swinging Age Mix." Two days later the Industrial Accountants of British Columbia heard all about "Debts and Credits of '69." "It's not a strain on me as I like people and enjoy meeting them. In fact I don't feel good if there's no people around. I like people around."

Almost ten years had passed since the Neys had moved to their larger office. It was now apparent to everyone concerned that those quarters were also becoming cramped. Recognizing that they were very well centered and established in town, they concluded it would be better off adding to their existing building than moving into a new one. The original building was not touched in 1975 when construction went ahead with a million dollar five story addition behind it. The new section with its walls of glass was designed to contrast and compliment rather than to copy the pillared core section of vaulted ceilings and Italian marble floor. The whole effect came across very well and the old building stood out as even more of a landmark than it had earlier. Frank settled himself into his big corner office and continued his work.

A fully serviced lot on Vancouver Island still cost only $10,900 in 1976. Frank's next push was to buy a full page ad in newspapers in neighbouring towns to explain "terms that make it so easy to own a piece of your own country. Terms like $109 down and $109 a month bring some of the finest land in B.C. within your reach." Horne Lake, Jingle Pot Lagoon and a number of other locations on the Island were being subdivided and serviced. A full list of properties was available. It was a happy time for the sales team as people bought into these wonderful opportunities without any hesitation.

Real estate is often a barometer of the economy. During down cycles when times got tough, the sales team at Nanaimo Realty thanked their lucky stars they were employees of this company. It was sometimes the only company in town that could get bank mortgages.A job at Nanaimo Realty was a good job to have in the boom days.When times were good there was lots of business, lots of money,and people had fun. Of the thirty or so secretaries, someone was always getting married, having a baby, retiring or experiencing some interesting turn of events. Once every six weeks the staff would be sent out to the Grotto or some other fine restaurant, where they would enjoy dinner and drinks at company expense.When times got tough in the 1980's, the boss covered the meal, but not the drinks.

Some type of ethnic Cultural Society wanted to build a center in a fairly decent part of town. They didn't have a lot of money and with taxes and everything it was quite a problem. Frank said, "Why don't you build a church, that way you don't have to pay any taxes." They did. Now they have a nice meeting place.

Anonymous

There was a small department store only a block away from the real estate office.This outlet carried an impressive selection of very cheap and tacky plastic toys. Frank did a splendid job of keeping these folks in business by purchasing bags and bags of trinkets.With all the hiring going on in his office he had to keep up his image and let the new people know what he was all about. One new secretary was completing her high school work experience program and was taking her job quite seriously. One day Frank quietly approached her desk from behind as she typed away.The entire staff was alarmed

by her shriek. Frank had dangled a plastic spider in front of the unsuspecting young lady.

In October 1975 I was looking for a job in a real estate office in Nanaimo. I was turned down by three firms. All depressed, I went back to Port Alberni.

The next day I went to see Frank at Nanaimo Realty. In his office on Front Street. I could not believe my eyes when I saw Frank holding two phones, one at each ear. And he was responding quite well to both people - of course with a cigar burning on his table, which he would puff on in between.

He asked me to wait for a few minutes. After hearing why I was there, he took me out of the office, walked a couple blocks with me, learning about me and my interests. When we came back to the office, he told the manager, "I think we should hire him right away."

I have been with the company since then.

Frank - A Great Guy!

Ash Pabbies

By 1976, Nanaimo Realty employed 376 island staff, including 250 sales people. Besides selling properties, the firm was involved in construction, land development and retail lumber. Its land bank grew to 3400 acres, including offices in eight cities. This made them the largest real estate company and land developer on Vancouver Island. The company's holdings took up six pages in the local land registry records.

The holdings of Frank's companies included hundreds of subdivided lots, farm land, industrial sites and good old fashioned raw land. Twelve of the twenty-nine apartment buildings were registered in Frank's name. Some people liked to read the records at the registry office and try to figure out exactly how much land this Mayor owned. By the time any reporters had a reasonable estimate worth writing about, the numbers would be jumbled from all the buying and selling.

Great National Land was securely established as one of the top 50 companies in B.C. Frank, being the chief shareholder among 3600 others, predicted that they would some day be producing $100 million per year. Land prices were rising as much as 30 per cent per year, and if the trend was to continue along those lines, Frank's visions would be visible for all to see.

The company was cautious about expanding too quickly. Frank said, "We could double the number of offices in six months if we wanted. We could buy them for $50,000 to $100,000 each, and we have the money to do it. There is more to expansion than that. When we open a branch, we want to be able to offer our customers a full line of services." He saw real estate branches like department stores. A customer had to be able to finance and construct industrial, commercial and residential buildings for sale or leaseback.

Mr. Ney was publicly secretive about his personal wealth. He always had enough work to keep his secretaries fully occupied. Often he would take one phone call with a phone in his other hand. Every week started with a close-typed list of engagements two pages long.

When I first became involved in business, Frank suggested that I be his designated driver and accompany him on his outings. In this way I could make some good contacts. I complied and was not disappointed.

There was a party for Miss Nanaimo, Theresa Delsal, who came in second for Miss Canada. I signed my name in the guest book as D. Strang. Frank took me aside and said, "Dave, can I offer you some constructive advice?" I gladly said, "Sure...." Frank continued, "You signed your name with an initial. There may be three D. Strangs here, there may be three guys behind you who don't know who you are. I always sign my name Frank J. Ney."

From that day on I changed my signature.

David J. Strang, RBC Dominion Securities

Frank never wanted to hurt anyone, yet some people insisted on taking shots at him. Just like anyone else, he was not immune to the everyday crooks and charlatans in our society. Being wealthy made him that much more of a target for the odd cheat or rip-off artist. Those who persisted had a good chance of taking him for a ride because he was not paticularly vindictive by nature.

His advice to never hurt people by legal encounters made it difficult for us because we always had to settle, even if settling was harmful to Frank himself.

Sid Clark, Frank's Legal Adviser

What some people failed to realize was the fact that besides being very wealthy, Frank was very well-liked. He had friends in all walks of life and government. A very well-liked rich man with international connections is a very powerful man. He had strong convictions as to what was right and what was wrong. To him, integrity was what his life was all about. He refused to abuse his power, stuck to his morality and never let things get him down.

When I first met the Ney family I was invited by his son Brad over to their house for dinner. Mrs. Johnson was the cook. There was a twelve foot oak table with a smorgasbord laid out on it. People were all around it. Frank was there with six or seven kids. I was sitting next to a guy who was only about nineteen or twenty years old. I asked him if he was related to Frank or how he knew the family.

He told me that he was hitch-hiking to Campbell River and this guy pulls up in a huge Lincoln Continental sled. The fellow said that he is the Mayor. Campbell River is a long way off so I should go have dinner with his family and afterwards he would drive me back to the highway.

The young guy next to me at dinner that evening was very happy to be there.

David J. Strang

Over the years Frank drove down to Victoria many times, and there are many people who remember being picked up as hitch-hikers. Two university students had their thumbs out when Frank pulled over to pick them up. They chatted and drove along until Frank said, "Oh, I must look at this piece of property," and pulled off to the side of the road. He got out of the car and said, "Well guys, do you like it? Should I buy it?" The young fellows humoured him and told him that it was great and he must have it. Frank appreciated their second opinion and bought it. On days like that Frank would walk into the office and announce what he had just bought. Jim Goodwin would ask how he was going to pay for it, and Frank would respond, "Jim, that's your job to figure it out."

Mr. Nanaimo just loved to make a deal. He had a saying, "If I have to get out of the car to look at a piece of property, I'm not going to buy it." Financing was often his afterthought and he would say, "Sure we can get the money! We can get the money somewhere, get it from the bank. Get it from the bank Jim. We'll get it from somewhere." This system worked quite well for them. They worked as a team. This pair used to go to meetings and interviews where Frank would hype everyone, and when people started to talk numbers he would introduce Jim. Frank had the sizzle and Jim had the numbers.

Frank had an envelope inside his pocket where he wrote down all of the numbers that he wanted to keep. That was the full extent of his bookkeeping. He never really kept track of his own affairs. He never filled in a financial statement, not even for mortgage companies. Never did he file his own tax return. He could read a financial statement, he knew how, but he just had no interest.

I very often ran into Frank socially at the RCMP hall or other functions. He never carried any money with him. I was never surprised when he would walk up to me and say, "Eileen, lend me $5, I want to buy so and so a drink".

I would have to tally up his loans in my head and collect from his accountant, Jim Goodwin. I figured that he made more money than I did, so I may as well collect it all back.

Eileen Hennessy, Royal Bank - Retired

I had to talk to him about problems with the company in the early days. Maybe they weren't major problems for him, but they were for me. I was the accountant and I'd say, "We have to have cash to pay this,"and I would chase Frank, literally chase him, to tell him these things. He didn't want to hear about it. He always wanted things to be positive. You would very seldom hear Frank talk negatively, and if you did, it would be a very private conversation. If I was negative he would try to talk me into being positive.

Jim Goodwin

If a salesperson was down and Frank was extremely busy, he would quietly ask another member of the staff to get together with the person and talk it up a bit. If Frank wasn't already being pulled in two directions, he would go to the sad salesman and say, "Come on, I have to go out to the Dairy Queen. Hop in the car." He would take the person out, talk about things and try to instill some confidence in him. Often He would give the salesman a lead to follow. This is what he did so well; this is the stuff that kept people working for thirty-odd years.

There is a cottage on Protection Island where Frank used to take his kids on weekends. A man had won a cabin in a Kiwanis draw. Frank bought it from him, cut it in half, and brought it over to Protection. For years it served as Frank's cottage. Later he sold it and built an octagonal one on the point. Jim, who had the cottage next door on Smugglers' Cove, found that this was the only place where he and Frank could really talk. Frank loved a bottle of rum and sometimes the two of them would relax there, while discussing solutions to problems and all the current real estate scenarios. That was Frank's relaxation. It was also very important to him that he spend time with his kids. The entire month of July each year was dedicated to his family at the cottage on Protection Island.

It was rumoured that Frank's goal was to leave a million dollars to each of his eleven children. To this Frank responded, "I think that would be the worst thing in the world. I may have to leave a million to the banker (laughs), but I think that would be a crucifix of destruction to each one of those kids because you give a kid or a twenty year-old a million dollars and by the time they're thirty, unless they're very exceptional children, I think their lives would be ruined because you have to know the value of a dollar. If you're born with a silver spoon in your mouth, I think you're going to face a lot more problems in the years to come than if you had the adversity while you were young, because then when you take each step you are stepping in the right direction. If you've got everything given to you all your life, you're just flip-floppin' all over the scene and not makin' any headway in any one direction. I would say this, the best thing that you can give your family is love and a good education."

My dad had a unique way of sussing my boyfriends when I brought them home to meet the parents. The wine tasting test in my dad's eyes was a sure way to see their true colours, character and level of honesty.

After the regular formalities of hand shakes, etc., Dad would proceed with the "be all and end all" and most inconspicuously, I might add. Two bottles would be sampled, one of high quality, the other low grade, which as far as I was concerned, tasted like the gas used for the Blue Girl. Dad would ask my gentleman friend his opinion on which wine he felt had the most body, flavour and aroma. Of course Dad would boost up the cheaper wine. Will they follow the Pirate's lead or stand their own ground? That's another story!

My sister Tami scored high with her man Ricardo, now married. I mean how could she lose. Ricardo was Dad's look-alike twin and Brazilian on top of that, so he definitely knew his wines!!

This is just one of the many caring and humourous ways in which Dad showed his love.

I love you, Dad.

Your middle daughter, Nicola

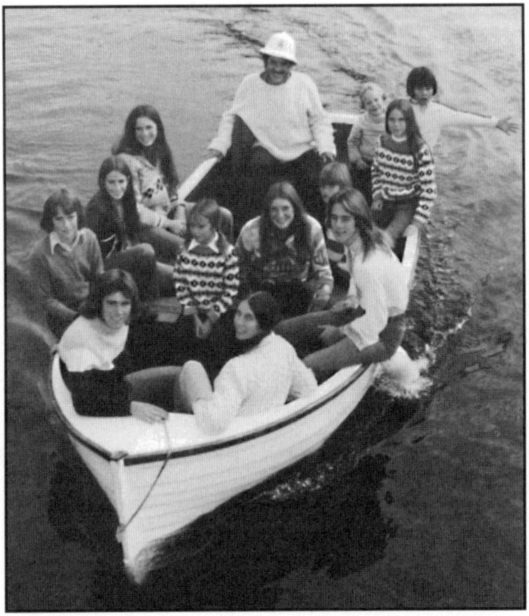

The mid 1970's saw the Ney family breaking all the maritime laws at sea. Mom is on the bow with Frank Jr.

There was a delicate balance between time spent with his family and time spent with his activities. He wanted to spend as much time as possible with his kids. Although he often wasn't at home when they got home from school, he would do the best he could to haul them off for some type of adventure on the weekends. If he had three parades to attend during a holiday weekend, he would not go alone! He never visited his friends on Christmas Day because the family valued this time together. On Boxing Day Frank would slip out to organize and host the Polar Bear Swim, which he did on the spur of the moment, and then he would load his family into the car and head for the ski hill. With some luck the heavy snows would trap him on a mountain with nothing to do but ski with his kids all day.

On one November 11th, after the Cenotaph Service, while at the Royal Canadian Legion, Frank approached me and said, "I would love to sit down with you sometime, and discuss the problems of trying to bring up a large family and how to cope." I had a large family, and it was obvious that he was very concerned about his family and was endeavoring to be a good father under very difficult circumstances. He was very concerned. We never had that conversation!

Pat Leahy

Frank became a single parent through divorce in 1977. His wife left with their neighbour, who was a mutual friend, business partner and lawyer. Frank was extremely sad at losing both a very close friend and his wife on the same day. This was a very dark moment in his life, although at the same time it marked the peak of his personal financial empire. It was a difficult time for him. Nine of his kids were still living at home at the time, aged 11 years and up. "I had never washed dishes or cooked in my life. For the first week it was kind of tough going."

Lost fortunes often accompany lost love in divorce settlements. Frank had owned some big items, but most of his wealth consisted of pieces of a number of ventures. He had mortgages out on plenty of properties with lots of different people. The debt load that he carried personally was based somewhat upon his positive net worth. When assets are removed from this type of a structure, the whole thing gets a little shaky. Providing the economy and interest rates stayed stable, a person in Frank's position could build it all back up again.

After his marriage broke up, Frank took an even greater interest in people. He became even more compassionate. Character-wise he found himself to be a stronger person, with a better understanding of people. He noticed more and more how many people are lonely and have problems. "I find when you're single, people open up more. I think they realize you have problems too and you're on the same level. I meet a cross-section of society in my travels. I have found that all people are pretty much the same, the same desires and ambitions."

Years ago I had my head shaved and played guitar. I squatted in a house in Nanaimo with punk rockers. The parties never invaded my bedroom as the door was locked and I would enter and exit through the window. We had lots of fun.

One day I answered a knock on the door and was face to face with Frank Ney. He said, "We have not collected any rent from this building in a long time." I told him that "Bob" just went to Nanaimo Realty to pay it. No problem.

Later on the hydro was shut off. He never did kick us out of the house, but I moved out soon afterwards anyway.

Keith Alce, Custom furniture manufacturer

As Frank adjusted to the life of a single parent, he said, "You know, I have a lot of children. When I leave the house, at least they have company. But when you're a single parent with one or two children, everytime you leave the house, and I know this because I talk to a lot of single parents, their conscience bothers them. They're worried about their children coming home to an empty home, or leaving them at night. You know if a girl's earning $900 or $1000 a month she can't even afford a babysitter. It's tough and there's more and more single parents coming along and I think the whole thinking of our society is going to have to change in the next few years if this keeps going on the way it is."

Frank developed a very strong admiration for the strength of the single woman who sacrifices for her children. "It makes it hard for her to go out to meet people. After a while she loses confidence in herself. That's tragic. It happens so often. Then quite often, because she's been living such a limited life, some guy comes along who takes advantage of her loneliness. That makes it a double hardship."

"Through Adveristy to the Stars"

"Well, you know, I've seen everything now. As a politician I get around and meet a lot of people. One thing I have found is that a lot of people are turning to Christ and I'm just surprised that some of these churches now, their congregations are just exploding with growth. I've met so many people that have said to me that religion has brought their family together and I'm told now that one in four in United States have turned to religion. I think you're going to find that there is going to be far more emphasis in orientation towards religion in our country in the next few years because of all the things people are doing to try to hold themselves together psychologically and the whole works. It seems to me that for what I have seen in my short span as a single parent, that religion is playing a dominant role in holding people together. I have difficulty going to church on Sunday because I ski. I go to every church because I think that every church is good and that they all have things to offer. I certainly have respect for the churches and what they're doing. They have a challenge ahead now because our society is changing and I think that's one phase of our society in which good things will happen because of the church."

Is the church a crutch for people who find life too difficult to tolerate on their own? To this question he responds: "Well, it could be to a degree but then what does it matter as long as it does the trick. They've tried everything else. Some go to drugs, some go to lovers, you know, some go to liquor. Well, I still feel very good about everything."

Because Frank was such a busy person, we met him in many different places. One thing that I will always remember about Frank is that he would come up to me and say, "David, how long's the service going to be?"

Archdeacon David Mckay

Like many other cities, Nanaimo lacked a proper recycling program. Some local citizens were becoming tired of the fact that nothing was happening and so took the matter before the City Council. These concerned people proposed to develop a facility that would be independent of the city. Through a series of visits to the council chambers they discovered that some of the aldermen had a less than encouraging attitude about the whole thing. Frank, on the other hand, was found to be very positive and helpful. He located and secured a building which became the recycling centre. And he was there cutting the cake at the grand opening, as he was for most every event in town.

Frank the consumer.

In 1979, I was a teenage clerk at Sears Nanaimo. Frank Ney came into my department to buy a gas barbecue. I knew it was Frank. I could't mistake his well-dressed style, good manners, and smile. My parents talked fondly about him often. And of course he was on the front page of almost every issue of the local papers.

He wanted to write a cheque. In cashier training, I was told that everyone who wrote a cheque must have two pieces of identification. I wanted to do a good job, so I asked him the same as I would ask anyone.

Mr. Ney, the Mayor, could't find one piece of I.D. He didn't bring up the fact that he was the Mayor, or that he wanted to talk to my boss. He just kept looking through each pocket of his trousers, his shirt, and his jacket for some form of identification. He didn't seem to have a wallet with him. Finally he saw that he had enough cash to cover the cost. He paid me, thanked me, and went on his way.

I often think of how young I was, and had it been now, I'd have taken the cheque, no questions asked. I respect him now for how he handled the situation without embarrassing me, a young store clerk. He was an exceptional personality.

Bill Costin, Musician

Frank's social life was active enough that he didn't suffer readjustment pains to the extent that many divorced men do when it comes to dating. Many different ladies accompanied him to different functions.One lady in particular became very fond of Frank and they dated on a regular basis. It was obvious that Frank was also taken with her, and some observers predicted another wedding. His girlfriend had the same thought when Frank called her up and announced that he was coming over with a gift for her. She excitedly awaited the man with a ring, and Frank then showed up with a washer and dryer!

Nanaimo was enjoying a major boom in the late 1970's. With only 52,000 residents there were five shopping centres and an eighty million dollar harbour development called Duke Point.

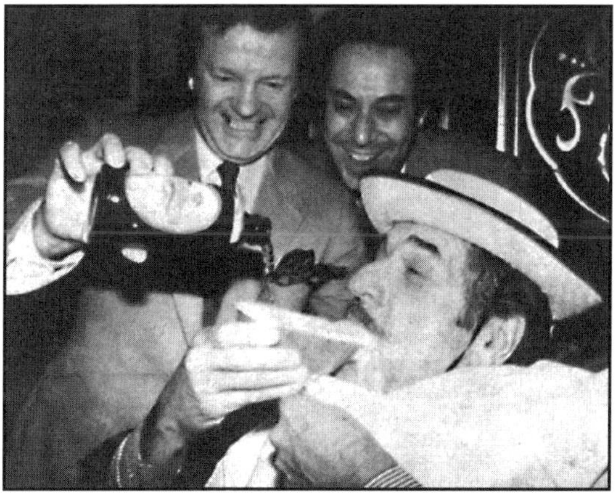

Frank's social drinking was a favourite topic for local gossip. Frank was a showman and liked to play everything up a bit.

Great National Land and Investment Corporation owned seven per cent of the land in Nanaimo in 1980. Frank said, "I always like to think that it's a Canadian company and Canadians are sharing in the growth of Vancouver Island, facing the challenges and doing what I hope is the best thing for the Island. We've had some very good developments over the years."

The boom years had been happy years for many. People were working and investments were paying off well. However, nothing lasts forever. Cycles will be cycles, and change was on its way.

Golden Years

He would always come and visit the restaurant and eat there. In 1980 he arranged to have Princess Alexandra dine with us. He supported all our functions.

At the time Nanaimo Realty was having a few problems. We were all in the same boat, facing ups and downs. A lot of his comments helped people carry on. He would just encourage us and tell us to plow through.

Chuck Wong, Diners Rendezvous Owner

THE RECESSION IN THE EARLY 1980's hit Nanaimo Realty and its parent company Great National Land very hard. A large number of holdings had to be liquidated. These transactions were not all to the best advantage of the shareholders, including Frank Ney, who suffered a great financial blow at this time. "I lost over a million dollars in twelve months. It was the first time in my life I ever really worried about financial things."

What had actually happened was that Frank's companies were burdened with a large bank debt; they had gotten into the subdivision market and constructed buildings with proper financing and proper leases. They simply never envisioned that a lease could be written that would cover the eventuality of higher interest rates on your mortgage security. What this means is that the mortgages were put in place at 9% and it became 22% upon renewal. Because the cash flow from the leases, which was a fixed amount, couldn't cover it there was a substantial short fall. The company had three large buildings, and a number of subdivisions in various stages of completion. Some which were complete stood empty because because the market was down. This created a tremendous drain on the company's cash. Assets of over twelve million dollars turned into seven or eight million as liabilities.

The situation was such that Frank had personally guaranteed loans for people and companies. He had said, "Either don't put any on or put a lot on," and he had indeed put his personal signature on numerous transactions. When everything collapsed, he had some major guarantees out there. To make matters worse, the properties that were foreclosed were done so at market value. There is a deemed disposition which creates tax, even though the owner doesn't make any money on it. Frank got caught in this net and wound up with a massive income tax debt.

He and Jim had gone to Vancouver to see some high-powered lawyers and bankruptcy people. These people had the advice, "Mr. Ney, you go to the Bahamas and leave it with us and we'll have you through bankruptcy in three months."

Frank said, "No, no no." He wouldn't do that.

I was standing in the lobby of a theatre during intermission at a rock concert and I saw this man wearing a great old-fashioned looking suit. I could tell that must be someone important because the crowd kind of parted as he walked by.

Gwen Fret, World Traveller

Bill, Frank's brother, retired from his position as Vice-president of Nanaimo Realty in 1983. He and Mary continued to live at their farm on Vancouver Island. Their three sons became successful in their respective trades. Bill was always supportive of his big brother. He is a big, friendly, soft-spoken man who had no problem leaving the role of the flambouyant frontman to Frank. To this day he speaks fondly of Frank and is still amazed at how naturally blessed Frank was as a promoter.

The smile that the public had become accustomed to over the decades never faded. It became his unspoken duty to be a cheerful host at the events he initiated as fun promotional activities. This was never a chore for him. It is what he loved to do. Standing on the stage at the Boxing Day Polar Bear Swim with a megaphone in his hand was the best therapy for shaking the worries from his mind.

Since it was so important to him that people enjoy life, he felt deep satisfaction in seeing a celebration in full swing.

Both the Protection Island swim and the Nanaimo to Sechelt marathon survived into the 1980's as annual events. These events were always regarded as being remarkable athletic achievements for the swimmers. It was, however, the Polar Bear Swim that consistently received the greatest national press coverage.

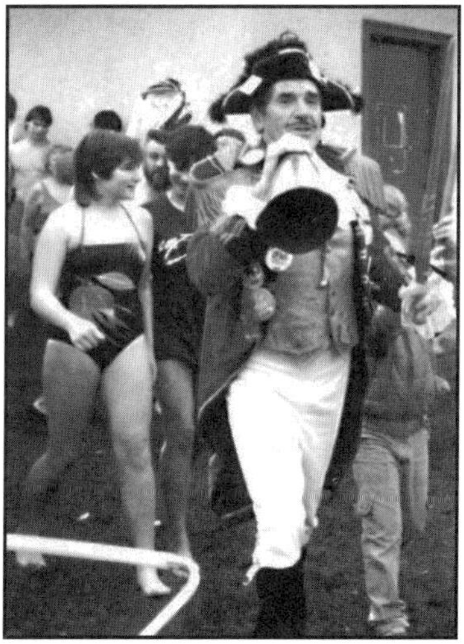

The Pied Piper of Nanaimo. The sword was held together with gaffer tape, the megaphone - an old cone from the '50's, but still they followed him to the shore.

A few hours before the Polar Bear swim in 1983, Frank cancelled the event. Because it was so cold out, he was concerned that participants might endanger themselves. To Frank's delight the sun came out and the swim was once again set to go. The swim of '83 became one that Frank would always remember. Much to the surprise and delight of hundreds of onlookers, he was carried off into the the 6 C water. It was the first time in twenty-five years that Ney got hauled in with the crowd. He took it well, appearing to be more concerned with getting his wristwatch wet than anything else.

The wet host was very pleased with the turnout and assisted Carnduff Scott in presenting City of Nanaimo medals to the other winter swimmers. Frank enthusiastically remarked, "I was only up to my waist so I didn't damage my $500 watch, nor my velour pirate coat. I think next year I'll go down to the beach with a sharper sword!"

When Cappy Yates Park was opened I was asked to compose a poem for the occasion. Frank really liked what I did and a year or so later he asked me to write a poem for the Polar Bear Swim.

I gave him the poem but it was a cold day with snow above the tide mark. Everyone was shivering and the Gyro Hall seemed not the right place for a poetry reading so the poem never got read, though I have always regretted my lack of fortitude.

Tim Lander, Poet

One of the companies of which Frank was president and major shareholder got into real difficulties in 1984. The mortgage company, which was a bank, pressed hard for repayment. But the market was down and there was nothing the company could do about it. There was still a fair amount of land left in the company that wouldn't sell. The vice-presidents of the mortgage company came over to Nanaimo to talk with Frank.

Frank took two officers and one company shareholder to meet the bankers in the boardroom. They spent all morning discussing ways to solve the dilemma. After a break for lunch at a hotel, it was back to square one again in the boardroom. One of the vice-presidents began, "Now Mr. Ney, we've got to get down to business." He slammed his hand on the table, "We want to tell you that unless this money is paid or something is done about it we're going to have to go after our personal guarantees and we're going to have to go after your personal assets. We will have to go after your income and take whatever measures we can to ensure our debt is paid." He went on pointing out all the options open to them, options that certainly did not favour Frank. In the end he said, "Well Mr., Ney, what have you got to say?"

Frank shot back, "Well, if I knew you were going to talk like that I wouldn't have bought lunch." It brought the whole thing down and that was the end of the conversation. The guys laughed and laughed. That was his way of dealing with a tense situation.

Problems didn't bother Frank, or if they did, he never let it show. He could be seen walking down the street cheerful as ever, shaking hands and asking people about their problems.

One time he came into a board meeting of the City Centre Association and offered to take us on the Blue Girl *for a ride. I thought it was really admirable that he would invite us when he was in such dire straits., but I guess that's the kind of man he was.*

June Luoma, Nanaimo City Centre Board Member

During these slow times the federal government sponsored a program called Katimavik. This was a work program for people in their late teens. Frank was asked to find a house for a gang of young people from various provinces across the country. Since his big waterfront house on Beach Drive was not inhabited to its capacity, he decided to rent it to Katimavik. Frank moved out and a mob of teenagers moved in. This showed an outstanding gesture of support for the program and once again a strong witness to his commitment to the younger generation. The people who lived in Frank's house were well aware that it was owned by a very prominant man. They respectfully had some very good parties!

During the early 1980's our church sponsored a Vietnamese family. My wife and I became acquainted with this family and enjoyed their company. In due time through them, we met other families of their nationality; they were so willing to become good citizens and obtain work. When they learned I was an upholsterer by trade, they asked me to teach them. I was most pleased to do so, but our biggest problem was that we had no building to work in. One day when I was having coffee with Frank, I shared my problem with him and he will-

ingly said we could have his building on Commercial St., known then as Charlie York.

Along with Carrol Mortimer, a seamstress, we set up an upholstery teaching shop, and thanks to Frank, it was rent free. Everything went along well, Carrol and I felt these eager workers were learning a valuable trade. Frank, who would pop in to visit, was pleased with what he saw. The students liked him and appreciated his interest in their welfare and progress. Unfortunately there came a day when we went to the shop and found it was ablaze. The fire destroyed everything we had in there, it was a sad day indeed for all concerned. Frank was a great guy and willing to do whatever he could to give help wherever it was needed.

Cliff Hobbe

After his divorce, Frank the bachelor had no problem getting dates. He was handsome, athletic and had an good sense of humour. Also he still had a reputation for being the richest man in town. At 66 years of age Frank was described as "Nanaimo's swinging single" in the premier issue of Companion West magazine. This was THE magazine for single people and Frank's story was perfect for the "Single Seniors" section. He had stated, "Life begins at 60 and I don't mean maybe." During the interview a lady called to check on their date. Frank confirmed that he would pick her up at 9:00 p.m., after officially opening a circus and making an appearance at a fund raising event. He said that he enjoyed being single, but "I think I will remarry. If I marry again I would like a person who is an active friend and a person who is alive, adventurous, and has the enthusiasm to go out and discover the world."

Some years previous, he had met a lady named Tina Leach in at the Tally-Ho hotel where he often appeared as a guest speaker at various functions. Tina managed the catering department which she and her first husband owned. Originally born in Holland, her family had moved to Manitoba. She married early and became involved in the hotel industry in Vancouver. Her first marriage, like Frank's ended in divorce.

Tina was crazy about Frank. Everywhere he appeared, his friend also appeared. She recalled, "One day he called me in Vancouver and asked if I wanted to go out for dinner. I thought, why not? So we went out and I found him interesting, a lot of fun and very knowledgeable." The two had been talking about marriage, but had not set a date. And then, Tina recalls, "One day Frank told me he bought a marriage licence. I told him he hadn't asked me yet." He did.

Frank always admired her sense of humour and found that they really did complement one another. She raved about his loyalty and caring towards people. "He does a lot for people that sometimes no one is aware of. He is super loyal to his kids." His wedding ceremony to the 41 year-old Tina was followed by a reception at the Tally-Ho with 400 invited guests.

A few days before the wedding Frank said, "When I got divorced I was very upset about it. After the divorce there was quite a change in my lifestyle. I had 11 kids, 9 of them at home. It's kind of hard to adjust... and it worked out fine. I must say, I didn't find single life that bad."

"I never thought I'd get married again. I suppose everyone is nervous when they get married because everything changes. I'm certainly going to have to become more domesticated. Actually it's quite exciting. I think it's important to have the courage in your heart to do what you think is right, and my heart tells me to get married."

Tina wasn't concerned that he was an older gentleman. "Age is not a factor. Frank is not 66. He has a lot more on the ball than a lot of younger men I've gone out with. He's got an incredible amount of energy."

Frank planned to take more time off to enjoy life after the wedding. "Sometimes we work too hard and we don't see the forest for the trees. I find that people in my office who take good recreational holidays are more successful in their work. People owe it to themselves to take time off for recreational enjoyments. My longest holiday was two weeks because I've been so busy. But all work and no play makes Jack a dull boy. In the next few years I will try to work myself into a situation at work where I can take more time off."

"I won't retire until I'm 80. I couldn't even think of retiring right now. I have too many financial commitments to think about. I like being active. I couldn't sit around doing nothing. If you're not active your body starts to rust. A lot of people think that when you get older your life is over. I'm figuring on living another 30 or 40 years. If you take care of yourself, look at things positively and with a spirit of adventure, life can be very exciting."

"I don't profess to be an expert at marriage and my track record is certainly not 100%. I'm just a normal person with all the frailties of the human race. Anyone who gets married and it turns out to be Utopia is lucky. Marriage involves a lot of compromise, understanding and unselfishness. It's something you have to work at."

.....June 23, 1984 was the day that Frank was remarried. A new club was started in Nanaimo called Hub City Lions Club and on that day Frank was invited as the guest of honour. We did't realize it was his wedding day of course. In the afternoon my husband and I saw Frank downtown and he said, "It's my wedding day but I will see you later for sure." I really laughed it off because obviously he was not available that day. My husband also expressed his doubts on seeing Frank that day, but suggested we pick up a bottle of champagne to celebrate his wedding night. We bought the bottle and brought it to our ceremony.

Much to everyone's surprise Frank did show up. He said, "I will never let you down." We had a really nice evening. He had brought with him a special book about Nanaimo and a ceramic bathtub, which he he presented to my husband and me. My husband was the first president of the club. Frank was our special guest and we still talk about what a special person he was.

Peter and Renee Thomas

Frank's new wife was not interested in living in the same house where he raised his kids. His financial problems had so far resulted in a new mortgage being placed on the big waterfront house and it was being rented out. He was faced with the fact that he had to sell his home and move on.

The newlyweds moved into an apartment until Tina was able to have a new house built under her name. Frank was happy to be in a house again and had keys cut for all of his kids, even though they were all grown up. Frank was always working and Tina was spending more and more time in Vancouver. The couple spent some good and bad times together until the day Tina packed up and left for good. They had been married for less than one year. It seems that they just drifted apart. After a few years they were legally divorced.

Frank managed to hang on to the new house by using his kid's names. These were difficult times, but as always, he was able to stay positive and focused. Many people were depending on Frank's businesses for their present and future survival. However, the interest rates were so high and the economy so bad that there was nothing more that he could do to save people's jobs. Through it all, he continued to show love and support to his family and friends.

Frank's optimism drove him on towards what he saw as being a better future. His enthusiasm alone bought him press coverage. Reports of true economic doom and gloom were lightened by his quality quotes such as, "You know what Nanaimo is? Nanaimo is a sleeping gazelle. It's about the fastest animal alive."

One of Frank's favourite mottos was "Per Ardua Ad Astra" or "Through adversity to the stars." Commenting on it, he said: "As the years go by, I'm very much aware that it's only through adversity that you strengthen your character, and I think that anyone that's born with a silver spoon in their mouths are going to find life a lot tougher than people who have the hardship when they're younger."

I knew Frank both personally and in business for many years. Like so many others, I was happy to call him a friend. That Frank was a character comes as no news to anyone. He was unpredictable and unflappable. If he was ever self-conscious or embarrassed, I never saw it.

Frank Ney A Canadian Legend

Frank was always in a hurry, and he had a habit of walking with his head tilted forward, with his eyes on the ground. I expect he was usually planning his next great escapade. One time his hurry and his posture caused him to drop in on my wife and myself, quite unexpectedly.

We were living in Seascape Manor apartments and Frank was living two doors away, on the same floor. We often visited in the hot tub or while riding the elevator.

It was Christmas and Frank had been to one of the many functions of the Season. He was all dressed up in a tux with a white silk scarf and he was in a hurry. He came down the hall headed towards his apartment but he must have been looking at the floor because he put his hand on our doornob and pushed. Ollie and I were sitting in the living room reading. Suddenly Frank was there in the room with us. He had up such a head of steam that he got into the apartment and down a twelve foot hallway before he sensed that he was not in his home. He looked up and saw me. Most people would have been shocked into serious embarrassment, but not Frank.

He looked at me and said, "Reg, I must have come in the wrong door." Ollie and I were both speechless, but again, not Frank. He laughed and made an excuse about being careless and held out his hand and shook mine while saying, "Well, since I'm here anyway, I might as well wish you both a Happy Christmas." With that he crossed the living room and shook Ollie's hand. Then he was gone, as quickly as he had come.

I don't know anyone else who could barge into someone else's home by mistake and turn the event into a memorable occasion.

Reg and Ollie Quist, The Mutual Group

Most of Frank's assets had disappeared in the economic recession but a couple key possessions still remained in his life — a cabin on Protection Island and a boat to take him there. This was his place of guaranteed peace. He had always been open to the idea of skinny-dipping in the ocean at night. Some people were quite surprised by this, thinking that a man of his position would be a little more subdued. The truth is that Frank never swam naked to shock anyone, quite the contrary. Always the gentleman, he would guarantee the privacy of his guest by swimming outward while the other swimmer entered the water. He exercised a similar courtesy when his guest came out of the water.

Jumping off of the Blue Girl *could be a chilly sensation.*

After about six months of hard work painting my house and having a new roof put on, I was just finishing off my new Japanese garden. A car drove up and it was Frank Ney. He said, "I just had to stop to tell you how lovely your garden is. It is the nicest garden in Nanaimo!" What a compliment and what a kind gesture on his part.

Clare Mosher

One of Frank's daughters was with the Royal Ballet for a time, but as she grew too tall, she became a dancer at the Lido in Paris. He put her picture in his office even though her costume was topless. He had this to say on the subject: "Some people thought that it was a girlfriend of mine. When I tell them it's my daughter I don't think they believe me. I guess some people probably think it's a little risque but of course I don't look at it that way. To me it's just a beautiful picture and I'm very proud of her. So I have no compunction about displaying that picture. Now some people may be shocked when I do that but I don't mind. I'm quite happy about it and that's the way I am."

> *Whenever he came by the store, he always bought a cigar and talked to a few of the out-of-town customers. He would welcome them to the city and invite them to sign the guest book at city hall. He was a phenomenal ambassador for the city.*
>
> Andy Wizinsky, Nanaimo Marine Charts

Although Nanaimo Realty was Frank's life, he showed an impressive commitment to all organized real estate. He admitted that he preferred business to politics. "I prefer business because that is where I make my living. Also politics is like playing Russian Roulette. You never know when you are going to get knocked out. and the day you are knocked out you are forgotten. You do your job and once you do it, it's over. If you do something today, people ask you what you are going to do tomorrow. Broken down politicians don't just happen. There have been many people who have given up careers in business to go into politics and have become very disappointed people." He had never gambled his livelihood on the possibility of achieving higher positions in government. He preferred being the Governor of the Real Estate Institute of British Columbia as well as the President of the Vancouver Island Real Estate Board. In 1982 he was awarded the Board's "Realtor of the Year Award." His talents did not go unnoticed.

Frank would say, "You know, in real estate, there are three words for success - location, location, location. Nanaimo has the location and is becoming one of the most beautiful cities in Canada, environmentally, culturally and socially. The area from Seattle to Vancouver will become to the Pacific what New York is to the Atlantic. Nanaimo will get the overspill of that growth. We have to be careful to manage the tremendous growth ahead in the next few years to make sure we can retain our clean environment."

Tourism was always on Frank's mind. He felt that Vancouver Island was still the country's best kept secret, and that once the secret was out, the holiday money would flow. If the developers and industrialists could manage to preserve the beauty of the Island it could remain a tourist destination indefinitely. "Tourism and retirement are going to be a big factor. We enjoy the best mean average temperature of any city in Canada. As a council, we started promoting tourism and industry. We felt they could live in compatibility, and we still feel that."

"I remember the old days when the smell of septic tanks came across the lawns at night. That's all gone now. We've become a beautiful, modern city."

Mr. Ney was at a party put on by the German Cultural Society. He was with a woman who was just brutal. She was kicking him under the table all night. I guess she had a problem or something. He paid no mind to that, he just smiled and laughed and had a great time.

John, Fisherman

The old pirate put out a call for 4000 volunteers for the 1985 B.C. Summer Games. After fighting for years to have the event staged in his town, he had finally won. He felt especially rewarded by the number of volunteers who came forward, all helping make the event an absolutely unqualified success. Frank was at numerous events waving his sword and promoting the town to every camera lens that pointed in his direction.

The local Terry Fox Run to raise money for cancer research was attended by a multitude of fitness enthusiasts. Frank was there to host the event and perform his regular duty of letting off a marine flare. As the red cloud of smoke emerged from the device, the participants all coughed, choked and wheezed on the fumes. A whole crowd of asphyxiated runners can attest to the fact that it was a day to remember.

Often we met him strolling along Commercial Street, greeting store owners and people on the street; shaking hands, joking, always leaving people smiling as he went on his way.

Mary E. Urquhart

Frank came to know hundreds of local people by name. He would greet them on sight, and always remembered their occupation, often relating it to whomever his companion happened to be at the time. Strangers also received a greeting from Frank, and he avoided brushing off anyone with complaint. Sometimes he was cornered by very abrasive individuals who let him know exactly how unsatisfied they were on a variety of topics. Frank patiently weathered these complaints without letting them disturb his peace of mind. He cared what these people had to say and felt he could always learn something from what they were going through.

There were plenty of things for Frank to be happy about in the early '80's. Most importantly he and his family were in good health. He could enjoy the benefits from the improvements he had added to his town and for the first time was referred to as a "Living Legend." Children who had grown up in the town with the pirate mayor were now seeing him as a regular man going about his work. He didn't appear to have slowed down one bit over the years. He had affected everyone's life in some way or another and as a result was looked upon as being someone special. Often he was approached by strangers who simply wanted to shake his hand and say "Thank you." Perhaps the most effective way that people had of showing respect and gratitude was by organizing plenty of parties and dinners in his honour.

There was plenty of love, camaraderie, esteem and laughter filling Nanaimo's banquet halls in the 1980's. Hundreds of citizens assembled at the banquets, parties and roasts that paid honour to Mr. Ney. He was talked about, laughed about, and presented with thousands of dollars worth of gifts and services. Frank had certainly never asked anyone to sponsor such events in his honour and appeared to be rather bewildered by it all. "This is not a eulogy, but a spring training camp for the rest of my exciting, topsy-turvy life."

One Sunday night after a showing of a film by the French director Alan Renais, I ran into Frank and as we walked to his car, he asked, "Are the films all of this calibre?" We discussed the film we had seen until he reached his car, where he opened the trunk and got out a beaded leather jacket. "Now I have to be at quite a different kind of function," he said.

Tim Lander

There were many opportunities for Frank to bring a guest amongst the dozens of events he was attending each week. In the same spirit of his earlier days of bachelorhood, Frank was not shy about inviting a lady friend. One day he asked a friend named Joyce MacMillan. She is a very lovely lady; lively with a great sense of humour. He hadn't known her very long when he asked her if she would like a hamburger. She politely declined, as she doesn't eat wheat. He said, "I'm going to take you out and get something to eat." He took her to McDonalds, where he bought a hamburger and asked, "Well, would you like half of my hamburger?" The humour of the situation was not at all lost on Joyce. She found him to be a very fascinating man.

Another time he took her to a fast food joint late at night. As always when Frank was out in public, he would see people he knew and of course others whom he didn't know would also want to talk with him. Eventually he brought the food back to the car and was ready to head home. Suddenly a young man appeared at Joyce's window. When she rolled it down to speak to him, he asked where they were going. Frank told him, "We're going home now."

The young man explained, "Well, I've got all these hamburgers and everything for my kids and my wife. Could you give me a ride?" Frank told him that they are not going very far because they lived only a short distance away.

The determined fellow continued, "My hamburgers are going to be cold by the time I walk all the way there." Frank looked at Joyce and then told the man to get in. The couple soon found out that this late night diner lived right on the other side of town. By the time he arrived with the dinner, his family was very happy to see him. Naturally, when Frank and Joyce got home they were the ones with the cold dinner. But they always found it was worthwhile to give someone a hand while at the same time having a unique story to share afterwards.

Frank would not let anyone down. He would stop for hitch-hikers with huge dogs. The first time Joyce shared such an experience, they were both dressed to the nines, being on their way to some important event. A young man with long hair and beard was standing beside the road with packsacks and a gigantic dog. Even the dog was loaded with luggage. The couple had a puzzle to solve; where was everything going to fit? As always, they would arrange the trunk and eventually all passengers and luggage would be secure and ready to roll on down the highway. Even if their big old Linclon whizzed by anyone on the side of the road, Frank would stop and back up for them.

One day I was walking down the street carrying my guitar in the rain. A big car pulled up beside me and it was Mr. Ney offering me a ride. Inside the car he said, "I hate to see a musician caught out in the rain." He drove me right to my door.

Keith Alce

After the downtown Safeway closed and before "Thrifty's" came to town, there was a time when I used to walk up to Overwaitea with a backpack once a week to buy groceries for my family. One time I was there just before closing time and Frank was in making a small purchase. When he saw me at the check-out he said, "Come on, I'll drive you home." So he drove me down to the south end, despite the fact that he lived only a couple of blocks from Terminal Park.

He was a man who really enjoyed the company of people. You never got the feeling that his kindnesses were charity, but a genuine enjoyment of you as a person.

Annonymous

It was with Joyce that Frank finally got to go on those holidays he had been talking about. She got him to sit on a bus for two hours on a trip around the Baja Peninsula. They saw Europe together and also had many laughs at home with video movies.

Joyce tells us that there was never a dull moment with Frank. One night he exclaimed, "I was just about killed by two wild beasts!" Joyce laughed and asked if they were blondes. Frank's face was grey as he pleaded, "You laugh and I was just about killed by wild beasts!"

Frank was having a rather humorous reaction to his experience of taking out the garbage. It was about ten o'clock at night and he had just thrown two bags into a big dumpster when two huge raccoons jumped out at him. One went by his left ear and the other one landed near his right shoulder. Frank was not happy to see his new furry friends!

When our family moved down from Gold River we had to get a notary public to sign an agreement of sale - Frank did it for free! Our son later chummed with Frank's son, both named Todd, and was taken on a fully paid holiday on the Blue Girl.

Hewitt Reavley

Why did he do it all? It was not simply because he loved the limelight. He suggested, "I guess if you really psychoanalyze me, it must be a certain amount of ego, but what creates ego? I guess it's a searching for security. Maybe that's what it is. I think everyone has a certain amount of insecurity. In fact I know in my own case in the last few years when I've had a few ups and downs, when I really get to meet people, and I've become more interested in people over the last few years, I meet very few people in any walk of life that don't seem to have some problems. When you really get to know them and sit down and talk to them, the wealthiest, the healthiest or what appears to be the happiest people....When you really get to sit down and talk to them, everybody has problems." It was people that he loved the most. He loved to help everyone have a good time. Frequently he would rush into city hall to borrow twenty dollars from an associate so that he could give it to a needy resident who showed up on the steps. He continued to feed the poor and needy as long as he lived.

People with problems whom Frank had met brought tears to his eyes on occasion. Some situations he encountered were very difficult to help. He realized that good, fine people through no fault of their own met up with hardship. He ran into human suffering more often than the average person just by the sheer number of people he met every day. There was no end to the visits and phone calls from people who felt that he could solve their problems, and some of which were really tough.

The one other thing that could spark an emotional display in Frank was a simple "thank you." He nearly cried when he opened a homemade thank you card sent to him by a young girl. It received a place of honour in his office among the pictures of famous people he had met over the years.

A man who had just experienced his wife's passing brought his two children to a community festive dinner. Having just moved to town, Frank wandered over to greet them. He was told of the family's misfortune and sat down for the entire meal with them. They left in far better spirits.

Shirley Faldwell

Since Joyce loved to dance, she was an ideal evening partner for Frank. He had been a wonderful dancer all of his life and got out on the floor whenever he could. This of course didn't mean that the couple danced together all evening. They both agreed that Frank was to dance with all of the ladies. Being incredibly social, he enjoyed the opportunity. This certainly didn't leave Joyce out in the cold, for she was also asked to dance with the many men at the dozens of functions they attended.

I never ceased to marvel at his stamina. I remember once we had fifteen functions in one day, starting with a ribbon cutting at 9 a.m. We had dressed a certain way for that and then went home and changed. We were off to Victoria for a lucheon. After that we turned around and came back in time for another function at 2 o-clock and from then on it was functions right through until dinner time. We changed our clothes a couple more times and then went on to eight banquets. I don't know if we ever did have dinner. It was quite amusing because each place we went to we'd either just missed the appetizers and they were into dinner and we could grab sort of a quarter of dinner and get on with the speeches, then out the door and onto the next one, where we may have gotten there in time for dessert or something.

By the end of the day we had indeed changed our clothes five times and been to fifteen functions. We arrived home at about 2 in the morning absolutely giddy, fell backwards on the bed and marvelled, "My God! Did we actually do that?"

Joyce MacMillan

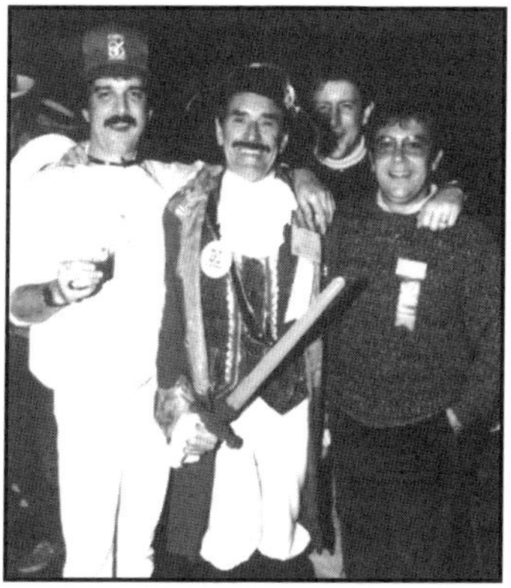

Many parties were in full swing by the time Frank arrived. He always caught the spirit instantly.

One day I saw Frank attend and change costumes for three different appointments. There was a black garb for a local funeral, his pirate suit at the city's first Kentucky Derby and his formal attire for a community wedding. He was truly a people's mayor.

Jack Whitlam, Businessman

Frank was well aware of his position in society. It was true that the ladies loved to dance with this charming fellow. It was not his style, however, to search out a partner who looked like a movie star or to compete for the girl who was already surrounded by men. Dancing was not a competitive game or an ego-trip for Frank. He danced with the young and the old, the skinny and the rotund. If a lady knew a paticular dance very well they would make a show of it. If a lady had trouble with her feet or could not move too easily, he would dance on the spot with her. Frank was always the perfect gentleman. And when he and Joyce went out together, they were showpiece of style. They were a pleasure to be around and were always welcome everywhere.

Frank always had an "out" before he went anywhere. He would show up at your house, party or whatever and say, "I have a meeting to attend, so I can't stay very long." Having said this, he could leave at any time and not offend anyone. If he was really having a good time the other "meeting" would be forgotten.

Don Swaine, Calgary Alberta

It was not always understood why Frank was so often late for the many functions he would attend. However, there could scarcely be another person in this world who was as supportive of so many events as Frank. Often an immediate request would be placed on top of a scheduled one and events would overlap. If he were going to a ceremony, he might stop off at the hospital on the way to wish someone's grandmother a happy birthday. Often he would not stay to the end of each event as there was always another one waiting. In between engagements there was travel time to consider as well. One particularly sad story involves the drive to an event at the Norwegian Hall.

Frank and Joyce were going down a steep hill on Pine Street when a 5-month old puppy ran out under their moving vehicle. Frank was devastated. The man across the street came out and joined the lady who was driving behind them. They both said that they saw what had happened and that there was no way that Frank could have avoided hitting the little dog. Frank and Joyce could do nothing but watch the dog's demise as its lungs had been ruptured upon impact. Frank wanted to take the pup to the SPCA to see if there was any way to save her, but he was told that there was no hope as the dog drew its last breath. Frank was very upset. Had there been a chance to save her, he would not have been concerned with his clothes, his car, or the function he was to attend. He would have done whatever needed doing.

He's the type of man who, no matter how busy he was with functions, the city, his children, his employment, he always had time for any kind of business or personal problem.

Whenever the office suffered internal strife, he always called a meeting to allow us to air our concerns. He was willing to listen to everyone's opinions, no matter how much they conflicted. He became my friend at work. His kindness influenced many others at work besides myself.

Frank was one in a million. No one else will ever fill his boots.

Liz Nicholet, Nanaimo Realty for 12 years

Once twelve years ago or so, when I walked downtown with my sons, the youngest had a plastic sword bought in Chinatown. There was Frank Ney in his pirate costume in the middle of Commercial Street directing traffic with his sword. So Frank and Arthur, my son, engaged in swordplay in the middle of the street.

Tim Lander

Jim and Frank managed to keep their business going until 1985, when they ran out of cash. Some building lots had dropped to a value of under $10,000 and some houses sold for as little as $20,000. These are unheard of prices in light of the $163,000 average house price in Nanaimo at the present time (1995). The average city lot today is $73,000 and the low end house is $49,500. The only problem with that particular house, (apart from being next door to the train track), is that it has already been burnt down. It is obvious that a dollar was a very powerful and valuable tool in the mid-1980's. Frank advised all entrepreneurs, "Buy the biggest home you can, more than you need. With our shrinking dollars, inflation will protect you." He was, of course, right with that statement!

Nobody could ever say that Frank didn't work hard in trying to get the economy to shape up. One evening he was on national television as a curiosity because he had been mayor of his town for so long.As always, a camera in his face sparked off his usual sales pitch. He was telling everyone out east to sell their houses and move to Nanaimo. He got excited and told the viewing audience that they could buy a very nice house for $57,000 and put the rest of their money in the bank.Who knows how many Canadians looked into the idea? One thing is for sure: everyone who followed his advice found regular assessments substantially higher when prices went crazy less than ten years later.

I always remember Frank Ney as a man of uncommon courtesy as well as of surprising and unflaunted culture.

I remember once seeing him as he walked out for his morning coffee at the Modern Cafe, impeccably dressed. As he was passing a couple of panhandlers on the street corner, "Good morning, boys" he said to them with genuine spirit and good humour.

Tim Lander

During the time that they were struggling to pay off the banks there was a lot of advice being offered to Frank. Real estate-oriented people would say, "Well, you've got all this debt.Why do you bother? Why don't you just go across the street and start "Frank Ney Realty? "You'll make a lot of money!"This was probably true. Frank had had thirty successful years in real estate, his name was very well known and his reputation was strong.With the combination of his connections and low prices, he could have made a whole lot of money during this period. Frank, however, stood his ground and said, "We have a lot of shareholders and we owe it to them. Let's just keep it going.These people put their money up and we owe it to them."

Frank also created loyalty amongst his staff and worked hard to keep these people happy. He went to every sales meeting when salespeople were down because of market conditions. A salesman's confidence is a very fragile thing if he doesn't sell for a while and Frank would go and help them out as best he could. He would encourage them and put a colourful spin on his words so that they were uplifting.

Things got so bad that the manager of a bank had a big box of keys dumped on his desk one day. The manager was told, "We ran it, now you try." The bank manager convinced the company take the keys back.

In 1985 Frank had to suspend his operations. He had to let twenty-eight long-term people go, including Jim Goodwin who had been with him for twenty-eight years. Frank had to sign a letter that laid off everyone except himself and a controller. For two years Jim and other senior members of the staff had to seek work elsewhere. At one point Jim was receiving a fee from the bank for his work in disposing of assets.

Those guys were selling lots for less than than it had cost to buy and subdivide. It was sell! sell! even at a terrible loss.

Anonymous

Frank was receiving Canada pensions and his war pensions. This was all that he had to live on. He knew that his younger partners were caught in the same financial trap and quietly offered his friends help in the form of a couple hundred dollars from his pension cheques. That's what he was about. Polititions and real estate people have sometimes earned themselves a bad name in our society. Frank defied all of that with his strong sense of morality.

I never saw Frank get mad, but I did see him perturbed. I walked into his office and said, "Hi Frank, how are you?" He answered "I'm broke." I told him that I already knew that.

His bank in Vancouver had just changed managers and the new one didn't know him. He had sent Frank a rather nasty letter that basically said, "Pay up or we will forclose on everything." Frank was not impressed by this. "They know they're going to get paid."

Frank got on the phone and gave the new manager a piece of his mind. "If you want ten cents on the dollar, just keep this up." He said that he was in it to the tune of $18,000,000.

Frank knew a lot of people in Vancouver, and the new manager soon realized that. He quickly made a trip to the Island to help bring about a reconciliation. They came to an understanding.

Annonymous, Reporter

All the loyal people suffered, but not as much as Frank, since he had the largest investment. Because of the fact that he stayed behind and faced the music nobody could say, "Oh that crook lost my money for me!" Frank had said "We did it once, we can do it again," and his enthusiasm helped people through it all.

He was always calling me a "scurvy wench." He had this ability to take something that would be miserable or blah to other people and make it exciting. How many people are thrilled to wake up at ten past four in the morning to a voice bellowing, "Wake up you scurvey wench! I've brought your grapefruit!" It was pitch black out, and while we normally would wake up very early, like six or quarter past six, usually the sun would be peeping out somewhere and you could see light through the curtains. It was pitch black, so dark out that I couldn't get my eyes going. When you wake up at that hour you're not quite with it. As I struggled up a bit, he left the room for a minute saying, "I'm going to get the paper."

He came back in a minute, turned on the light and said, "Wake up! What's the matter with you? You gonna sleep all day while I slave away in the kitchen? Here, I've made your breakfast now wake up! Wake up and eat it!"

He turned on the lights and complained that the paper wasn't there. With the lights all on my eyes definitely had to try to open. I leaned over and I squinted at the clock. I couldn't believe it. I said, "Frank it's ten past four!"

"No", he said "It's six."

"No, it isn't. It's ten past four."

He said, "Well that doesn't matter. Eat you're grapefruit you scurvy wench. I've slaved away in the kitchen all morning."

There was a grapefruit cut in half. You just had to get up and laugh.

Joyce MacMillan

The bank asked Jim Goodwin if he would come back in 1987 to restructure the company with Frank. The outcome of their work is a company now called Great National Investments. It is a successor corporation which owns all of Nanaimo Realty and residual assets. The new company was restructured with the assistance of the Royal Bank, but there were five banks in all that held debt. Four million dollars was converted into preferred shares in lieu of debt and it was arranged that the banks would get another 2.1 million over time. This was negotiated over a two-year period. Frank put the whole thing in front of his own personal fortune.

There was a sustantial number of shareholders at that year's meeting. In his report Frank said: "I am very happy to report to the shareholders that our company is starting to look like it has a future. Just recently five major banks have taken a position in our company!" That is a very positive and humorous way of saying that they took shares because there was no other way they could get any money. How could anyone get mad?

The reporters wanted to know what was happening to his empire. "I've gotten over that hump now. It made us tighten up the business and made me work harder. I've just refinanced seven million dollars worth of debt, with eastern financiers, at a savings of $290,000 a year."

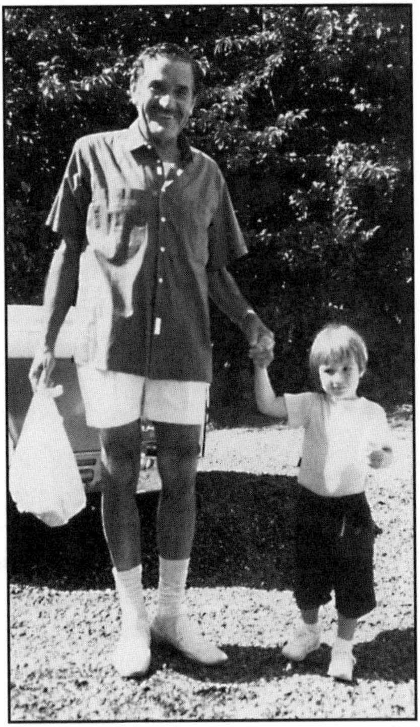

Papi taking Alex out for ice cream. Frank loved both.

Frank cared for his family very dearly and during his last years he tried to arrange his affairs so that he would leave an estate when he was gone. Joyce saw him through some severe personal financial problems and through continuous hard work they managed to overcome them. Frank never did declare bankruptcy and by the end he had paid all of his debts. He was still working everyday, and soon even the Federal Government had all of the money they wanted from him.

The majority of people who saw Frank around town during the hard times knew nothing of his misfortune and still saw him as an incredibly weathy man. One man had borrowed $20 or $40 from Frank every month to see him through the last few days until he got his pay-cheque. This went on for years and Frank marveled at the fact that the money was always promptly paid back. Frank respected and admired this man because of his honesty and pride.

He never spoke of his tales of generosity. Not once did one of his personal acts of kindness get recognised in the press. The majority of people who knew him never got to know what he was really like.

The telephone at Frank's house never stopped ringing. In his later years he enjoyed relaxing in front of the T.V. as much as anyone. It was usually on these evenings, or when he was asleep in the middle of the night that people would call him. One fellow called in the middle of the winter and said that he had no oil for his furnace and that his house was very cold. He also had children that were not at all well. Frank asked, "What is your address? I'll see if the delivery guy can come out right away." Frank hung up and after a few phone calls found one company that could deliver oil first thing in the morning. Frank paid the bill as he had done every winter for years with this man.

Over the years there were many distress calls from parents with freezing houses. At midnight one night a call came in from a man whose child had pneumonia. Again Frank would tried to get an immediate delivery to the caller's house, until a promise of 6 a.m. satisfied him. With a typical oil bill ranging from $100 to $200, there is no way of calculating exactly how much Frank spent on stranger's heating bills over his lifetime.

Some hillbilly couple called Frank and wanted him to pay their phone bill. He spent as much time as he could discussing it with them and then paid it. They were so out-of-it that they didn't realize that Frank actually paid their bill out of his own pocket. They just figured that he was so powerful that he could just talk to someone or flick a switch somewhere and the account would be waived. Because of that they never did pay him back.

Tom McConnell, Bartender

There were always calls about hyrdo and telephone bills. Some people used electric heat, and some people were going to lose their phones. Frank did not ask for the money to be returned in situations that were obviously emergencies but would request re-payment from those who needed to learn a lesson. He was kind, but never a fool. How many people paid him back, and how moch money is still owed to him will forever remain a mystery.

Someone always needed money at every point of the year. Other types of phone calls included those from a regular assortment of people who were dissatisfied with the services they were receiving from the city, or who simply disliked developers. Unfortunatly these people would not call the switchboard at the city hall and get connected to the right person during the day. Instead they would wait until the day was over, and often when the bar was closed, and give Frank Ney a call at home. He heard it all from "My streetlight is broken!" to "There's a hole in my road!"

Where did Frank got the patience to listen to over twenty years of weird phone calls? If the caller was really yelling, Frank would just hold the earpiece out and look at it. There was no reason why any of this should have bothered him personally, and he refused to take it that way. He loved people and always assumed that their intentions were good ones. At the end of a frustrating encounter - whether it was strangers yelling or his kids fighting - he would always turn to his partner and say, "Well, what do you make of that?"

One thing everyone agreed on; you could always count on Frank.

At any function of ours to which Frank was invited, he always managed to put in an appearance, even when tardy. (He often was late!)

My fondest recollection of Frank occurred in May of 1989. Our association was hosting a Naval Veteran's Reunion, a three-day affair, with some five hundred veterans and their spouses in attendance. As a matter of course, we invited Frank to grace our head table at the Saturday evening banquet.

The next day was "Battle of the Atlantic Sunday", and a huge parade had been organized, with senior naval officers invited to take the salute at the dais.

I was Parade Marshall, and in the press of organizing bands, veterans groups, a platoon from H.M.C.S. Restigouche, and cadet groups, I completely forgot to ask Frank, as Mayor, to take his rightful place on the saluting dais.

While preparing to give the order to march the parade off, who appears but His Honour, Frank Ney. He gave me a little wave and a grin, then quietly placed himself unobtrusively among his fellow veterans, and paraded with us.

Now that was class!

Ernie Doctor, Past President R.C.N.A Nanaimo Branch

Joyce's Sunporch Restaurant often had a pirate in the galley.

One of Frank's old girlfriends called one night when he was at home with Joyce. This was 1992 and his old friend was living out of town and seeing some bad times. She needed to borrow money to pay her phone bill. She had sick children in another province and her phone bill was really high. Frank asked her, "How much?" and wrote a cheque. He explained to Joyce that he used to go out with her and that she was really very nice. He knew that she would pay it back someday. Frank and Joyce had a good understanding between them. As two mature people - grandparents - and deeply in love, they communicated very well, and were perfectly honest with each other.

A knock on Frank's door would often mean someone was selling something. More often than not it was children. Frank did not always want to buy whatever the product might be, but he never let it show. He would give them what change he had or hand over a $2 bill with some encouraging words. He never turned anyone away, ever. He bought a lot of stuff, not only at his door but also from small businesses. He stuffed everything into their "gift cupboard" and whenever he felt like giving a present he would say, "What have we got in there?"

I had my art on display and Frank looked it over. It was all for sale. Frank bought a little ash tray for $2 that my daughter had made. He was so happy. I guess he felt that he just simply HAD to buy something.

Anonymous Local Painter

Frank looked out onto the street when he sat in the kitchen in the morning. Very often there was an old lady waiting outside for the first sign of him before she knocked on the door. She lived nearby and showed some signs of mental illness. Her usual request was for money for cigarettes. He would smile at her and give her what change he had. Sometimes he only had a $5 bill, and that's what she walked away with that day. He was not thrilled about contributing to what he considered to be a detriment to her health, but still could not turn her away.

Golden Years

By this time, the couple were experts at attending functions. They had developed a system whereby they would split up as soon as they entered the room and then circulate in different directions. They would meet on the other side, continue the circle and quietly depart. No one knew that they had left as they had created the illusion that they were still circulating. It was an exciting time for both of them as they were both free, happy and popular.

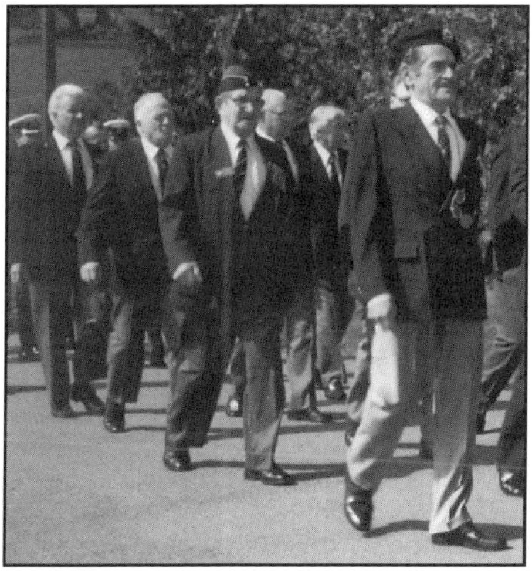

Frank remained a public fixture throughout the 1980's and early 90's. His schedule remained busy and he continued to gain new friends and new fans, becoming a true legend in his own time and receiving the much deserved love and respect from the people to whom he had given so much of himself over the years. He felt that he had made the best of his life and had not wasted much of his time. He delegated work for years and had created a lot of jobs for thousands of people. He had made many people happy without hurting anyone. He had good health and was thankful that his children were all healthy. All in all, Frank considered himself very lucky to have lived such a rich life. "Some people at 40 are very, very old, while I find other people at 80 have more enthusiasm and energy. I think you have to take the initiative in liking people, have a twinkle in your eye, a warm smile and a friendly handshake."

I will always be a fan of Frank Ney's. From the moment I met him in 1992 I was always happy to hold a brief conversation with him whenever our paths crossed. I say "brief" because Frank was forever in a hurry. I remember one day last June when I was stopped for a red light at the intersection of Comox Street and the highway, I saw Frank as I will always remember him — in a hurry to get to his next engagement or meeting.

A small yellow car came speeding down the hill from Front Street, turning the corner heading north. The top was down and the windows were rolled all the way up. There was Frank, leaning into the wheel, bearing straight ahead, Joyce beside him hanging onto the seat. As they came alongside me I saw a good six inches of Frank's kilt caught in the closed driver's side door, and flapping in the breeze.

Brenda Bird

June 3, 1992, was a typical day for Frank. He spent some time at Nanaimo Realty in conversation with Jim Goodwin and then went out to participate at a local function. It was a busy and happy afternoon for Frank as he stood behind the counter at a local fast-food restaurant and served burgers and fries to customers as part of a promotion to raise money for charity. Other dignitaries had also been invited to participate in this charitable event. Frank was surrounded by many of his favourite things including friends, strangers, charity, and of course, milkshakes.

Frank was suddenly stricken with a seizure. He became disorientated and was quickly rushed away for medical aid. He was later diagnosed as having a malignant brain tumor.

In the early part of his illness, Frank knew his future was limited, and was determined to keep his company going. He and Jim made some changes which involved corporate appointments and a larger directorate so that the company would continue. Frank had always been the president and the inspiration behind Nanaimo Realty, while Jim was always the treasurer. When Frank transferred the presidency title to Jim, he objected, "Frank, I can't operate the company, I don't know anything about it." Frank answered, "It's simple. There's nothing to it. You be fair to your clients, you be fair to your staff and to your competitors. It's easy!"

I returned alone when I learned Frank was terminally ill. We spent a wonderful couple of days together. Of course we went out on the boat which he allowed me to steer, we swam in the harbour. I'll remember Frank Ney from that visit, as clearly as I recall our first meeting in the Modern Cafe 37 years ago.

Malcolm Barr, travelled 5,000 miles
to attend the unveiling of Frank's statue.

I worked with Frank for thirty-five years, eight or ten hours a day. Frank and I went out for lunch and at that time Frank's memory was getting a little slow. He would say to me, "Allan, what about Mr. So and So?" I'd say, "I'm sorry, Frank, he's deceased."

"Well, how about Mrs. So and So?" I'd say "She's gone as well. Frank, it's kind of unpleasant and uncomfortable, let's not talk about people that have passed on."

Frank, as he could do, got a little angry. He said, "Allan, what are you talking about? When I go I would love to have people remember me and talk about me!"

Alan Lupton, Nanaimo Realty

Against the advice of his doctor and to the amazement of many, he showed up at the bathtub parade. Black Frank sat up on the back seat of a convertible and raved about bathtubbing though his megaphone. He was his usual self through the entire bathtub weekend. He proudly stood on the bow of his boat, waving his plastic sword and yelling at other boaters. Frank had certainly gained respect for his bizare public performances. This is what he truly loved. Here he was again, participating in the opening segment of the TSN telecast, distributing dozens of hats and signing numerous posters. Not only did the pirate show up at the start of the race; he even hit the beach in Vancouver. All this despite the fact that he was seriously ill and heavily dosed with medicine. He was in danger of having another seizure at any time.

The summer of 1992 was Frank Ney's last one on the west coast. He wasn't working, so he got to spend more time with his family. He was out on the *Blue Girl* often at that time, where he could still be seen smiling, shaking hands and hosting parties. Nanaimo's harbour was closely dotted with anchored boats and the *Blue Girl* would have a number of other boats tied to her. Passers-by would shut off their engines and add their boat to the floating party. Frank looked great as he shouted greetings at everyone, offered them rum and invited them to join him for a swim in the ocean. As usual, he was having the time of his life.

It was 4 months after Dad's first seizure. He had lost most of his recent memory but could recall things if they happened 10-15 years ago or later. Here is my story: Life was great!

It was a hot late August afternoon in 1992 and I was sitting with Dad on his bed, having a conversation about anything and everything. We were both having fun. He said to me in a confused voice that there was something wrong with him, but did not know. So he asked me and I told him the truth. He then asked if he was going to die. I said, "Yes, it appears so."

He then said, "Oh God, I'm too young to die." So I replied, "You're not that young, Dad. I asked him how old he thought he was, and he said, "61 or 62." (Hence the memory lapse of 10 - 15 years). I told him that was not correct. He then asked me how old he was. I told him 74. His response was..."74! Well if that's how old I am then I think its OK to die. I've had a great life and lived it to the fullest. I feel so much better now that I'm 74." He then said, "Let's go get some ice cream at the Dairy Queen." (one of his favourite hangouts!)

I have never seen an individual take such advantage of every minute in a day, and since that day I am trying my best

> *to live my life to its fullest so I too will have a positive attitude like my dad when it's my turn.*
>
> Todd Ney, Denver, Colorado

As fall approached Frank was still getting the odd call from strangers asking for help. One lady called him at home and spoke of her inability to cover her fire insurance. She was getting bills from the insurance department at Nanaimo Realty and couldn't pay them. Frank told her, "It's O.K., I'll get right on it tomorrow." He was starting to forget things and the bill went for a while longer without his giving any attention to it. The lady was persistent, calling him back again and again.

Great respect was shown to the man with the presentation of the first ever "Canada 125 Medal" in recognition of his outstanding citizenship. This award commemorated Canada's 125th birthday and was comprised of a certificate and silver medal. It was presented by his old political rival Dave Stupich during a quiet luncheon with a selected audience on September 30, 1992. With a certificate of appreciation from the government in hand, Frank decided not to take all the credit for the town's accomplishments for himself: "Nanaimo is on the move today and it's because of the hard work of many people. Keep the ball rolling. I was just one of the many people."

> *When we were young we didn't think he was anything special. We took a lot of ribbing because of him. I think they used to call me the "Son of the Man About Town." During the last year I've really seen how much he means to so many people. I've been pretty touched by all this."*
>
> Frank Ney Jr.

Frank and Joyce went out to the Legion Hall one evening. The people of Nanaimo were well aware of his condition, and there was a solemn air of admiration in the air. Joyce had a glass of wine and Frank had a non-alcoholic beverage while the band leader dedicated a song to the couple. They were the only ones on the dance floor while the 1932 romantic melody "Fascination" filled the hall. When the final note faded, the croud burst into applause. The couple knew, and the audience sensed, that this was their last dance...

Frank astonished everyone one more time on Rememberance Day. He was told that he was not well enough to participate in the ceremony, and people were not expecting him to be there. When he heard the music, he started to march with the other Veterans. He had an extremely deep respect for his fellow Vets. There he was, marching with a legion platoon, chest out, eyes straight ahead and medals shining. This was Frank Ney's last public appearance.

On the afternoon of Wednesday, November 18, he was hospitalized for the last time.

Farewell old friend.

Joyce had been taking care of him up until that point. When Frank was in the hospital, she spent as much time as she possibly could with him. They communicated by way of writing notes to each other in a booklet. This way Frank didn't have to depend on his now fading short term memory. He could read that she had been there in the morning, and that everything was taken care of. He could only remember and speak of the good times in his life. Frank loved life, and was positive right up until the end.

Frank James William Ney passed away in Nanaimo hospital on Tuesday morning, November 24th, in the presence of Joyce MacMillan and his children.

His large office at Nanaimo Realty sat empty; a cluttered testimonial to his years spent living a varied public and professional life. The worn and faded pirate suit, complete with boots and hat, rested in the corner where it was hastily dropped after its last appearance. In another corner of the office sat a pair of snow shoes, an old cricket bat and a beautiful Indian headdress. The floor and table were lined with piles of business and seafaring magazines. A collection of books remained stacked in places where they could be easily reached had Frank ever had the time to read them.

A series of filing cabinets had served their purpose of holding documents on years of transactions as well as supporting dozens of framed photopraphs. Along side of pictures of Frank with his famous friends stood pictures of some of the good times aboard the *Blue Girl*. This office contained a collection of items that seemed to document the rich life of the man, providing a reminder of the many things he cherished in this world. There was no shortage of bathtub memorobilia, but one facet of his life stood out above the rest. Businessmen usually have a photo of their kids on the desk, but in Frank's case, the photo display was like a gallery.

The old pirate was gone. Even with all the dozens of interesting things to see in his office, it was still empty. For many people that empiness extended into their own lives. Frank had given so much of himself to so many that a void was left when he died.

A private funeral service was held, followed by interment in Cedar Valley Memorial Gardens at Cedar B.C. The funeral procession had stopped briefly at Nanaimo's City Hall where staff lined up on the front steps to pay their last respects. Local flags were at half mast for a couple weeks to follow.

Frank Ney A Canadian Legend

Large newspaper ads were published inviting all residents of Nanaimo to attend a celebration of the life of Frank James Ney at 11:00 a.m., December 12, 1992 at the Frank Crane Arena. This ninety-minute event was attended by thousands of people. Nine friends shared their memories of him with the emotional crowd. Naturally there were lighthearted moments, since this event did celebrate a man that was not without humour. Music was provided by the Malaspina Choir, Scottish Pipers and the Nanaimo Concert Band.

Lloyd Bertram sang a fitting lyric "The Winds of the Straight" to the melody of the hymn-song "Kings Fold." Ken Gogo, moved the crowd to tears with one of Frank's favourite songs, "My Way," accompanied by his wife Theodora (Dodie) on piano, and some of his family as backing. Perhaps the most emotional musical moment occurred during the lament and cannon firing. A solo trumpet followed by the bagpipe reverberated through the chilly winter air into the hearts of many.

Henry Wong provided tables of cookies and coffee for everyone to enjoy. Those who could not attend watched the service at home via the broadcast provided by the local cable telvision camera crew. The stage itself was set with flags and a banner and the sound system left no room for improvement. The entire service was without a hitch, and we can all be proud to have paid that fitting tribute to a man that touched all our lives.

"My way" was Frank Ney's favourite song. It's become my favourite since the first time I heard it, which was at the Frank Crane arena. The song touched my heart about as much as Frank Ney did. His smiling face was at most events doing things for everyone, being here and being there. I think that if it weren't for Frank Ney, many people, adults, or kids would be missing a part in life. A Mayor who is also a friend.

One year at the walkathon he gave my friend a ride to the finish line because she felt sick and couldn't walk. I, like many others grew very fond of Frank Ney. I even have my own little flag, which I bought wanting to be just like him. When I heard he had died, I lost a special "one of a kind" friend. I was so sad because I'd known him since I was about 9 years old, maybe even younger.

Ang Wilson, at 14 years of age

During this time the school board announced the plans to build a new elementary school to be named "Frank J. Ney School." The Victoria B.C. architect Chow Fleischauer conceived 250 student building next to city property in the north end of Nanaimo. It is hoped that this will be a community based project with the possibility of the city building a recreational facility next door. The school will cost four million dollars to build.

A "Name the street" promotion in 1993 was won by lifelong Nanaimo resident Larry Lemmon. He came up with "Blue Girl Way," thus naming a new waterfront private lane after Frank's boat. Thirty suggestions, each bearing a twist on Ney's name had been suggested, including "Ney's Way" and "Neyburry Street." The *Blue Girl* itself was bought from Frank's estate by Frank Ney Jr. He cruised her down to his home in Washington State. He faithfully brings her back up the coast every year for Bathtub Weekend.

Nanaimo Realty continues with a number of offices, with staff numbering some106 realtors and about 50 support staff. There are some fine people working in those offices since Frank had hand-picked his staff and put together some terrific teams. The Great National Land building still stands and witnesses numerous transactions everyday.

The city of Nanaimo still has some of Frank's coloured sidewalks. His palm trees also do quite well. Nobody could really imagine how the town would have turned out if Frank had not shown such an interest in it. His impressions are everywhere. All of the fire trucks in Nanaimo are still red. Other cities painted theirs yellow, but Frank didn't like that at all and insisted that red is the contemporary classic colour for fire trucks.

Frank was brought down to the waterfront of Nanaimo during his twilight days. He was asked where a dedicated bench should go.

He pointed to two possible spots where the race begins. And thus it came to be that Frank's name became a fixture on both of these locations. At Swy-a-lana lagoon his bench can be found within view of a tribute of a classical proportion. Thousands of Frank's friends and fans gathered on a magical evening during the 1994 Marine Festival to witness the unveiling of the 12' high 225kg (500 lb.) bronze statue of "Black Frank." It was an emotional moment for the huge crowd as the cover was lifted and the giant pirate stood proudly with sword held high.

A lot of love for this great man filled the hearts of many people that evening. Speeches were read and cameras flashed. Hot dog vendor Frank O'Neill commented on the fact that he had never seen as many people show up for an event during his ten years at the park.

No sooner had the statue been unveiled when a beautiful rainbow appeared as a backdrop. The west coast was basking in its third week of summer sun, when, from the sky came not rain, but an amazing multi-coloured frame for old Black Frank. It reminded many of the rainbow that graced Frank's last bathtub race.

Frank has been sculpted in a number of materials over the years. Free standing busts are displayed as are a variety of tin, wood and ceramic statues. Somewhere there exists a beautifully carved head of Black Frank from a huge arbutus trunk. Frank's famous smile and pirate outfit have also graced the front of thousands upon thousands of postcards sents to all points of the globe by people impresessed with the Island he persuaded them to explore.

Every year brings a fresh new display of Frank Ney T-shirts and posters. His face has become synonymous with bathtubbing. The future will undoubtedly bring tributes to the man who made everyone smile.

Perhaps the best tribute we can offer is to carry on his tradition of bringing happiness to others. We can also enjoy many of the things that he left for us. Every summer hundreds of people swim in the ocean off of Nanaimo, which remains clean, thanks to his farsightedness. Every day the walkway along Nanaimo's waterfront brings tranquillity to the many folks who enjoy its magical west coast beauty.

Frank Ney became a legend in his own lifetime. His name is etched into our lives here on Vancouver Island. We thank him for all that he has done for us and assure him that he will never be forgotten.

Postscript

He loved people and many, many people loved him. To have known him and shared his friendship was a great privilege which enriched the lives of all who knew him.

Major A.E. Swaine, Great Britain

The wife and I were in London, England seven or eight years ago and we came out of a place called Sussex Garden. I held out my hand and a taxi pulled in. "Where to?" I said, "Victoria station, please." Same old line, "Where you from?" Oh, I says, "Canada." "What part of Canada?" "Oh, the west." He said, "What part of the west?" I said, "Vancouver," and then my conscience bothered me and I said, "No, actually Nanaimo." He said, "How's Frank Ney?"

I first met Frank in 1947 while doing a real estate deal, and later when he became Mayor he automatically became my boss, and a good fair boss he was. I spoke to a number of the Nanaimo retirees and these are some of the comments I received: he was a people person with respect for all, he had good intuition and was a good businessman, he was fair minded..., he had a fantastic memory, he never said "no" and he certainly understood numbers. Everybody that I spoke to had nothing but good to say about Frank.

Albert Dunn

I don't think I ever saw him get mad. If he did, he didn't sound off too much. Just very, very, very cool. It was a laid-back office to work in. You got your work done in a friendly, not tense, office. You couldn't have it any better.

He made it a happy office to work in. He had a good sense of humour and he always had that twinkle in his eye whenever he greeted anybody. He was very likeable and the best guy in the world to work for. Just marvelous. I can't say enough about him.

Gordon Theedom,
Early Nanaimo Realty, Now Retired

Frank Ney was a rare and great figure on the British Columbia political landscape...who had a remarkable career. Characteristic was his untiring and enthusiastic boosterism, in the best sense of the word - of being proud of his community, of bringing thousands of people together, to have that same pride in Nanaimo. Colourful and full of character was Mr. Ney, especially through his efforts on behalf of the annual Nanaimo to Vancouver Bathtub Race.

He took defeat with a twinkle in his eye, and good humour. I remember when he was defeated in 1990.....Frank Ney said in his colourful language: "In South America, they shoot the old Mayor when they want a new one. I prefer this system".

He was a wonderful and unique British Columbian. We came from different sides of the political fence...but he was a friend and I was honored to have known him and to participate with him in activities like the royal and ancient bathtub society race, where he'd get us dressed up in costumes to participate in the Nanaimo celebrations after being dragooned over there in his pirate ship.

I know we will never see another one like Frank Ney.

There was no other mould. There was only one Frank Ney.

Mike Harcourt, Premier British Columbia

My Memories of Frank Ney.

The first time I ever met Frank Ney was during the late 1970's. I was downtown walking with a couple of friends, when he dashed past us like a blue streak. "Morning Gentlemen," he said to us. As Frank Ney was the first personality, I ever came in contact with, I was rather thrilled. I was very impressionable then.

A few years later when I was employed at Caprice Cinemas as an usher, Mr. Ney came in one evening and saw the film "The Sting II". Before he went into the theatre, he asked me a question. He couldn't recall at the time what style of music was performed during that period of history. I replied, "It's Ragtime music." "Yes, yes, that's right. Good evening, sir," he said to me, as he sauntered into the theatre.

While I was attending N.D.S.S. we had a milkrun for some cause I don't recall now. At any event most of the students participated in the run. At the finish line every student received a carton of milk of our choice, whole, 2%, skim, or chocolate. All the leading dignitaries were there. They all spoke, and we all listened. Mayor Ney was the last to speak. Many of the students began talking amongst themselves and were ignoring our mayor. I felt this was disrespectful and rude. I made an effort to listen to him anyway. Mr. Ney's reputation for fun preceded him. That's what I remember most about him, his sense of fun and humour.

Vincent Wells, Actor

You just couldn't ask for a better guy. He went to every damn thing going on in this town. He must have had one hell of a secretary.

Robert Ball,
Remembers Frank at his Aunt's 50th anniversary

Frank was a very, very dear friend, a very close friend to many of our people. He was highly respected and highly honored. That respect and honor was shown to this man over twenty years ago by the members of our community when we made him an honorary member of our band and he was given an Indian name. That's something that isn't done very often.

The name Frank was given translates to "killer whale." He was given that name and there was a lot of thought put into it before it was done. The reasons were: because the killer whale is a very high held creature in our society and in our culture, because of its socialness, because of the way it reacts with its family and the rest of the animals that it's with. In its pod it's a very close knit social creature.

Frank will always be remembered by the members of our community for his work and for helping us with everything we asked him for. He was always there for us...He's a man we'll always remember and respect.

Chief Robert Thomas

Things will never be the same on Protection Island. He was our most prominent citizen. We all knew of Frank Ney's prowess in the political field and his business know-how in real estate and there is nary an Islander who cannot relate a tale or two about the man.

Most of the stories, however, tell of a human being in cut-off jeans and an old T-shirt, playing the Pied Piper to a bunch of kids, frolicking on the beach or sauntering through the woods.

Islanders also tell of his renowned hospitality; if you dropped by his place, you would most certainly be invited to share a drink and a bite to eat.

Frank Ney was also a charter member of the Protection Island Lions Club and seldom missed out on a social event! He never needed much prompting to climb on his soapbox and deliver one of his famous speeches.

The Lions Club will plant a tree on the Island as a living tribute to this man of vision, supporter of change and progress.

I would like to think that his spirit will linger, looking after the Island's welfare and well-being and, if we look closely, I'm sure we'll see him at the helm of his beloved boat, sword in hand, cheering the bathtubbers along.....

Anonymous

The colour and exuberance which he showed for his community is something that will warmly be remembered, not just by the citizens of Nanaimo, but by all those who came in contact with him....I did admire the positive and enthusiastic approach he had to all projects that he took on and ultimately successfully completed....

Gordon Wilson, Liberal Party Leader

I had the pleasure of starting to work with Frank more than twenty years ago as a young boy. Frank was a life member of the Nanaimo Figure Skating Club and he and I used to do comedy routines and ice shows. We later graduated to comedy in the council chambers...it always strikes me as very interesting in reflection to think that Frank did not come to city hall 'till he was fifty years old. Think about that. I always thought that he was born to the role, that he created the role, that he was the role and I think that's the essence of Frank Ney. Being Mayor for Frank was not a title, it was a persona that he lived 24 hours a day, 365 days a year, for more than two decades. He was the quintessential protocol male Mayor and he always had time to lend an ear to individual concerns. He never had a lot of time for agendas or for reports or for meetings...I think Frank's favorite motion for many years was "Let's adjourn and go home."

Gerald D. Berry, Nanaimo City Administrator

Mr. Ney was a champion of his province and of his community and someone that British Columbians were very, very proud of.

Jack Weisgerber, Reform Party Leader

Frank and his death will mark the passing of someone who has made his mark on the world and many, many friends he has made during his lifetime. Frank will always be remembered in a kind and friendly way because that was the type of person he was throughout his life.

Don M. Ross, Kirkotti Fife Flyers 1939

Whenever I walked into his office, he'd say, "Oh, here comes Mr. Safety!" He had a memory on him like a steel trap. He could pass someone on the street and he'd know their name and what they did for a living. Just an amazing capacity for recalling things. As far as I'm concerned, he was a real great guy. I don't suppose any of us can walk on water exactly, and I guess Frank had his problems along the way, but he was a great guy.

Mike Severn, Former Woods Foreman

Frank Ney was known variously by the nicknames "Mr. Nanaimo" and the "Captain of the Bathtub Races."

I ran against Ney in three provincial election campaigns, winning the first and third, and losing the second to Ney.

In the first campaign, in 1966, he phoned and said there was a cheque waiting in his office for a contribution to my campaign fund. It wasn't a large amount of money, but he made a point of giving to all the campaigns. What I will treasure is the indomitable one-of-a-kind spirit, the ever present ebullience, the optimism and the energy.

It's hard to talk about Frank without saying Frank loved Nanaimo. But to him Nanaimo was not just an area of land with a ring around it representing the city limits; there was no boundary to Nanimo...he loved people, he loved individuals. He was always ready to find the time, despite how busy he was, to listen to someone who had a problem. And it didn't matter how lowly in station that person was.

Three years ago on Canada Day three of us were invited to speak at the Evangelical Church; myself as MP, Dale Lovick as MLA, and Frank as the Mayor, representing the three levels of government. We were asked to speak to their congregation about our feelings towards Canada. Frank was last and he wound up his remarks by saying something to this effect: "We have to keep Canada together, we have to save our country. Look at all the young people in this congregation. For their sake we must succeed." That's my fondest memory of Frank...

Dave Stupich, Former MLA for Nanaimo-Cowichan

Frank was known by many here at Keyport and will be missed. He was a very valued friend of the U.S. Navy.

E.L. Surgest Jr., U.S. Navy Commander

In January, 1991, in the Ecumenical Centre, Frank Ney gave a eulogy on behalf of his employee and close friend, Glen Galloway. He remembered how Galloway had come to him with the idea of a bathtub race.

Shortly after the funeral he took the time to come to the church and thank me for the service. I remember Frank Ney for his faith and enthusiasm in unlikely projects and for his thoughtfulness and kindness in showing apreciation.

Rev. Stanley A. Woodcock

THE PIRATE GHOST

This will be his first appearance, the ghost of whom I speak,
He won't scare us with a boo, or make the floorboards creak.
Halloween is new to him from the other side,
But I'm sure that he will be here, in his costume full of pride.

Perhaps you'll see him on the bay, atop his giant tub,
Or over the hills of City Hall, or at the Davy's Locker Pub.
Wherever there's a party in Nanaimo on this night,
You'll know Black Frank will be around, so keep your drink in sight!

Ada Ravnborg

The thing that touched us (aldermen) was not his flamboyancy but his sensitivity. Frank often said that in order to be in politics you had to be thick-skinned, but he was anything but thick-skinned; in fact he was very sensitive and never vindictive. I remember a statement in the press made by one of his opponents which was less than charitable and I expected that he might retaliate. Instead he said, "Don't worry, the fellow really means well." That was Frank.

At my first UBC convention in Penticton, Frank had to attend to some business in Edmonton and he was then to join us later in Penticton. On his return flight the stewardess gave him a newspaper to read. They had to stop in Calgary and then move on to Penticton. When the plane landed, Frank put down his paper and rushed off the plane to get a cab. Frank always rushed, he never walked. When he got in front of the terminal there was total darkness and there wasn't a cab to be found. There was just one little old man. He walked over to that little old man and said "Aren't there any taxi cabs in Penticton?" The little old man said, "Yup, there are a lot of taxi cabs in Penticton, but you're in Cranbrook."

His sense of humour and the compassion that he had for others is what endeared him to so many....

Gino Sedola, Nanaimo Harbour Commission

The Chinese Society had a New Year's dance for nine years and he never missed one. He was always there, regardless of how busy he was, for anniversaries, birthdays and funerals.

The Chinese community remains indebted to Mr. Ney for his efforts to secure and maintain the city's old burial grounds for former mineworkers. We consulted with Frank in 1973 through the Chinese Society and the city decided to convert it to a memorial park in commemoration of the Chinese pioneers who helped build the community.

Chuck Wong

Although I am an enemy of overpopulation, development, growth and immigration, I still liked Frank Ney.

I remember one time I rushed off the B.C. Ferry and got a taxi to Beban Park to attend a boxing event. After the boxing was over, I thought: "How in the hell am I going to get home?"

Then I saw Frank Ney and told him my predicament. He says: "Don't worry; I'll drive you home." Just when I got home, Frank says: "You've got a sense of humour."

I say: "Yeah, Frank, I'm a clown like you," and jumped out of the car. I hope I thanked him for the ride home. So I sincerely hope you rest in peace, Frank.

Bill Zelley"Royal City Red"

I will never forget Frank Ney.

I knew him for only 10 short years, but Frank made an impression in that short decade which will remain with me forever.

I suppose it was my chosen field of journalism which brought me into close contact with the man who was mayor when my family and I arrived in Nanaimo in late 1982.

My first encounter with the Mayor of Nanaimo came within a short time of moving to this city. It was the annual polar bear swim in Departure Bay, and I was one of the brave and foolish who had made the decision to dash into the frigid waters on Boxing Day. I was told the mayor was in charge of the festivities, but the only person I saw at the microphone was this wild and crazy guy, dressed up like a pirate, bragging about importing ice cubes to lower the water temperature, and blowing ships' horns to keep the whales away. Then I learned he was the Mayor.

When I first began working for this newspaper, all reporters took a regular turn at weekend duty, covering and photographing each and every ribbon cutting, political event, shopping centre event, you name it.

That could sometimes turn into a 20-25 appointment weekend, enough to run even a young buck ragged. But Frank attended virtually each and every one of them, even during the two-year term when he wasn't the Mayor. I often kidded him that we could really car pool for the weekend.

If my weekend schedule was heavy, I could always chat with Frank and he'd list the wedding anniversaries, birthday parties, christenings and other private functions he chose to attend on top of all his regular duties. And his boat, The *Blue Girl*, was the venue of many official and unofficial events, whether it was dignitaries, Big Sisters, Boy Scouts and ordinary citizens on tours of his beloved city. A number of those tours turned into adventures, as Nanaimo Search and Rescue can attest.

When you reflect on the life of a man as active and involved as Frank Ney was in his community, the list can go on and on, but a few stick out among the others.

In the early 1980's the annual convention of the Canadian Federation of Municipalities was held in Winnipeg, my former stomping grounds. Winnipeg was also the city where Frank Ney grew up, so that made it only natural that we should revisit some of our old haunts. So with a friend of mine we tore through Winnipeg's famous Chinatown, savouring the delights of a not-small selection of restaurants.

But for Frank there was something special he had missed for years, the taste of Winnipeg Goldeye, a fish delicacy only former prairie dwellers would know about. And maybe it's just as well, Goldeye is an ordinary-looking grey bottom fish from the Assiniboine and Red Rivers. The secret of its success as a much sought after delight is the fact that it is smoked and then dyed a bright red before serving.

It was quite a search, but in the wee hours we found Winnipeg Goldeye in the posh dining room of the venerable old Hotel Fort Garry.

Just recently Frank and I reminisced about that night in Winnipeg , and even though his illness was affecting his memory at the very last, he remembered just about every detail of that weekend. When I go back to Winnipeg for a visit, I'll retrace our steps of that night.

There are many other memories, like some of the city council meetings I covered as a reporter, but these are personal memories, just one extremely minute part of what made up Frank Ney. He was known world-wide for his promotional antics, he was criticized by some for what they interpreted as a lack of a dignified manner for a mayor, but he put this community on the map.

I'll never forget his optimistic outlook. Negativity was not in his make-up, no matter how dark it might be, he always saw the light at the end of the tunnel.

Perhaps the greatest tribute of all, I never heard him say one bad word about anyone.

Yes, Frank Ney was my friend. But most important, Frank Ney was everybody's friend, you couldn't help but love the man.

There's no more fitting tribute to Frank Ney than to quote his own famous, "Eight bells and all is well..."

Merv Unger, Nanaimo Daily Free Press

I knew Frank for many years and I believe I knew him well. As his legal adviser for some thirty-five years, I encountered two problems with Frank. First, the impossibility to sit down and talk for more than five minutes at a time. He was continually on the go from one project to another, with his mind always running before his body. You know, the question "How do you hold a moonbeam in your hand?" posed in the musical, "The Sound of Music" were asked of us today, I believe it should apply to Frank Ney. Secondly, his advice never to hurt people by legal encounters made it difficult for us because we always had to settle even if settling was harmful to Frank himself. On various occasions Frank referred to me to his American visiting friends as "a brain surgeon from Martha's vineyard in Massachusetts," when really I was a law student or "the world's tallest professional midget basketball player", when really I wasn't, and to a great group of people in California I was "the commissioner in and for British Columbia, something like you're Governor." But this gentleman truly was a friend. Even though he tried to kill me the way he drove his car on those freeways in Los Angeles...

I've toasted and roasted Frank Ney so often in the past that it's very difficult for me to realize that this will be the last time. But our mutual friend is gone and we should be grateful for the fact that he was allowed to live amongst us and for the many, many things he did for us. I say he's gone but with a word of caution - if you're at a wedding or an anniversary or any celebration in Nanaimo and you think that the wind has blown the door open somewhere, please don't be quick to close that door, because I think Frank's spirit will be around here for a long time. So it's time to say good-bye to an old friend and I say "eight bells and I hope all's well where ever you are."

Sid Clark, Provincial Court Judge
Eulogy at Frank's Memorial Service
December 12, 1992

The Frank Ney Challenge

Frank's challenge is a challenge to us and to our youth—a challenge to us and to kids to see if we can outdo him in our lifetime at serving our Community with more innovation or more intensity.

-a challenge to leave our Community a better place for their presence.

-a challenge to take much needed leadership in the Community, Country and Province and to stride through the criticism and sacrifice that comes with it. Frank's genius was his recognition that if you are really serious about life and about your Community, you must learn to laugh so people will take you seriously.

-if it's not fun it's not worth doing.

-if it's not fun, make it fun, then do it.

That is the "Frank Ney Method."

Frank was serious and dedicated to both people, fun, and serving Community. Frank has told us in his own way what he wants us to tell youth:

Fill your life with experiences.

Fill your life with joy.

Fill your life with friends.

There are few people you will meet who were loved by so many people. I have no doubt that over the next year, the Chamber will be involved in ways of assuring that Frank's memory, his message, his challenge to us and to our youth are never lost. Take from Frank his Challenge. Take his Genius. It leaves Greater Nanaimo even Greater. Frank's challenge has left us with a legacy that will grow forever.

Thanks, Frank.

David N. Spearing, Architect
President Greater Nanaimo Chamber of Commerce

Dear Dad,

Thank you for my life you gave.
Thank you for the inspiring things you would say.
You were strong, you were thoughtful,
and you were always optimistic.
You were compassionate, you were fair,
you were giving, you were adored.

But perhaps most of all, you were loved, Dad.
Thanks for the wonderful times we shared;
the boat trips, the ski holidays,
the cougar hunts and all,
were things that you shared that showed that you cared.

Thank you, Dad, for being there,
you always seemed to find the time to spare.
Thank you for teaching me such wonderful things:
the love for life, the love of the earth.
These are surely things we should be thinking of first.

I love you, Dad.
I know at this time, you may think I am sad,
But this feeling I have is just in the moment of grief.
To know you are at peace brings me the greatest relief.

As I am sure you would all agree,
conclusively and incontrovertibly,
Frank Ney, my father and my friend,
is truly number one.

From the sun porch of Canada,
the jewel of the West,
Thank you Dad and aloha.
(which means "until we meet again")

Michelle Ney

Somebody once posed the question, "Is there such thing as the typical parent?" Nobody thought of asking me that question; after all, how many kids ever had a pirate for a dad? As far I know, he was the only one on Beach Drive where we grew up. I don't know how or when Dad became a pirate but I remember that before he was a pirate he was a Mississippi gambler. He didn't actually become a Mayor until I was a young teenager, and I have to admit life became much more interesting after he became a Mayor, for it was just about at that time that his family stopped growing. Eleven seemed like a good number.

Some of you might be wondering how it was that my dad, who was able to attend the multitude of weddings and funerals and ceremonies and meetings and the thousands of other things he did in this community - still had time for his family. Well, I think sometimes it did catch up to him. In fact the other day somebody was telling me about the time when he arrived late as usual to a funeral. He arrived at the back and leaned over to the fellow beside him and said, "Well, you know old Charlie, he was really such a great guy." The fellow standing beside him whispered, "Frank, this isn't Charlie's funeral, it's Fred's funeral." My dad, he never got embarrassed. He just came back and replied, "Well Freddy Who?" (answer) "Freddy so and so." My dad goes back, "You know Freddy, he was such a real great guy." And you know what, I know Dad meant it. As far as my dad was concerned, both Charlie and Fred were really both great guys.

Going back to how it was that Dad had time for the family. The truth of the matter is that he didn't have much time for us during the weekdays. On the weekdays he didn't have time to make us breakfast, but I tell you on Wednesday he would bring home a giant family bucket of Kentucky Fried Chicken for dinner and that always served us well. Sundays were different. I remember him in his pyjamas fryin' up eggs and bacon and tomatoes and serving them for anybody who was around. Sunday was also our day with our Dad, much to the relief of our Mother. He loved the outdoors, he loved nature, he loved the mountains, he loved the islands, the ocean, the trees, the rain and the sun. A lot of the times we spent with Dad were outdoor activities. He'd pile us up in the old "suburban" and along with half the neighbourhood or anyone else we happened to come across, we'd be off for a trip up to Green Mountain or a trip on the boat to the cabin on Protection Island.

To get a sense of life with Dad, imagine this. You've invited a friend to accompany you on one of those Sunday boat outings and the Pontiac Parisienne covertible is loaded up with most of the neighbourhood and we've all been waiting and waiting. We did a lot of that with Dad. And then he comes out of the house wearing one of those bright coloured pirate's costumes, waving his sword and blowing on that whistle of his. Well, as younger kids, I think most of us would be a little embarrassed by this whole performance but what we noticed was that our friends, who by this time my dad would be calling "You scurvy swabs", they seemed to be enjoying it. It was kind of a cross between Captain Kangaroo and Barnum Bailey's three-ring circus and we all had the front row seats. I mean think about it, how often do you get the chance to go on a boat with a raving pirate? But the thing was because my dad seemed to be enjoying it so much he got us all in the mood, and somehow magically, but not without adventure and mishaps, we managed to end up at our destination safe and sound.
A few hours late, of course, but we got there.

Dad enjoyed adventure, he enjoyed excitement, he always had fun, and so did we. It was the occasion that he liked sharing most - sharing time with others. His attitude reminds me of the song, 'We're here for a good time - not a long time" He never stayed anwhere for a long time; his was the law of perpetual motion.

In his last days Dad told me that he had but one regret in life. He said that he thought that he expected too much out of life. But if this was his regret it was also his uniqueness. He did expect a lot out of life. He lived every day to its fullest, every day. Except for a few expensive suits and a good guitar, Dad's tastes were hardly extravagant. In fact thay were modest. He would brag about getting Chilean wine on sale at the local BC liquor store or he'd come in bragging about how cheap he got the strawberries or peaches on sale at Thrifty's. And you know what else, when he went grocery shopping or to buy gas for that gas-guzzling 1976 Lincoln Continental, he'd use coupons. That's what made it fun for him.

In his later years his greatest delight was to see how many of his kids he could get to live with him. While this might sound peculiar to some of you, he genuinely liked having as many of us around as possible. I haven't lived in Nanaimo for about fifteen years or so but even up until a month ago it was not unusual for Dad to phone three or four times a week just to say "hi" and to tell me what he was up to. I know his children meant a great deal to him and I remain impressed by his caring attitude, as are my brothers and sisters. We are very proud that he is our father.

Tara Ney

In the beginning, when I first started going with Frank, it was his compassion for everyone that struck me. Anything moving, or even if it wasn't moving, if it was an old house, he revered it.Feelings. You could feel the emotion that he had for everything. I don't know if you could actually put into words the aura that exuded from Frank. It made you feel alive just to be with him. It made you feel like it was a truly wonderful thing to be breathing and witnessing whatever was happening. There was a presence when he walked, the way he carried himself. I don't know whether it was "old world", the way he was taught, I don't know what it was but there was something in the way that he carried himself that you knew right away that he was a man who had something to do in this world. He was going somewhere and doing things, not necessarily for himself, but to make it a happier and more wonderful place for those people who were around him.

He walked into a foyer in a hotel and people recognized him right away. It gave life to the whole area. It's almost like Frank was a part of the environment and he brought life to wherever he stepped. In didn't matter where we were, in airports, in hotels, wherever we went people could feel this well-being that he gave. He was so dynamic that he actually made other people feel good. Wherever we went people would almost trip over themselves in order to be able to come and speak to him. People would always have the most wonderful accolades like, "Do you know what this guy did for me once..." They wanted to tell you about him. Everyone had such good things to say, but things that you would never hear from Frank. Frank never ever was one to do things for the sake of blowing himself up. He didn't talk about the things that he did.

He truly had the greatest compassion for anyone in need. He would do it because that person had a need, and whatever he could do, whatever he had in order to make someone else's life more complete he would do it.

When we went to Mexico we were at the bottom of the Baja at Los Cavas. While we were there for the six and a half days, Saturday to Saturday we met at least eight to ten people who knew him. After the first two days when we'd run into three or four couples, he said to me over breakfast one morning at 7:30 when a couple from Gabriola had just spotted him - "It's a good job we're not trying to hide!" It was really quite funny because you couldn't hide. With Frank Ney you'd have to get in a box and keep the lid on.

In France it was the same thing. Not as many, but still travellers from California and Arizona spotted him. When we spent a week in Quebec City I can't even think of how many people we saw who knew him from something he had been involved in somewhere, somehow. Always they were truly happy to reacquaint. It made you feel so alive to be with him because he had this happy exuberance.

You know, you go through life and most people are good people, but Frank just totally, constantly gave of himself. Really he never wanted to slight anyone, hurt anyone's feelings. When people came to work on the house he would always say to me, "I hope you gave them a cold drink." I grew up with a father who was from the old country and who was pretty much the same way. I would always tell him, "Yes, I took a jug of lemonade out." He was always a little surprised that I would think to do that, but then I had grown up that way. He would even phone, with all his busy days, and say, "How are they doing? Is there anything they need? Are you looking after them? Did you give them a cold drink?" He gave to everyone, he truly did.

It was a very fulfilling and satisfying feeling to be a part of his days. Very rewarding to know someone who was so basically wanting to be so good to others. Most people are good, but Frank worked at it!

You read in the paper about the odd one who writes something about "the developer Frank Ney." Well he was a developer, but they don't expound on it. He was a man with vision who never ever forgot one simple thing. I was not going out with him very long when he drove me by and stopped outside of the very first house he ever bought in Nanaimo. We parked in front of it and he told me about his time inside that house, how much he paid for it, what year it was et cetera. That was way back in the forties, and when I met him it was 1982. Those feelings from that time of his life still remained with him and he shared that.

Frank had a very quick mind, and I think some people found it too quick, because sometimes his brain really danced ahead of everyone. That's a part of the vision that he had. I think that's what made him work so hard with the city of Nanaimo. He could envision all of the things that the environment could give back to the people.

I'm sure that there are few people who spend their life wanting to contribute the way he did. Every day was like, "What are we going to do today?"

I really feel very fortunate in having shared a part of Frank's life. I feel that I am the fortunate one, having had that special time to witness how very compassionate and good some people really can be. We don't all get that opportunity. We hear about it, we watch T.V. and witness how people live and what they do. But I had a personal share in witnessing the life of a truly great man, and I just feel so fortunate in having had those days.

Joyce MacMillan, Frank's Spouse

Index

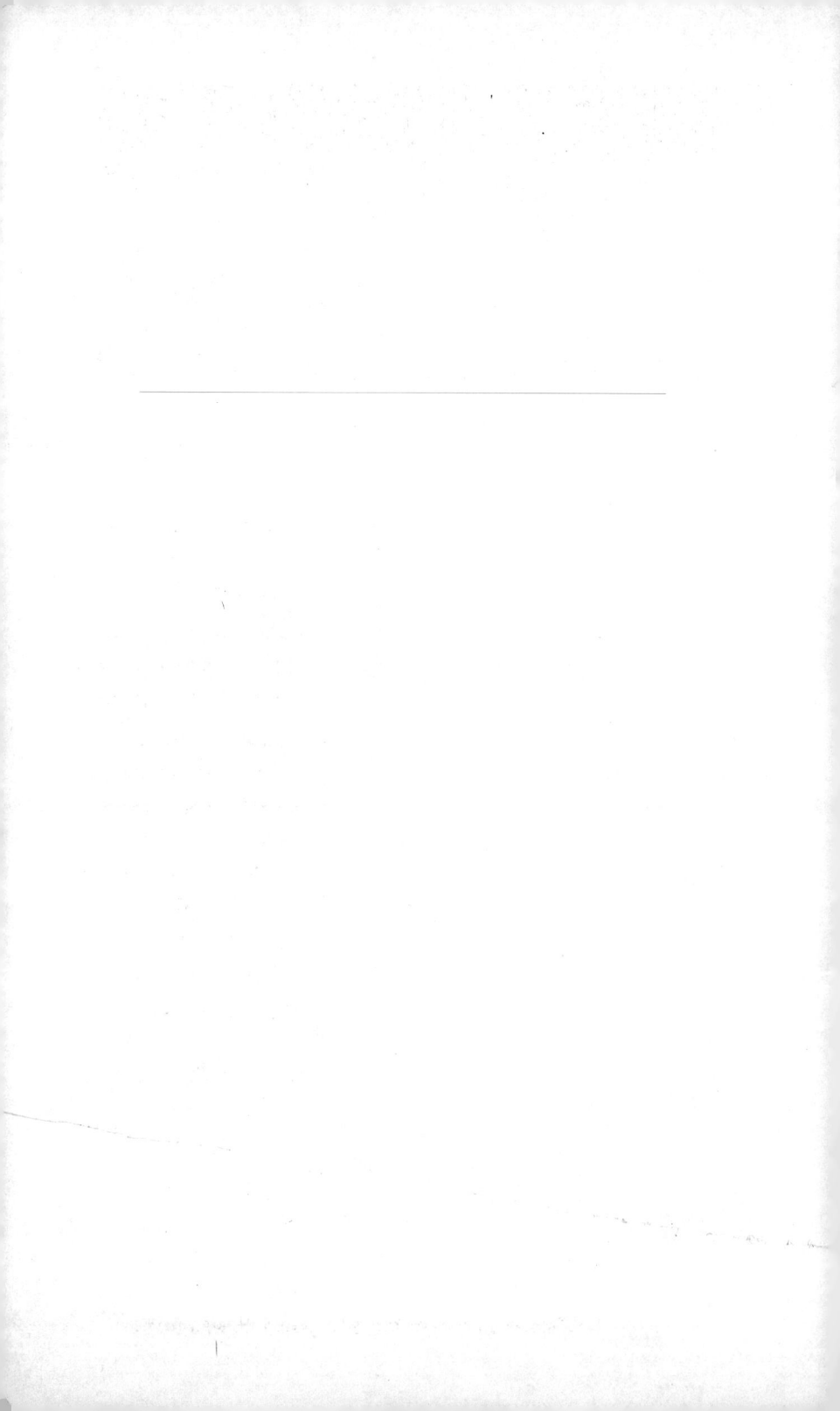